Writing Islands

WRITING ISLANDS

Space and Identity in the
Transnational Cuban Archipelago

Elena Lahr-Vivaz

UNIVERSITY OF FLORIDA PRESS

Gainesville

Publication of this work made possible by a Sustaining the Humanities through the American Rescue Plan grant from the National Endowment for the Humanities.

27   26   25   24   23   22   6   5   4   3   2   1

Library of Congress Cataloging-in-Publication Data
Names: Lahr-Vivaz, Elena, author.
Title: Writing islands : space and identity in the transnational Cuban
    Archipelago / Elena Lahr-Vivaz.
Description: Gainesville : University of Florida Press, 2022. | Includes
    bibliographical references and index. | Summary: "Analyzing works of
    contemporary Cuban writers on the island alongside those in exile, Elena
    Lahr-Vivaz offers a new lens to explore the multiplicity of Cuban space
    and identity, arguing that these writers approach their nation as part
    of a larger, transnational network of islands"—Provided by publisher.
Identifiers: LCCN 2022020660 (print) | LCCN 2022020661 (ebook) |
    ISBN 9781683402701 (cloth) | ISBN 9781683403296 (pbk) |
    ISBN 9781683403180 (pdf) | ISBN 9781683403319 (epub)
Subjects: LCSH: Authors, Cuban—Cuba—20th century—History and criticism.
    | Exiles' writings, Cuban—20th century—History and criticism. | Cuban
    literature—20th century—History and criticism. | Identity
    (Philosophical concept) in literature. | Personal space in literature. |
    BISAC: LITERARY CRITICISM / Caribbean & Latin American | LITERARY
    CRITICISM / Modern / 20th Century
Classification: LCC PQ7378 .L34 2022 (print) | LCC PQ7378 (ebook) | DDC
    860.9/97291—dc23/eng/20220609
LC record available at https://lccn.loc.gov/2022020660
LC ebook record available at https://lccn.loc.gov/2022020661

UF PRESS

UNIVERSITY
OF FLORIDA

University of Florida Press
2046 NE Waldo Road
Suite 2100
Gainesville, FL 32609
http://upress.ufl.edu

To my family, near and far

Contents

Illustrations

Acknowledgments

First and foremost, my thanks to the writers and artists who so graciously shared their insights with me as I researched and wrote this book. Reina María Rodríguez, Antonio José Ponte, Ramón Hondal, Ricardo Alberto Pérez, Caridad Atencio, Rito Ramón Aroche, Julio Moracen, Dolores Labarcena, Léster Álvarez, Luis Enrique López-Chávez Pollán, Roberto Zurbano: I cannot begin to tell you how much I have appreciated our conversations and your ongoing *apoyo*, be it in offering clarifications or in helping me track down difficult-to-find texts. *Writing Islands* would not have been possible without you.

My thanks as well to those who talked to me about this project during my trips to Cuba and Spain, including Antonio Armenteros, Ismael González Castañer, Emily Maguire, Julio Mitjans, Pedro Marqués de Armas, Michel Mendoza, Erick J. Mota, and Desiderio Navarro; and to Yanila Estrabao Ballester and Acelo Hernández Méndez, who always made me feel at home when I visited their Casa Verde. As always, special thanks to Kristin Dykstra, whose superb translations and great generosity never fail to inspire me; and to Carlos J. Alonso, for organizing the first trip I took to Havana.

I was fortunate to participate in the Rutgers Center for Cultural Analysis Seminar on Archipelagos (2015–2016) as this project began to take shape. I am indebted to Seminar participants for a year of rich conversations on all things archipelagic, and, in particular, to Seminar organizers Yolanda Martínez-San Miguel and Michelle Stephens. Special thanks as well to Seminar fellows Enmanuel Martínez, Kathy Lopez, and Anjali Nerlekar for reading early versions of chapter drafts as well as the book proposal; and to Rachel Burk, Tania Gentic, Jaime Hanneken, and Dierdra Reber for our conversations in Havana and Philadelphia.

Elisabeth Austin and Meredith Broussard read various iterations of the book manuscript in its entirety more than once; their suggestions unfailingly made it better, and their belief in the merits of the project always buoyed me. Camille Andrews was there every step of the way, bringing her librarian's expertise to my analysis and her good cheer to everything: I can't begin to express my gratitude. My fellow Northeast Senior Fordies gathered with me on Saturday mornings for writing retreats and motivated me to keep going; my "Blue Group" at Rutgers and my Faculty Success Program group at the National Center for Faculty Development and Diversity (NCFDD) offered support and encouragement as I finished the final round of edits.

My colleagues at Rutgers–Newark enthusiastically supported my research: my ongoing thanks to Jennifer Austin, Javier Castro-Ibaseta, Jason Cortés, Jennifer Duprey, Isadora Grevan, Kimberly DaCosta Holton, and Stephanie Rodríguez, as well as Jennifer Ansbach, Natalie Borisovets, Aarón Lacayo, and Laura Lomas. I am fortunate to be in such good company. Also at Rutgers–Newark, my thanks to Vice-Chancellor John Gunkel, who helped me sort through the logistics of traveling to Havana for research; to Rafael Osorio, who offered invaluable assistance with interview translations; and to Raydel Rijo, who read portions of the book and gave insightful suggestions. I remain indebted as well to my students, who helped me think through my ideas in class discussions and office hours and invariably made them better.

At the University of Florida Press, my thanks to editor Stephanye Hunter, who supported the project from the beginning and offered her expert advice throughout the process, as well as project editor Eleanor Deumens, who shepherded the book through to publication. As I worked to make my deadlines, Jordan Gonzales came through more than once to help make sure the manuscript was ready to go to press. Jessica Freeman and Christine Preston completed the copy editing and proofreading for the book; Eunice Rodríguez Ferguson and Elisabeth Lunz made time in their busy schedules to read the project and offer incisive feedback. Allison Hunt at the Perkins Art Center digitized the artwork on the book's cover: a painting by an unknown artist that I purchased in Havana. The anonymous readers of the manuscript offered excellent suggestions that helped me to round out my analysis.

This book is dedicated to my family, near and far. My partner Brent and my daughters Hannah and Emmy unfailingly offered their support and encouragement as I wrote, be it by bringing me coffee, listening to me talk through my ideas, or allowing me the space and time to write. Thank you! My in-laws

Rick and Judy helped make my research trips to Cuba (and everything else) possible with their help. I am forever grateful. My family was always there for me, as were my friends: a big thank you to Dora, Beatriz, Deidre, Maria, Emilio, Karena, Dianne, Betsy, Sigmund, Anne, Reyna, and Philip for keeping me afloat both as I traveled to conduct research and as I wrote from home. I am so grateful for you all. My father passed away as I wrote this book—I continue to miss him greatly.

Writing Islands has been supported by grants from the Rutgers Center for Latin American Studies, the Rutgers University Research Council, and the Rutgers Center for Cultural Analysis, as well as the Dean's Office at Rutgers–Newark. I am grateful for this support, as well as for a research leave from Rutgers that afforded me valuable time for research and writing. Preliminary versions of the book's chapters have been presented at Rutgers University, Swarthmore College, and Vanderbilt University, as well as at conferences hosted by the American Comparative Literature Association (ACLA), the Asociación de Estudios de Género y Sexualidades, the Latin American Studies Association, the Modern Language Association, the Northeast Modern Language Association, and the Southeast Modern Language Association. My thanks to all those who offered helpful suggestions in these fora, and especially to Christina Karageorgou-Bastea, who invited me to participate in a research workshop on "Poetry and Its Others" at Vanderbilt, as well as César Salgado and Juan Pablo Lupi, who invited me to participate in their illuminating ACLA seminar.

Portions of chapters 2 and 3 were published in an earlier form in a chapter titled "Birds of a Feather: Reina María Rodríguez and the World Republic of Letters" included in *La futuridad del naufragio: Orígenes, estelas y derives*, editors César Salgado and Juan Pablo Lupi, Almenara Press, 2019. This material is reprinted here with permission. Portions of chapter 6 were published in an earlier form in "Timeless Rhetoric, Special Circumstances: Sex and Symbol in *La nada cotidiana*," *Revista Canadiense de Estudios Hispánicos*, vol. 34, no. 2, 2010. This material is reprinted here with permission of the *Revista Canadiense de Estudios Hispánicos*. Excerpts of poems from Ramón Hondal's *Diálogos* and *Scratch*, and from Ricardo Alberto Pérez's *¿Para qué el cine?*, are reprinted here with the permission of the authors (and my gratitude); interviews included in the book's Appendix are included with permission of interviewees.

I never imagined when I began to write this book that I would finish it during a global pandemic. It occurs to me as I do so, however, that the issues I analyze are perhaps even more germane now, as we are asked to fundamentally, and seemingly continually, reimagine our negotiation of space and identity. It is thus my hope, now more than ever, that this book will contribute to a larger conversation on the issues of community and change that underlie and inform my analysis in the pages that follow, both in the transnational Cuban archipelago and in the wider seas of the Caribbean and beyond.

Introduction

Seen in an aerial shot, the main island of Cuba curves sinuously through an expanse of blue sea. With fin-shaped outcroppings of land jutting out from below, the elongated shape of Cuba's best-known landmass suggests a maritime creature making its way through the surrounding Caribbean waters. Just below the main island, a smaller spot of green is visible: the Isla de la Juventud, or, as it was once known, the Isla de Pinos. Multi-hued, aquamarine water cuts between this Isla and its larger neighbor; wisps of white clouds stand out against the darker backdrop of land and water.

In common parlance, an archipelago is defined as a "group of islands," or as "any sea, or sheet of water, in which there are numerous islands."[1] Based on this definition, Cuba *is* an archipelago from a geographic standpoint: although it is frequently thought to be a singular island, it is in fact composed of some 1,600 islands, islets, and keys. In this book, I show that these Cuban islands not only form part of a geographic archipelago, but that they are part of a larger, transnational constellation, and that the landmasses and the waterways that connect them comprise a transnational archipelago.

Employing an archipelagic approach to analyze the work of writers who have remained in Cuba alongside that of those who are in exile, this book proffers a new lens on Cuba's multiplicity, bringing texts that are often not considered together into conversation. Although their perspectives (and politics) differ in myriad ways, the Cuban writers whose work I analyze converge in implicitly contesting any attempt to limit the space of the nation to the space of the island(s)—or, indeed, the Caribbean. Suggesting the larger contours of a constellation that continues to shift and morph, the writers highlight the transnational ties that increasingly join Miami and Havana, Madrid and Matanzas, Nueva York and Paris;[2] and, in so doing, craft spaces that—as is true of the constituent islands and waterways of an archipelago—offer a glimpse of a whole that is larger than the sum of its parts.

Utilizing the trope of the archipelago throughout the book illuminates Cuba's plurality of islands. The book's title, *Writing Islands*, refers not only to the multitude of spaces that construe Cuba as archipelagic in world atlases and cartographies, but also—and more metaphorically—to seemingly disparate writers' creation of spaces that are both scattered and interconnected. By bridging seas and surpassing sightlines, these spaces together comprise a transnational archipelago, underscoring the connections (rather than the divisions) between spaces and individuals separated by geopolitics.

With the concept of the singular island no longer adequate to describe the spaces inhabited by transnational communities in the 1990s and 2000s, new hermeneutics are necessary to better understand the rich histories of the interconnections that exist between them.[3] Cuba is, of course, already known by many names that draw attention to these interconnections. In cogent studies of Cuban culture, for instance, Rachel Price writes of *Planet/Cuba*, Marta Hernández-Salván refers to *Mínima Cuba*, and Ruth Behar and Lucía M. Súarez describe Cuba as *The Portable Island*. In my own analysis, I use the neologism *arcubiélago*: the term riffs on the Spanish *archipiélago*, at the same time that it incorporates a reference to *Cuba*, writ large, and invokes the spaces that writers craft both on the ground and in print.

In coining the term *arcubiélago*, combining *Cuba* and *archipiélago*, I provide a shorthand for easy reference to Cuban writers' creation of a transnational, archipelagic space that functions both materially (or *in situ*) and metaphorically (in poems, blogs, essays, novels, and songs). As a portmanteau, the term embodies the concept it denotes: in the same way that *arcubiélago* is simultaneously two (truncated) words and one (combined), the transnational Cuban archipelago exists both as a singular entity and a multiplicity. More broadly, the term *arcubiélago* also evokes the plurality of dimensions in which space and time are negotiated throughout the transnational Cuban archipelago, and points to the need for a decolonizing methodology that unwinds the fantasy of insular singularity that persists from the colonial era on. As poets, authors, and essayists write islands, they work in two dimensions to create a space out of time; as they walk the streets of Havana or gather in New York, they work in three, connecting in real life as well as on the page. Be it in writing or in traversing islands, moreover, the poets, authors, and essayists whose work I analyze signal the array of perspectives implicit in the multifaceted cube or *cubo*, including the six-sided

"Rubik's Cuba" invoked by Cuban author Gustavo Pérez-Firmat in his poem "Bilingual Blues"; and the Cubist paintings of twentieth-century artists who sought to portray three dimensions in two, such as Cuban Wifredo Lam (1902–1982) or Spaniard Pablo Picasso (1881–1973).[4]

Endeavoring to reimagine the possibilities of space and time across the *arcubiélago*, I employ a decolonizing approach in my work. Following scholar Nelson Maldonado-Torres, "Decolonial thought tends to demonstrate the importance of interstitial spaces, edges, borders, diasporas, migrations, archipelagos, ancestral territorial relations, and connections of peoples through spaces and times that resist incorporation into a continentalist geopolitical imaginary [. . .]."[5] More specifically, my approach stems from the work of scholars in the nascent, interdisciplinary field of Archipelago Studies. With its origins in the Italian "*arci*-chief, principal" and "*pélago* deep, abyss, gulf, pool," the term *arcipelago* first appeared in print in a 1268 treaty between the Venetians and the Byzantine Emperor Michael Palaeologus: "Item, quod pertinet ad insulas de Arcipelago" [Also, as regards the islands of Archipelago].[6] As its etymology makes clear, the term is thus tied to the long history of European colonialism. Indeed, following scholar Yolanda Martínez-San Miguel, archipelagos remind us of the need for the decolonizing methodology referenced above, as they may be construed, historically, as "grupos de islas, puertos, ciudades y lugares en los que se articulan formas de poder colonial/imperial sobre zonas que ostentan discontinuidad territorial" [groups of islands, ports, cities and places in which colonial/imperial forms of power are articulated over zones that hold territorial discontinuity].[7] The transnational Cuban archipelago that I describe here is no exception, and, as I will show in the chapters that follow, the legacy of Cuba's colonial history (and postcolonial present) reverberates through works published in the 1990s and 2000s.

Recognizing the need to rethink the longstanding colonialist dichotomies that privilege continents over islands, land over sea, and singularity over plurality, I join scholars in Archipelago Studies who endeavor to destabilize oft-held assumptions about the relationship of (smaller) islands to (larger) continents, and of terra firma to salty seawaters. What might it mean, for instance, to think of islands as interconnected rather than isolated? What are the implications of contemplating waterways as intrinsic parts of a larger whole? Asking questions such as these, scholars in Archipelago Studies employ a range of disciplinary perspectives in their work. For instance, in Yolanda Martínez-San Miguel and Michelle Ann Stephens's recent edited volume, *Contemporary Archipelagic*

Thinking: Towards New Comparative Methodologies and Disciplinary Formations, South Asian literature professor Anjali Nerlekar discusses archipelagos in the context of the Indo-Caribbean; geography scholar Jenny R. Isaacs uses the trope of the archipelago in her study of shorebirds' migration along the Atlantic Flyway; and ethnomusicology professor Jessica Swanston Baker analyzes "archipelagic listening" in the Caribbean.[8] Considered in concert, these and other scholars in Archipelago Studies aim, in the words of geographer Elaine Stratford et al., "to understand how this 'world of islands' (Baldacchino 2007) might be experienced in terms of networks, assemblages, filaments, connective tissue, mobilities and multiplicities."[9]

While scholars in Archipelago Studies work in a variety of locales, the Caribbean has long been a fecund site for theorizing islands and archipelagos. Scholars Brian Russell Roberts and Michelle Ann Stephens signal the importance of the region in this regard, noting, for instance, that as early as the 1950s, "Trinidadian intellectual C.L.R. James was advocating for the federation of the British West Indies around the principle that they too functioned culturally as one interrelated unit."[10] The Caribbean has also been fertile ground for decolonizing projects more generally. As Maldonado-Torres writes, "With the longest history of exposure to modern Western colonialism and the longest history of opposition to it [. . .] it should not be surprising that the Caribbean counts with some of the most important and influential voices in the decolonial turn [. . .]."[11]

Cuba in particular has been described in a multitude of ways that draw attention to the connections between its often far-flung spaces and peoples, and I build on this scholarship in the pages that follow. Iván de la Nuez reminds readers that Cuban anthropologist Fernando Ortiz described Cubans as "aves de paso" [migratory birds],[12] and that other terms used to demarcate the space of Cuban culture have included "palimpsestos" [palimpsests], as well as "el éxodo, [. . .] el trasiego, o el viaje" [the exodus, [. . .] the movement, or the trip].[13] In all these instances, writes de la Nuez, there is a recognition of a refiguring of space and identity, as "Se ha perdido el centro" [The center has been lost].[14] Here, as in the transnational Cuban archipelago, or the *arcubiélago*, the nominal center no longer holds.

In my research, I consider how Cuban poets, novelists, and essayists inaugurate new, archipelagic spaces of identity for interconnected communities of readers in the 1990s and 2000s, and I analyze how these spaces function both materially (*in situ*) and metaphorically (in poems, novels, blogs, and songs).[15] It is of course true that all cartographies of material formations are themselves metaphoric constructions: human minds create, and human hands draw, the lines that divide waters into seas, and land into nations.[16] I use the term *materially*, though, both to acknowledge that Cuba is considered an archipelago, as defined by geographers, and to analyze the ways in which the writers and artists whose work I analyze create interconnected spaces on (or, in some instances, above) the ground in the 1990s and 2000s. I use the term *metaphorically*, by extension, to signal the ways in which writers also create a parallel series of interconnected spaces in their work.

In detailing how Cuban writers and artists underscore what might be described, following Stratford et al., as the "mobilities and multiplicities"[17] of islands and waterways, poetry and prose, I draw as well on Martinican writer Édouard Glissant's cogent theorization of what he terms the poetics of Relation. As Glissant writes:

> What took place in the Caribbean [. . .] approximates the idea of Relation for us as nearly as possible. [. . .] a new and original dimension allowing each person to be there and elsewhere, rooted and open, lost in the mountains and free beneath the sea, in harmony and in errantry.[18]

For Glissant, Relation allows individuals to be in more than one place simultaneously, as they inhabit both land and sea. More generally, as is true as well of the archipelago, Relation eschews the *rooted*, with the focus on origins that this implies; and embraces instead the *rhizomatic*, which foregrounds decentered interconnections.[19] Relation also allows (and is predicated on) *errantry*, which, in contrast to what Glissant describes as the "arrowlike nomadism" of conquest and colonization, connotes a decolonizing interdependence with others.[20]

Living in Havana and Jaruco as well as Madrid and Miami, the writers I study in this book create a transnational, archipelagic space that offers a glimpse of the possibilities of the poetics of Relation. Some of the authors whose work I analyze are well known, and, as such, the islands they write into existence might be considered mainlands (or mainstays) of the *arcubiélago*:[21] Reina María Rodríguez, Antonio José Ponte, and Zoé Valdés have each received multiple awards, honors, and recognition for their work, and are well known throughout the transnational Cuban archipelago. Others whose work I analyze are less known, and the islands they write might be considered to be emerging formations of the *arcubiélago*: Ramón Hondal, Ricardo Alberto Pérez, and the Grupo de Palenque are key voices of their generations but have received less critical attention to date. While some islands thus receive more ink than others, all are equally important, as, following Glissant, "With archipelagic thought, we know the rivers' rocks, without a doubt even the smallest ones . . ."[22] In contradistinction to continental thought, archipelagic thinking such as that in which I engage here emphasizes the importance of tiny rocks that tumble along rivers alongside the landmasses visible from airplanes.

. . .

As they write islands, the authors I examine create a transnational constellation of spaces that are simultaneously one and many: the *arcubiélago*. This space exists both materially and metaphorically, even as its contours are constantly shifting in time and space, and extends rhizomatically to surpass the bounds of any one island or nation.

I collected material for this book between 2013 and 2020, visiting Cuba seven times to conduct research in person. Many of the texts that I studied are ephemeral, housed on websites that might disappear, or available only in used bookshops or private collections due to limited print runs. In addition, books published by Cuban presses are often only readily available in Cuba (and are often not available at all in the United States, due to the longstanding embargo). As such, I have relied here on what scholar Shalini Puri terms "literary fieldwork," both to locate important literary artifacts and to acquire what Puri describes as "knowledge and expression unavailable in print."[23] In addition to conducting literary fieldwork in Cuba as I researched and wrote the book, I was fortunate to be able to meet with the writers whose work I studied in Barcelona and Madrid, as well as in Newark, New Jersey; New York City; and Philadelphia.

The texts that I study date primarily from 1995 to 2014, and, as such, center on the key years of transition preceding (yet often overshadowed by) U.S. President Barack Obama's 2014 announcement of renewed U.S.-Cuban relations. Written during a time of sea change for Cuba, the texts that I examined span the middle years of the Período especial en tiempos de paz [Special Period in Times of Peace], an epoch of severe economic depression in Cuba that followed the 1989 collapse of the Soviet Union. They span as well the first years of Raúl Castro's formal leadership, after he assumed the presidency long occupied by his brother Fidel in 2008. I should note, however, that these bookends are not exact: as is true of the constituent islands, islets, and keys of the archipelago, which shift and morph depending on the whims of sea and sand, the texts and cultures that I discuss here have moved in time and space as I have written this book. Texts that I first analyzed in manuscript form (such as Ramón Hondal's *Scratch*, analyzed in chapter 3), for example, are now published in print and thus date from after 2014. The November 2016 election of U.S. President Donald Trump, the death that same month of Fidel Castro, and the April 2018 election of Cuban President Miguel Díaz-Canel have also all resulted in changes in policy and cultural programming that are unavoidable referents as I finish this book (and as you read it). This is equally true of decolonizing projects more generally: as archipelagos shift, so too do decolonial histories, which acknowledge the possibility of movement and the reality of impermanence.

In the chapters that follow, I theorize how Cuban authors, poets, and essayists write islands into existence in their work; and I analyze how texts travel between and among the constituent islands of the *arcubiélago*, be it through state-sponsored events such as the annual Feria del Libro [Book Fair] or more clandestine means. The Feria represents a fecund exchange of ideas both on the page and on the ground, yet this is only part of how identities are negotiated between and among the constituent islands of the *arcubiélago*. At times, as occurs with the gatherings of poet Reina María Rodríguez, books from private collections are passed from one person to another, as writers reference what they are reading in a bid to establish transnational ties. At times, as occurs with the blog "Del Palenque . . . y para . . ." ["From the Runaway Slave Settlement . . . for/toward . . ."], favorite pieces are posted online, then photocopied (or downloaded to a USB) for those who do not have Internet access, as Cuban writers living in Europe endeavor to forge and retain ties with friends in Latin America and elsewhere. In each instance, the lines that nominally separate one space from another are blurred, as writers forgo the solitude more traditionally associated with the island to forge more interconnected, archipelagic spaces with (and for) a transnational readership.

Chapter 1, "Islands and Archipelagos," establishes the theoretical framework for the project and situates the works that I analyze culturally and sociohistorically. Here I offer a succinct summary of recent events in Cuban history and I detail how space has long been considered central to the identity of Cuba, a nation whose population is often seen as sharply divided along political and geographical lines. Here, too, I provide an overview of existing research on Cuba as island and diaspora and theorize the archipelago as a critical term that I use both materially and metaphorically in my project.

Each of the remaining chapters is designed to build on the next and to illuminate another island in the *arcubiélago*. In chapter 2, "Birds of a Feather," I explore how Cuban poet Reina María Rodríguez crafts an archipelagic space in which like-minded readers and writers might gather. Rodríguez is an award-winning poet who is known not only for her written work, but also for the gatherings she long hosted in Havana for fellow writers and artists. In her gatherings, I suggest, Rodríguez creates an archipelagic space for a public residing in Havana. Outside the Cuban capital, the territory that Rodríguez claims for her archipelagic out-croppings can also be found in the references and rhythms of her prose poem . . . *te daré de comer como a los pájaros* . . . [*I Will Give You to Eat as to the Birds*] (2000), or in the poetry collected in her anthology *Bosque negro* [*Black Forest*] (2013). This text-based, poetic archipelago, I argue, is open to all like-minded in-dividuals—all birds of a feather—whether they live on the island or in the larger, transnational archipelago that Rodríguez evokes and envisions.

Chapter 3, "Artistic Collaborations from Jaruco to Habana," shows how poets Ricardo Alberto Pérez and Ramón Hondal collaborate with artists to commu-nicate with a wider, archipelagic public. Pérez's *¿Para qué el cine?* [*For What Purpose Cinema?*] (2010), for instance, is a collaborative venture with artist Ezequiel Suárez that offers readers two texts within one, with underlined words in each poem offering a second possible reading. Hondal's *Scratch* (2018), addi-tionally, signals the importance of music in forging transnational, archipelagic ties, while his collaboration with artist Léster Álvarez highlights the myriad ways in which books do (and do not) circulate throughout the *arcubiélago*. Mixing media in these ways, I contend that Pérez and Hondal demonstrate the ongoing need for what I describe in chapter 2 as the archipelagic space envis-aged by Rodríguez.

In chapter 4, "Blogging on (and Beyond) the Palenque," I continue the dis-cussion of how Cuban poets craft alternate spaces of identities for themselves and their readers through an analysis of the blog "Del Palenque . . . y para . . . ," active from 2007 to 2014. In this blog, the Afro-Cuban poets associated with the "Palenque" group craft a space that supersedes racial categorizations at the same time that it underscores their existence. The difficulties of navigating race and identity in Cuba are highlighted not only in the blog, but also in the controversy that resulted from the publication of Palenque poet Roberto Zurbano's polemic 2013 *New York Times* op-ed, "For Blacks in Cuba, the Revolution Has Not Yet Begun." I juxtapose the blog alongside the firestorm that followed Zurbano's op-ed to signal the depths of the troubled waters that surround race in a nation that has long maintained its color-blindness; and I trace the ties between the virtual Palenque and physical spaces such as book fairs and parties, where poets gather in Havana to celebrate their birthdays.

Chapter 5, "Rankling José Martí," turns to the consideration of exiled writer Antonio José Ponte's essays on José Martí. Ponte, who has lived in Madrid since 2007, is known for his lucid nonfiction, as well as his short stories, novels, and poetry. While Ponte is associated with the space of exile, I read the author's work through an archipelagic lens to signal the connections between the myriad spaces of the *arcubiélago* from the nineteenth century to the present. Analyzing Ponte's essays on José Martí alongside his work on ruins, I argue that the writer seeks to create a wider, archipelagic space in his writing. For example, when Ponte reappropriates Cuba's national hero José Martí in his well-known essay titled "El abrigo de aire" ["The Coat of Air"] (2003), he suggests that the space of the Revolution is not closed and static, but, rather, that it must be rankled and remapped to remain relevant.

Chapter 6, "Timeless Rhetoric, Special Circumstances," takes a step back in time to consider the early work of exiled author Zoé Valdés. Through a critical discussion of the novels *La nada cotidiana* [*Yocandra in the Paradise of Nada*] (1995) and *Te di la vida entera* [*I Gave You All I Had*] (1996), I argue that Valdés offers a trenchant critique of the Castro regime for readers in countries such as France, Spain, and the United States while also seeking to establish an alternate, archipelagic space of identity through her use of a rhetoric of timelessness. The continuing need for such a space, as well as the difficulties in any such project, is underscored in Valdés's *El todo cotidiano* [*The Daily Everything*] (2010), which I consider in the last section of the chapter.

The conclusion closes the book with a brief discussion of developments throughout the *arcubiélago* in the years between 2014, when Obama made the historic announcement of renewed U.S.-Cuban relations, and 2020, when the global COVID-19 pandemic upended the world as we knew it. Here I discuss how Jorge Enrique Lage's *Archivo* [*Archive*] (2015) emblematizes the changes of these years, and I detail as well the ripples that followed the February 2021 release of the rap video "Patria y vida" ["Homeland and Life"].

1

Islands and Archipelagos

Each year, Cuba's capital city of Havana hosts the international Feria del Libro. This book fair is part scholarly conference and part carnival, and typically draws thousands of attendees.[1] In February 2016, I attended the Feria for the first time, after hearing about it for years. I was staying in a *casa particular* [in-home inn] in the Vedado neighborhood of the city, an area known for its stately homes and lush greenery, and much of the Feria was being held in the Morro, a colonial-era fortress (and now tourist attraction) located on a small island just off the coast of Havana.[2] Since it was too far to walk, I took a taxi down Calle 23, along the Malecón (a seaside promenade that circles Havana), and through the tunnel that leads to the Morro. After my taxi driver dropped me off at the bottom of a small hill, I walked past tents selling snacks, drinks, and toys to reach the gates to the Morro.

As I entered the Feria, I was struck by the number of people in attendance, and by the range of offerings: books were sold alongside art and school supplies, and restaurants offered food and drinks. (See Figure 1.) Young couples strolled along, hand in hand, perhaps planning to stay for one of the concerts offered in the evening. Academics and avid readers attended book talks and browsed in the stalls of national and international publishers. With small children in tow, parents searched for coloring books or merchandise emblazoned with Disney princesses. Cuban poet Ramón Hondal would later tell me that no one came to the Feria for the books, but books—or at least books published by Cuban presses—were reasonably priced, and I often had to wait in line to complete my purchases.

Dating to 1937, the Feria begins in Havana, then travels (albeit in a smaller form) throughout Cuba. At the Feria, an international group of writers gathers to read their work and exchange ideas; and readers and editors from across the globe attend literary and cultural events, browse bookstalls, and rub elbows with

Figure 1. Havana's annual Feria del Libro (Book Fair). Photo by author.

the literati.[3] Each year, furthermore, the Feria showcases the culture of a different "país invitado de honor" [invited country of honor]: recent "invitados," for example, have included Brazil (2005), Venezuela (2006), and Argentina (2007), as well as Angola (2013), Ecuador (2014), and Uruguay (2016).[4]

The Feria represents but one instance of how texts circulate in Cuba, and, as is true of all the spaces I discuss in the pages that follow, it is complex and far from utopian. The circulation of texts in Cuba is often tightly controlled by the government—there is no Amazon or Barnes and Noble, for instance, and private printing presses are not allowed—and while some books are readily available each year at the state-sponsored Feria, others are released in extremely limited quantities, and yet others (such as those written by exiled author Zoé Valdés) are rarely available at all.

Nonetheless, this internationally recognized book fair in many ways emblematizes the connections between the spaces of the *arcubiélago*, or the transnational Cuban archipelago. Cuba is often considered an island, and yet—as my trip to the Feria made clear—it is in fact an archipelago that comprises some 1,600 islands, islets, and keys.[5] The largest island (called "Cuba") is the best known, but the Isla de la Juventud located to its south is home to some 100,000 people, and the Morro is considered an integral part of Cuban history and culture. You can see the Morro from Havana, and Havana from the Morro; and the water separating the two islands often splashes up along the Malecón, as though to suggest that the divisions between land and water, as well as between one island and another, are largely arbitrary.

In this chapter, I theorize about islands and archipelagos and provide an overview of recent Cuban history. Cuba is frequently construed as isolated and isolationist due to its geography and history, despite the fact that it has been connected to the continents by cultural and commercial exchanges since at least 1492, when Christopher Columbus took possession for Spain.[6] Drawing on the recent decolonizing research of scholars working in Archipelago Studies, as well as on the foundational work of Édouard Glissant on the poetics of Relation, I seek to reconnect the spaces of Cuban island(s), as well as the waterways between, to underscore the longstanding transnational ties of the *arcubiélago*.

Archipelagic Assemblages

Although it may seem like a truism, it bears noting from the start that the island has long been considered key to Cuba's identity, even as this space has been contested and reconfigured in various ways over time. Indeed, it remains common for people to refer to Cuba as "la isla" [the island] in everyday conversation, and for scholars to write of Cuba in the singular in their work, despite widespread recognition of this nation's archipelagic geography. (See Figure 2.) For, as professor Oscar Rodríguez Díaz states in *Compendio insular: Islas del mundo* [*Insular Compendium: Islands of the World*], Cuba is not only an archipelagic nation, but also forms part of the wider Caribbean archipelago known as the Antillas Mayores, or the Greater Antilles, which comprises Cuba, Hispaniola (the Dominican Republic and Haiti), Jamaica, and Puerto Rico. He describes the Cuban archipelago:

> Archipiélago perteneciente a las *Antillas Mayores*, ubicado en el océano Atlántico, entre las dos Américas y a la entrada del golfo de México. Está conformado por más de 1 600 islas, cayos e islotes formados en cuatro grupos insulares adyacentes a la isla mayor (*Cuba*), la cual se reparte 95,5% de toda la superficie emergida (105 006 km²). Le siguen en importancia

la *Isla de la Juventud* (2 204 km²) y los cayos Romano (777 km²) y Coco (370 km²).

[Archipelago belonging to the *Greater Antilles*, located in the Atlantic Ocean, between the two Americas and at the entrance of the Gulf of Mexico. It is composed of more than 1,600 islands, keys, and islets formed in four insular groups adjacent to the largest island (*Cuba*), which occupies 95.5% of the emerged surface (105,006 km²). Following in importance are the *Isla de la Juventud* (2,204 km²) and the Romano (777 km²) and Coco (370 km²) keys.][7]

A nation of islands within the Greater Antilles, Cuba is thus construed by mapmakers as an archipelago twice over: an archipelago, that is, within an archipelago.

Cuban writer Virgilio Piñera's 1943 poem "La isla en peso" ["The Weight of the Island"] is often invoked as articulating the difficulties of what is described in

Figure 2. A Havana mural proclaiming an individual's love for a singular *isla*, or island. Photo by author.

the poem's opening line as "La maldita circunstancia del agua por todas partes" [The cursed condition of water on all sides]. Confined to a space in which "el agua me rodea como un cáncer" [water surrounds me like cancer], the space of the island is for Piñera a space of postlapsarian loss:

> Una taza de café no puede alejar mi idea fija,
> en otro tiempo yo vivía adánicamente.
> ¿Qué trajo la metamorfosis?
>
> La eterna miseria que es el acto de recordar.
> Si tú pudieras formar de nuevo aquellas combinaciones,
> devolviéndome el país sin el agua,
> me la bebería toda para escupir al cielo.
>
> [A cup of coffee will not erase my fixation,
> in other times I lived like Adam.
> What brought about the transformation?
>
> The eternal misery of the act of remembering.
> If you could shape again those combinations,
> giving me back the country without the water,
> I would drink it all to spit at the sky.][8]

Inhabiting this *isla en peso* rather than the Eden of yore, Piñera suggests at one point that drastic action is necessary:

> Hay que saltar del lecho y buscar la vena mayor del mar para desangrarlo.
> Me he puesto a pescar esponjas frenéticamente,
> esos seres milagrosos que pueden desalojar hasta la última gota de agua
> y vivir secamente.
>
> [You must jump out of bed and seek the major vein to bleed out the sea.
> Frantically I fish for sponges,
> those miraculous creatures that can soak up the last drop of water
> and live dryly.][9]

In offering the radical proposal of bleeding the sea dry as a means of escaping the *peso* of the island, Piñera describes the island's identity as doubly (and problematically) insular: "of or relating to an island or islands," the *isla en peso* is at the same time also "standing alone; detached; isolated."[10]

Such portrayals of Cuba as an isolated *isla en peso* hearken back to a long-standing colonialist discourse on islands. In colonialist discourse, islands are, as scholar Elizabeth DeLoughrey writes, "simultaneously positioned as isolated yet deeply susceptible to migration and settlement."[11] On the one hand, islands are adrift in wide-open seas; on the other, they are ripe for settlement. In the present as well, islands are frequently associated with both isolation and mobility. Consider, for instance, the stock cartoon image of a shipwrecked man, gazing out to sea as he stands beneath a lone palm tree. It is the island that condemns him to solitary confinement, yet this solitary confinement would not have been possible without the mobility that brought him to its shores (and that might one day carry him away again).

More broadly, such depictions of Cuba as a singular island—an isolated *isla* rather than an archipelagic constellation of landmasses and waterways—contribute to the postulation of identities that are binary rather than plural, and to the envisioning of spaces that either stand out for their singularity or, conversely, shrink into the background in comparison with larger continents. As analyzed by geographer Elaine Stratford et al., such characterizations result in a limiting optic, but are nonetheless frequently employed in extant scholarship in island studies, eliding other possibilities:

> What remains largely absent or silent are ways of being, knowing, and doing—ontologies, epistemologies, and methods—that illuminate island spaces as inter-related, mutually constituted, and co-constructed: as island and island.[12]

Arguing that such outdated and inaccurate models of insularity must be revised to better account for the reality of more fluid relations between islands and continents, scholars in Archipelago Studies employ an interdisciplinary, decolonizing approach to rethinking space and identity. As such, they aim to address the limitations of established hermeneutical frameworks through inter-island comparisons, and to "move beyond restrictive national, colonial, and regional frameworks"[13] to engage in the practice of what DeLoughrey terms "archipelagraphy": "a historiography that considers chains of islands in fluctuating relationship to their surrounding seas, islands and continents."[14]

Underscoring interconnectivity and multiplicity, an archipelagic approach gestures toward the need for a decolonizing methodology that seeks to uncover what Aníbal Quijano terms the "coloniality of power." As Quijano demonstrates, globalization remains rooted in colonialism: "the culmination of a process that began with the constitution of America and colonial/modern Eurocentered capitalism as a new global power. [. . .] the model of power that is globally hegemonic today presupposes an element of coloniality."[15] Employing a decolonizing methodology that centers on the interconnections of islands and waterways, I follow writer and anthropology professor Epeli Hau'ofa, who proposes in his seminal essay "Our Sea of Islands" that the Pacific be rethought as "'a sea of islands'" rather than "'islands in a far sea.'"[16] As occurs as well in the *arcubiélago*, such a reconceptualization more accurately depicts a space that is interconnected and replete with sea as well as land, replacing the previous (and mistaken) notion that islands are tiny and isolated.

The history of Cuba as an *isla* is thus both specific and general, given its long history of colonialism and imperial nationalism.[17] As Dara Goldman details in her study of Cuba, the Dominican Republic, and Puerto Rico, for instance, the conflation of nation and (singular) island is not unique to Cuba, but is true of the Hispanic Caribbean more generally. Even though the bounds of the nation are increasingly recognized as more fluid and porous than such characterizations would suggest, Goldman writes, the island continues to be used as a marker of national identity in the Hispanic Caribbean and its literary and cultural production.[18] More generally, as DeLoughrey reminds us, the imagery of the island is often yoked to the depiction of tropical, "exotic" locales, be it in a bid to promote tourism or in an attempt to gain geopolitical leverage: "Although islands are scattered all over the globe, the spaces that signify as islands are generally the small landmasses close to the equator, lands associated with tropical fertility, former colonies and outposts of empire that are deemed remote, exotic, and isolated by their continental visitors." Even though the continents are also surrounded by water, Cuba's status as a former and "fertil[e]" colony—not to mention a strategic imperial "outpost"—associates it with the hallmarks of Caribbean island identity in the popular imaginary.[19]

Emphasizing the significance of the archipelago as a shifting whole that is larger than the sum of its parts, the archipelagic framework that I employ foregrounds the oft-elided connections between individuals and spaces, in recognition of the limitations of binary oppositions between (small) islands and (large) continents, as well as between those on and off *la isla*. In this regard, I point to the archipelago as a constellation-like assemblage.[20] To quote Stratford et al. once more:

The significance of the assemblage is ontogenic: it is not simply a gathering, a collection, a composition of things that are believed to fit together.

Assemblages act in concert: they actively map out, select, piece together, and allow for the conception and conduct of individual units as members of a group.[21]

With islands grouped "*in concert*," the transnational Cuban archipelago reaches from Havana to Jaruco, and from Miami to Madrid. Like the Big Dipper or Orion, the *arcubiélago* can be considered an assemblage, with constituent components that exist both individually (as do the stars in the sky) and together (as do the constellations), shifting, in both instances, according to the perspective of the observer.

Analyzing how writers and artists negotiate the *arcubiélago* in the 1990s and 2000s, I draw not only on the seminal, interdisciplinary work of scholars in Archipelago Studies, but also on Martinican writer Édouard Glissant's theorization of what he terms the poetics of Relation. This concept refers, in brief, to the interconnections and interrelations exemplified in the archipelago, and is foundational to Archipelago Studies.[22] In explaining the idea of the poetics of Relation, Glissant acknowledges his debt, in turn, to theorists Gilles Deleuze and Felix Guattari, and reminds readers of the distinction that these theorists establish between the *rooted* and the *rhizomatic*. That which is rooted, Glissant writes, is singular and single-minded, existing for itself and itself alone. That which is rhizomatic is, in contrast, multiple and interconnected: "an enmeshed root system, a network spreading either in the ground or in the air, with no predatory rootstock taking over permanently." For Glissant, the poetics of Relation is rhizomatic, for here "each and every identity is extended through a relation with the Other."[23]

If the Relation that Glissant theorizes is rhizomatic, implying an interconnected, enmeshed network, it is also important to note that it is tied to what the Martinican writer describes as *errantry*. Errantry, for Glissant, is possible when there is no longer a singular root, but, rather, an understanding of identity as relative, and as in relation to others: "the thought of errantry is also the thought of what is relative, the thing relayed as well as the thing related. [. . .] The tale of errantry is the tale of Relation."[24] Errantry stands in contradistinction to what Glissant describes as the "arrowlike nomadism"[25] of the era of conquest and colonization, and implies a wandering of sorts that, in turn, is related to the destructuring of national entities and the multilingualism that accompanies the lack of a singular tongue.[26]

In Relation, as in the *arcubiélago*, there is no longer a center or a periphery, as space is reconceptualized as rhizomatic and interconnected, rather than rooted and singular. This is manifest not only in the ways in which Cuban writers craft and negotiate spaces of identity in their work, but is also apparent, more broadly, in the ways in which they inhabit and create space in the world. Generating archipelagic, interconnected spaces that function both materially and metaphorically, Cuban writers draw on the poetics of Relation and, in so doing, emblematize the *errantry*, the wandering and multiplicity, with which it is associated. As such, the writers whose work I analyze here reject what Glissant terms filiation, or the "hidden cause (the consequence) of both Myth and Epic" in the Western World. Rather than adhering to the linear timeline associated with filiation, with "its work setting out upon the fixed linearity of time, always toward a projection, a project,"[27] Cuban writers embrace instead the rhizomatic interconnections of the archipelagic, often appealing to a space out of time with no set chronology rather than projecting their work forward toward a fixed future destination.

The archipelagic, rhizomatic approach that I employ builds on scholar Antonio Benítez-Rojo's postulation of the "isla que se repite" [repeating island] in his well-known book of this title, at the same time that it departs from its rhetoric of singularity. For Benítez-Rojo, the Caribbean is a "meta-archipelago":

> the Antilles are an island bridge connecting, "in another way," North and South America. This geographical accident gives the entire area, including its continental foci, the character of an archipelago, that is, a discontinuous conjunction (of what?): unstable condensations, turbulences, whirlpools, clumps of bubbles, frayed seaweed, sunken galleons, crashing breakers, flying fish, seagull squawks, downpours, nighttime phosphorescences, eddies and pools, uncertain voyages of signification.[28]

Publishing his book in 1992, the quincentenary of Columbus's arrival to the so-called New World, Benítez-Rojo's idea of the "meta-archipelago" is foundational, at the same time that it suggests a series of repetitions that discount the variations within and among islands and waterways.[29] As Stratford et al. pithily note, "Thus 'repeated islands' and archipelagos are not the same thing."[30] Making a similar point, scholar Jonathan Pugh also critiques the idea of the "isla que se repite," writing that "Too easily it suggests shared island experiences repeating across the chain. [. . .] The real force of the Caribbean island archipelago movement is a metamorphosis that emphasises invention and creation." In contradistinction to "la isla que se repite," repetition is replaced by novelty in the *arcubiélago*, with a shift in focus and intent to what Pugh variously describes as "movement," "metamorphosis," and "invention and creation."[31]

Foregrounding the rhizomatic, archipelagic interconnections of identities that are far from rooted, my approach overlaps with those of scholars working in Diaspora and Exile Studies, at the same time that it departs from central precepts of these fields. As emblematized in professor Yomaira C. Figueroa-Vásquez's *Decolonizing Diasporas: Radical Mappings of Afro-Atlantic Literature*, there are undoubtedly significant convergences between Archipelago Studies, Diaspora Studies, and Exile Studies. Employing a decolonizing approach, Figueroa-Vásquez convincingly maps the ties between Equatorial Guinea, Puerto Rico, the Dominican Republic, and Cuba to reveal the "Afro-Atlantic Hispanophone diaspora as a palimpsest, as an archive of overlapping histories and incommensurable differences."[32] Her work reveals the palimpsestuous and at times archival ties between a transnational constellation of authors, and her methodology to some degree coincides with that which I employ in this book, particularly in the analysis of the Afro-Cuban poets who belong to the "Grupo del Palenque" [Palenque Group].[33]

While there are significant convergences between Diaspora, Exile, and Archipelago Studies, an archipelagic framework is better suited to foregrounding the rhizomatic interconnections of a whole that is considered larger than its parts. An archipelagic framework emphasizes the *rhizomatic*; a diaspora- or exile-based framework centers on the *roots* of an originating home or homeland. This emphasis is manifest in the standard definitions of both terms, and ripples out into the fields of study to which they give their names. According to the Oxford English Dictionary, the term "diaspora" refers to "Any group of people who have spread or become dispersed beyond their traditional *homeland* or point of origin [. . .] the countries and places inhabited by such a group, regarded collectively," while the term "exile" is defined as a "Prolonged absence from one's native country or a place regarded as *home* [. . .]" or "Banishment to a foreign country, or [. . .] to a remote part of one's own country."[34] In the specific case of Cuba, many writers have indeed been exiled from the country they consider "home," and I use the terms exile and diaspora in acknowledgement of this fact and its repercussions. At the same time, the archipelagic methodology I employ marks a departure from an optic that privileges the search for origins, to emphasize instead the rhizomatic interconnectivity of the *arcubiélago*.[35]

In writing on the *arcubiélago*, I thereby join an interdisciplinary group of scholars who point to the shifting coordinates of space and time for land and sea alike, signaling the tenuous nature of national and transnational formations, as well as land and sea masses.[36] For, as is true of the sea, which washes away the sands and rearranges the shorelines, the ongoing negotiations of space and identity across the transnational Cuban archipelago point to the changing connections between individuals over time and across space.

Revolutionary Insularity

The texts I consider in *Writing Islands* date from the 1990s and 2000s, and as such follow the 1959 triumph of the Revolution by more than thirty years. Yet while pictures of Disney princesses may greet visitors to the Feria del Libro in the early 2000s, the *peso*, or weight, of 1959 remains heavy for writers across the *arcubiélago*. In this year, Fidel Castro and his comrades forced out longtime Cuban dictator Fulgencio Batista. Shortly thereafter, the United States, concerned about the existence of a socialist-communist state so close to its southern border, imposed an economic embargo on the nation that crippled Cuba's economy for the next sixty years. The ongoing *peso* of 1959—and the rhetoric of Revolutionary insularity employed by a government seeking to break from the colonial and neocolonial past—is evident today in the seemingly ubiquitous Revolutionary slogans and murals in Havana, as well as in the ongoing importance afforded to patriotic figures such as Ernesto "el Che" Guevara, Fidel Castro's Revolutionary comrade, and José Martí, the nineteenth-century patriot portrayed as a forerunner of his twentieth-century counterparts.

The rhetoric of Revolutionary insularity is manifest not only in Cuban murals and monuments, but also in Fidel Castro's 1961 "Palabras a los intelectuales" ["Words to the Intellectuals"]: a well-known and oft-quoted speech, delivered at a meeting with writers and artists held at the Biblioteca Nacional José Martí [José Martí National Library].[37] Stating that the Revolution was to be the principal concern of all citizens, Castro emphasized in his "Palabras" the importance of crafting a new identity for the nation:

> Nosotros señalamos que el estado de ánimo de todos los ciudadanos del país y que el estado de ánimo de todos los escritores y artistas revolucionarios, o de todos los escritores y artistas que comprenden y justifican a la Revolución, es qué peligros puedan amenazar a la Revolución y qué podemos hacer por ayudar a la Revolución.

> [We signal that the mindset of all the citizens of the country and the mindset of all the revolutionary writers and artists, or all the writers and artists who understand and justify the Revolution, is: what dangers might threaten the Revolution and what can we do to help the Revolution.][38]

Lest this seem unnecessarily limiting, Castro assured the assembled writers and artists that there was no need to worry about artistic freedoms or liberties, as "all" would be permitted, provided it was "within" the Revolution:

> Esto significa que dentro de la Revolución, todo; contra la Revolución, nada. Contra la Revolución nada, porque la Revolución tiene también sus derechos; y el primer derecho de la Revolución es el derecho a existir.

> [This means that within the Revolution, everything; against the Revolution, nothing. Against the Revolution, nothing, because the Revolution also has its rights; and the first right of the Revolution is the right to exist.][39]

"Within" the space of the Revolution, all was to be allowed; there could be nothing permitted, however, "against" it. The potential contours of what Castro vaguely articulated as "dentro" [within] and "contra" [against] the Revolution in his 1961 "Palabras" were somewhat clarified a decade later, with the 1971 "Caso Padilla" [Padilla Affair]. The "Caso" began in 1968 when the Unión de Escritores y Artistas Cubanos (UNEAC) awarded poet Heberto Padilla a prize for a collection of poems titled *Fuera del juego [Out of the Game]*; the book was published with a disclaimer by UNEAC leadership. Some years later, in 1971, Padilla was imprisoned after giving poetry readings that were deemed counterrevolutionary. Released after a month in prison, Padilla was then forced to make a public confession of his supposed transgressions. "Fuera" [outside] the game was, it would seem, also "contra" [against] the Revolution, and as such impermissible.[40]

Castro's rhetoric of Revolutionary insularity in his "Palabras" is apparent not only in the binary opposition he establishes between "dentro" [within] and "contra" [against], but also in his two references to "la isla" in the speech. In the first reference, Castro mentions the Isla de Pinos (renamed the Isla de la Juventud in 1978):

> En cierta ocasión, cuando nosotros andábamos un poco peregrinando por todo el territorio nacional, se nos había ocurrido la idea de construir un barrio en un lugar muy hermoso de Isla de Pinos, una aldea en medio de los pinares—en ese tiempo estábamos pensando establecer algún tipo de premio para los mejores escritores y artistas progresistas del mundo—, [. . .] proyecto que no tomó cuerpo pero que puede ser revivido para hacer un reparto o una aldea, un remanso de paz que invite a descansar, que invite a escribir (APLAUSOS).

[On one occasion, when we were traipsing all around the national territory, the idea occurred to us of constructing a neighborhood in a very beautiful part of Isla de Pinos, a town in the midst of the pine trees— at that time we were thinking of establishing some type of prize for the best progressive writers and artists of the world—, [. . .] a project that was not realized but that can be revived to make a neighborhood or a town, a peaceful, quiet place that invites rest, that invites writing (APPLAUSE).][41]

To some extent, Castro's suggestion that the Isla de Pinos might serve as a retreat for writers and artists subordinates the (smaller) Isla de Pinos to the (larger) island of Cuba, and calls to mind the longstanding characterization of remote islands as isolated, paradisiacal sanctuaries for the weary and downtrodden. In referencing the Isla de Pinos, however, Castro also implicitly recognizes Cuba's archipelagic geography: the Isla de Pinos, as mentioned earlier, is Cuba's second-largest island, and is home to approximately 100,000 people.

Castro's second reference to *la isla* in his "Palabras" signals the importance of a single island, united, for a singular Revolution. Describing the accomplishments of the Revolution, Castro here states that "Se han organizado las escuelas, ya están funcionando, e imagínense cuando haya 1000 grupos de baile, de música y de teatro en *toda la isla*, [. . .] lo que eso significará en extensión cultural" [Schools have been organized, they are functioning, and imagine when there will be 1,000 dance, music, and theater groups in *all the island*, [. . .] what that will mean in cultural extension].[42] In referencing *la isla* in conjunction with this list of Revolutionary accomplishments, Castro in effect ties the Revolution to the island (both in the singular). Implying that one is synonymous with the other, he undercuts his earlier, implicit recognition of the nation's archipelagic geography—and, by extension, its multiplicity—in his reference to the Isla de Pinos, and emphasizes the unidirectionality of Cuban history, which moves ever onward to Revolutionary gains.

It might of course be argued that such references to Cuba as a singular island—an *isla* or an *isla en peso*—are functional rather than philosophical. The word "archipelago" is a mouthful, after all, and *la isla* might simply serve as a shorthand that allows speakers to refer more readily to a nation that comprises multiple islands. While this is undoubtedly true to some degree, such slippage between island and nation is nonetheless also representative of a portrayal of twentieth- and twenty-first-century Cuba as an isolated socialist enclave in a larger capitalist sea; and, additionally, as an island whose population is irrevocably fractured, divided across the chasm of straits and time. For while Fidel Castro implies in his "Palabras" that the Isla de Pinos is contained "within" the "territorio nacional" [national territory],[43] he long portrays Miami's "Little Havana" neighborhood—a metaphorical (and cultural) island of sorts—as a world apart, and those who opt to leave as traitorous exiles or "gusanos" [worms]. While this rhetoric changes in the 1990s, in offering such characterizations Castro recognizes the important and vexed history of Cuban migration only to establish those who leave as "contra" [against] the Revolution, as well as "fuera" [outside] the island with which it is often conflated.

Transnational Ties

Somewhat paradoxically, the characterization of Cuba as an isolated, insular island between 1959 and 1989 was propagated both by those in favor of the Revolution and by those against it, even as this stark portrayal was belied by Cuba's longstanding, and ongoing, transnationalism. This rhetoric shifts in the 1990s and 2000s, with the advent of the Special Period and the resulting changes in Cuban politics and practices.

The privileged position of the singular island holds steady in Cuba's Revolutionary imaginary of the 1960s, 1970s, and 1980s but changes in the 1990s. In this decade, professor Ottmar Ette writes, there is a burgeoning recognition of Cuba's multiplicity, and of what he describes as the many islands of the Cuban archipelago:

> la existencia de muchas y muy diversas islas (cubanas) en todo el mundo. [. . .] un proceso de comunicación intensificado a las distintas islas del archipiélago cubano—Cuba y Florida, España y México, Nueva York y París, e incluso cubanos de las Alemania oriental y occidental.

> [the existence of many and very diverse (Cuban) islands in the world. [. . .] a process of intensified communication to the distinct islands of the Cuban archipelago—Cuba and Florida, Spain and Mexico, New York and Paris, and even Cubans in East and West Germany.][44]

The depiction of Cuba as a small, precarious island destined to sink under its own weight (or, conversely, as a one-of-a-kind powerhouse capable of remaining afloat despite the odds) was due in no small measure to the embargo that the United States imposed on Cuba in 1961, following the unsuccessful Bay of Pigs invasion (known in Cuba as the Batalla de Girón). Yet even as the United States attempted to isolate Cuba economically and culturally, tourists continued to travel to Cuba from Europe, Latin America, and even the United States itself. During this period, furthermore, the Soviet Union offered the country critical economic support. As evidenced in many Cubans' Russian names (not to mention Havana's proliferation of Soviet-style architecture), the USSR profoundly influenced not only Cuban economics, but also Cuban culture. Those Cubans who left, moreover, forged new connections abroad even as they maintained their relationships with family and friends who remained.

Drawing new attention to the connections between "las distintas islas del ar-chipiélago cubano" [the distinct islands of the Cuban archipelago],[45] the Cuban government began to rethink its policies in the 1990s, when its economy underwent a dramatic downturn following the 1989 collapse of the Soviet Union. In 1990, Fidel Castro declared the advent of the Special Period, imposing a series of strict fiscal measures usually reserved for wartime and implementing a series of economic reforms to give new life to a sagging economy.[46] These changes, in turn, resulted in profound shifts in Cuban culture and society and contributed to a greater awareness of the archipelagic interconnections between geographically distant communities and spaces.

Contributing to a more archipelagic consciousness, the Cuban government began to actively promote transnational tourism in the 1990s in an attempt to gain access to much-needed revenue.[47] As the Castro regime turned to tourism to meet its sudden need for cash, furthermore, Cuban authors began to seek out publishers abroad in light of severe shortages at home, offering readers new access to their work through these non-nationalized releases. Glossy spreads in travel brochures and coffee-table books complemented these publications by providing easily accessible images of Cuba to would-be travelers, encouraging potential visitors (and readers) to delve deeper into *lo cubano*; the 1999 release of Wim Wenders's hugely successful documentary film *Buena Vista Social Club* again offered spectators iconic shots of *la isla* and its inhabitants.

The Cuban government also decided to implement a more mixed-market approach to the economy in the 1990s, allowing the privatization of some businesses. As a result, those who lived in the once-grand colonial-style homes for which Havana is known were able to open *casas particulares* [in-home inns]; those who had a knack for the culinary and a few extra seats they could place around a table could bill themselves as *paladares* [in-home restaurants], and thereby earn dollars or euros from hungry travelers. These policy changes benefited some, but not all, Cubans: the shifts in economic policy resulted in a needed influx of cash, but also led to greater economic disparities in a society that had long prided itself on its equality. These changes also marked a significant departure from previous policy. With the success of the Revolution, Fidel Castro had declared the end of the tourism that had largely fueled the economy under Batista. Associating tourism with precisely the capitalist abuses that he sought to eradicate in the name of a more egalitarian society, Castro emphasized instead the importance of education (through, for instance, his famous 1961 literacy campaign) at the same time that he sought to increase the nation's agricultural production in a bid to plant the seeds of a self-sufficient economy.[48]

With the upsurge in tourism in the 1990s, Cubans expanded their transnational networks as they forged and maintained relationships with visitors from Latin America, Europe, and the United States.[49] At the same time, the nation was, paradoxically, characterized once again as an isolated island in marketing materials and the popular imaginary. In a bid to encourage potential travelers to visit Cuba before it was too late, advertisements and articles highlighted what they portrayed as the need to act quickly to experience firsthand an island frozen in time. And indeed, this sense of urgency on the part of many potential travelers increased in 2014, with U.S. President Barack Obama's announcement of renewed U.S.-Cuban relations: a historic decision, albeit soon reversed by the subsequent Trump administration, that seemed to presage a new era of increased openness and accessibility.

Also contributing to a more archipelagic consciousness, Cubans who left *la isla* in the 1990s and 2000s relocated to an ever more diverse array of locales. Immediately following the Revolution, a first wave of exiles left Cuba in the late 1950s and early 1960s to escape what they feared would be the horrors of life in a socialist-communist state. These exiles, who were largely from the privileged upper classes of pre-Revolutionary Cuban society, relocated primarily to the United States (which then had an "open door" policy for Cubans), often settling in Miami.[50] In the 1990s and early 2000s, the majority of Cubans who left continued to relocate to the United States,[51] where they were able to remain on U.S. shores if they reached land due to the so-called wet foot/dry foot policy in place since the mid-1990s.[52] A significant number, however, opted to relocate to other countries. Following professor Iraida López:

In comparison with the United States, clusters of Cubans elsewhere seem small but not insignificant [in 2015]: there are roughly 90,000 in Spain, mostly in Madrid; 17,000 in Canada, especially in Toronto and Montreal; 9,000 in Germany, primarily in Berlin; 7,000 in France, above all in Paris; 3,000 in the United Kingdom, mainly in London; and about 20,000 in Venezuela.[53]

Those who had hesitated to leave for the United States, in particular, given fraught U.S.-Cuban relations, found opportunities to emigrate to "third countries" such as those detailed by López above.[54] At the same time, the Cuban government began to use less charged language to refer to those who left, opting for "the neutral term 'emigration' or 'the Cuban community abroad' in lieu of 'exiles'";[55] a notable departure from the divisive rhetoric long used to deride exiles as traitorous "gusanos" [worms].

Alongside these societal and cultural shifts that contributed to a growing archipelagic consciousness, Cuban writers began to publish for a more transnational public, both in print and online, in the 1990s and 2000s. The book had long occupied a privileged place in Revolutionary culture, but paper shortages during the Special Period contributed to falling publication numbers. As such, Cuban writers turned to established publishing houses abroad (in Spain and France, in particular) to release their work. Audiences throughout Europe and the Americas were thus able to read about Cuba in the fiction of writers—such as Antonio José Ponte and Zoé Valdés—whose work was seldom available in Cuba. In the 2000s, Cuban authors continued to publish their work with established publishing houses in Europe and the Americas, at the same time that they also turned to a slate of new presses founded in the early years of the new millennium. Forming what scholar Rafael Rojas terms a "mini-boom editorial de la diáspora cubana" [mini publishing boom of the Cuban diaspora],[56] these presses included Almenara and its imprint, Bokeh (founded in 2012 in Leiden, Netherlands); Hypermedia (founded in 2013 in Madrid); Casa Vacía (founded in 2016 in Richmond, Virginia); and Rialta Ediciones (founded in 2016 in Querétaro, Mexico). Publishing a wide range of titles, the presses of the "mini-boom" were inaugurated with an express commitment to publishing works by Cuban authors, regardless of their country of residence.

Online publications expanded significantly during the 1990s and early 2000s as well. Internet access remained largely limited in Cuba during these decades. Nonetheless, sites such as *La Habana Elegante* (www.habanaelegante.com;

launched in 1998), *Decir del agua* (www.decirdelagua.com; launched in 2002), and *Cubista Magazine* (www.cubistamag.com; launched in 2004) published the work of Cuban writers, again making it available to a wider audience.[57] As scholar (and *La Habana Elegante* editor) Francisco Morán writes of these publications, "Las revistas electrónicas contribuyen a desactivar los mapas al articular un cruce, una red de miradas que pasan, atraviesan la Isla [. . .] pero que también la perforan" [Online journals contribute to deactivating maps by articulating a crossing, a network of gazes that pass, and pass through, the Island [. . .] but that also perforate it].[58] Remapping the space of what Morán describes as Cuba.com, authors releasing their work online contributed to a greater awareness of the connections between the constituent islands of the *arcubiélago*.

Publishing their work in an increasingly varied assortment of venues in the 1990s and 2000s, Cuban writers thus forged new, interconnected spaces in their work. During the same years, shifts in migration patterns drew increased attention to longstanding transnational ties, leading to a more archipelagic consciousness. The spaces created by writers, at once singular and conjoined, together comprise the *arcubiélago* that is mapped, in part, in this book.

. . .

In detailing the rationale motivating a shift from a focus on the insular (or the island) to the archipelagic, Stratford et al. explain that:

> There is a need, then, to articulate new research agendas to explore alternative cultural geographies and alternate performances, representations and experiences of islands. Different relations need to be thought through, and established relations considered differently.[59]

The importance of employing a decolonizing, archipelagic approach to think through "different relations" in modern Cuban literature, and to consider "established relations" from new perspectives, was underscored during my 2017 research trip to Havana. In previous years, due to travel restrictions, I had booked a flight on a charter airline through one of the few U.S. companies authorized to do so. In 2017, with the changes in U.S. policy inaugurated under Obama, I was able to book my flight online through the American Airlines website from my home in New Jersey. On the day of travel, I showed my passport and visa to the ticket agent, received a "Cuba ready" stamp on my boarding pass, and climbed aboard the plane for a direct flight from Miami to Havana. Less than an hour later, I disembarked at the José Martí International Airport.

If Cuba is often portrayed as an isolated island, my 2017 flight highlighted its myriad transnational connections in the era of present-day globalization. The American Airlines flight arrived in the international terminal (rather than the smaller terminal reserved for U.S. charters), and when I entered the airport, I joined travelers from Europe and Latin America waiting to pass through customs.

In a reminder of the need for a decolonizing methodology in an era of increasing globalization, Cuban writer Roberto Zurbano also prodded me to recall the colonial and postcolonial history of oppression associated with the Morro during my 2017 trip. Designed by Italian Bautista Antonelli and constructed in 1589 with slave labor, the Morro is a colonial-era fortress that hosts many of the events of the annual Feria del Libro. The Morro was built to protect Havana's harbor but also served as a prison. Dissident writer Reinaldo Arenas was one of the most famous prisoners to be held in the Morro in the twentieth century, but Zurbano told me that his father had been imprisoned there as well. There is a whole history of oppression associated with the Morro, Zurbano stated, and this history is "de los negros" [of Afro-Cubans]. According to Zurbano, the colonial-era history of those of European descent is acknowledged in the Morro's nightly "cañonazo de las 9" [9 p.m. cannon firing], featured in guidebooks and set off by men wearing white wigs; but the history of Afro-Cubans has been largely elided.

The *cañonazo de las 9* offers a sonic metaphor for Quijano's concept of the coloniality of power. It signals the ongoing need for consideration of the ways in which islands are (and are not) written into existence, and it highlights the importance of a decolonizing approach to works produced throughout the *arcubiélago* during the Special Period and the "mini-boom" of the 2000s. This *cañonazo* sounds throughout the works analyzed in the pages that follow, and echoes throughout this book.

2

Birds of a Feather

Cuando el Malecón empieza a desbordarse
caen en la acera tablas del piano,
flores pintadas a mano salen a flote
no como decoración, sino como dolor.

[When the Malecón begins to overflow
piano planks fall on the sidewalk
hand-painted flowers resurface
not as decorations, but as pain.]

Reina María Rodríguez, "Resaca" ["Undertow"][1]

If the Feria del Libro offers one example of how the transnational Cuban archipelago functions *in situ* in Havana, so too does the Malecón, or seaside promenade, that winds its way around the capital city. On the Malecón, water pools on the sidewalk as the sea crashes over the bulwark meant to contain it. Looking from the promenade down into the sea, one can see eddies of water flowing around small outcroppings of land—miniature islands, as it were—just off the sidewalk, in the realm nominally ruled by the aqueous. The fragility of the coastal divide between land and water, moreover, is underscored by the damage that occurs when the sea takes over the land, rushing into homes and buildings that line the coast and pulling prized possessions—*tablas del piano*, or *flores pintadas a mano*—out to sea.

In many ways, the Malecón offers a street-level glimpse of the ties between sea and land that are visible from above: from the balconies of the buildings that line the Malecón, or from the windows of the airplanes that arrive and depart daily to and from Havana. These ties between earth and water, and between individuals from one island and another, are evident as well in the work of award-winning poet Reina María Rodríguez. Born in 1952, Rodríguez is known for her lyrical poetry, as well as for her seemingly effortless inclusion of theory alongside everyday experiences in her work. Rodríguez is also known for the gatherings that she long hosted in the *azotea*, or rooftop patio, of her Havana home. In the 1990s and 2000s, she greeted writers, artists, and others here in a soft voice as her cats roamed around her; she and her guests shared whatever meager refreshments were available in times of extreme scarcity, then launched into readings and discussions that lasted long into the night.

Through her poetry and gatherings, Rodríguez creates an interconnected, archipelagic space both materially and metaphorically. Rodríguez remained in Cuba throughout the Special Period of the 1990s and 2000s, and she suffered personally as she watched the exodus of many writers, artists, and intellectuals during these decades. The departure of many of her close friends resulted in a sense of profound loss that is reflected in her work, and scholars often employ the terms *exile* or *diaspora* to refer to this aspect of her poetry.[2] These terms are accurate, but the trope of the archipelago is more suited to theorizing the interconnected, rhizomatic space that Rodríguez calls into existence. Utilizing what Édouard Glissant terms the poetics of Relation, Rodríguez crafts a wide-open, archipelagic space that supersedes the binary divisions implicit in exile and diaspora. As Glissant writes of the poetics of Relation exemplified in the archipelago, in a description that might be applied equally to the space that Rodríguez imagines: "It is not merely an encounter, [. . .] but a new and original dimension allowing each person to be there and elsewhere, rooted and open, lost in the mountains and free beneath the sea, in harmony and in errantry."[3] This space exists both materially, in the gatherings Rodríguez held, and metaphorically, in the poet's work, and offers an evanescent alternative to the perceived divides of exile and diaspora, as well as to the difficulties of everyday Revolutionary life "(a)dentro" [within].

Reina María Rodríguez

Rodríguez is generally regarded as one of Cuba's preeminent living poets. Among her many awards and honors, she received Cuba's National Prize for Literature in 2013 and the Pablo Neruda Iberoamerican Prize for Poetry in 2014.[4] In its press announcement, the panel of judges for the National Prize for Literature summed up Rodríguez's important role in Cuban letters during her almost 40-year career, stating that the poet "ha llenado un espacio imprescindible en el panorama de la poesía cubana contemporánea, con alta calidad estética, ética y conceptual" [has filled an indispensable space in the panorama of contemporary Cuban poetry, with the highest aesthetic, ethical, and conceptual quality].[5] Rodríguez is a prolific writer whose collections of poetry include *La gente de mi barrio* [*The People of My Neighborhood*] (1976), *Cuando una mujer no duerme* [*When a Woman Does Not Sleep*] (1980), *Para un cordero blanco* [*For a White Lamb*] (1984), *En la arena de Padua* [*In the Sands of Padua*] (1992), *Páramos* [*Plains*] (1993), *Travelling* (1995), *Ellas escriben cartas de amor* [*They Write Love Letters*] (1998), *La foto del invernadero* [*The Winter Garden Photograph*] (1998; bilingual edition, 2019), . . . *te daré de comer como a los pájaros . . .* [*I Will Feed You as the Birds*] (2000), and *Otras mitologías* [*Other Mythologies*] (2012). Her most recent publications include *El piano* [*The Piano*] (2016), *Luciérnagas* [*Fireflies*] (2017), and *Achicar* [*To Reduce*] (2021).[6]

Rodríguez's poetry is often described by critics as "intimist." In the years following the Revolution, many Cuban poets employed a "conversationalist" tone in which "the lyric voice speaks as one with 'the people,' assuming a collective 'I' that sees itself as part of a project of historical (dialectical) development."[7] In contradistinction to this group, Rodríguez, along with other poets described as the "Nuevos" [New], employs a more intimist style and often shares details of her personal life in her poetry. At the same time, she speaks of her experience as an individual, rather than as a representative of a larger collective.[8]

In addition to her poetic prowess and intimist work, Rodríguez is widely recognized for creating a real-life space in Havana in which fellow literati might gather—an alternative space that exists alongside, and at times even "within," those spaces officially sanctioned by Cuba's post-1959 Revolutionary regimes.[9] In the 1990s, Rodríguez hosted popular literary salons in the *azotea* of her home located on Ánimas Street in Centro Habana [Central Havana].[10] In the 2000s, she tired of cleaning up after these gatherings, which often lasted into the wee hours. Rodríguez then organized salons and workshops in the Torre de Letras [Tower of Letters], a space for cultural events sponsored by the government-affiliated Instituto Cubano del Libro [Cuban Book Institute].[11] The Torre was originally located in the Instituto's building on the Plaza de Armas, in Habana Vieja [Old Havana]; when the Instituto relocated to the Calle Obispo (also in Habana Vieja) in 2011, the Torre moved to the ninth floor of the new building.[12]

Rodríguez's gatherings in Havana were particularly important during the Special Period. Actor and writer Pedro Roxy reminisces about the *azotea* in *Después de Paideia* [*After Paideia*], Mirian Real's 2011 documentary:

Hablarse de la casa de Reina es [. . .] [hablar] de qué cosa fue poesía en Cuba. No sólo porque ella fue la madre de los pollitos, como le decía yo cuando veía aquella cosa que después se llamó la diáspora, de los poetas cubanos que emigraron y los que se quedaron dentro, que vivían un in-xilio [. . .] aquel espacio [. . .] había sido creado como la única alternativa real que existía para la [. . .] joven guardia cubana.

[To speak of Reina's house is [. . .] [to speak] of what poetry was in Cuba. Not only because she was the mother hen, as I would tell her when I saw that which later became known as the diaspora, the Cuban poets who emigrated and those who remained within, and who lived an in-xile [. . .] that space [. . .] had been created as the only real alternative that existed for the [. . .] young Cuban guard.]

In the gatherings that Rodríguez hosted in the *azotea*, writers shared ideas with each other, read their work aloud, and swapped copies of difficult-to-obtain texts. For Rodríguez, these gatherings followed those of the aforementioned Paideia group, which brought together writers and artists in the Alejo Carpentier Center.[13]

In the 2000s, Rodríguez continued to offer a space for like-minded individuals to gather in Havana through the events she coordinated in the Torre. Although fewer attended, as many of those who frequented the *azotea* in the previous decade had left Cuba, Rodríguez remained committed to continuing to provide a space for those who wished to join. As she writes:

Mi idea era que los autores que todavía quedaban en la Isla tuvieran un sitio para leer, dar sus conferencias y publicar sus obras de una manera alternativa, sin propaganda de los medios, un sitio para trabajar y pro-ducir—también crear una biblioteca que fuera la biblioteca del escritor, con los libros más necesitados y queridos de algunos de ellos [. . .]

[My idea was that the authors who still remained on the Island would have a place to read, have their conferences, and publish their works in an alternative way, without the propaganda of the media, a place to write and produce—also, to create a library that would be a writer's library, with some of their most needed and beloved books [. . .]][14]

Thus the Torre functioned similarly to the *azotea*, although the gatherings in this space were more limited in size and scope.

In hosting gatherings in the *azotea* and the Torre, two airy perches offering a bird's-eye view of Cuba's capital, Rodríguez crafted an alternate space for writers and intellectuals that contributed to the larger formation of the *arcubiélago*. This archipelagic space resembled (although it was not synonymous with) what Franco Moretti describes in his discussion of modern European literature: "a *different* space: discontinuous, [and] fractured," that "functions as a sort of archipelago."[15] As is true of the European archipelago that Moretti describes, Rodríguez's Cuban iteration is, therefore, both singular and multiple. Embracing spaces that are simultaneously scattered and connected, Rodríguez's archipelago is *rhizomatic* rather than *rooted*, conjured, as it were, out of thin air in the *azotea* and the Torre, without an originating island.

The constituent spaces of Rodríguez's rhizomatic archipelago might be described metaphorically as nests, as well as islands.[16] In his 1958 *The Poetics of Space*, French philosopher Gaston Bachelard proposes that the nest is the very embodiment of shelter and home, at the same time that it is inherently fragile in nature: "A nest [. . .] is a precarious thing, and yet it sets us to *daydreaming of safety*."[17] In his book as a whole, Bachelard offers a "phenomenological inquiry on poetry" in which he studies "images of intimacy,"[18] such as attics and nooks, chests and drawers, nests and shells. Rodríguez mentions Bachelard in her work, and the *azotea* and the Torre recall his description of the nest, offering a rhizomatic, interconnected constellation of spaces in which all "birds of a feather" might gather, albeit briefly.[19] Marked by their ephemerality, these spaces are inherently "precarious," yet they are undoubtedly capable of inspiring "*daydreaming of safety*"[20] on the part of the writers, poets, and artists who gather there: "daydreaming" of community, and of home.

Embracing the multilingualism that Glissant associates with the poetics of Relation, Rodríguez continues to feather the nest in the present as she oversees the publication of a series of books published under the rubric *Colección Torre de Letras*. Rodríguez also launched a magazine, *Azoteas*, but published just seven issues.[21] To date, almost seventy titles have been published in the *Torre de Letras* book series, including Juan Carlos Flores's *El contragolpe (y otros poemas horizontales)* [*The Counterpunch (and Other Horizontal Poems)*], José Kozer's poetic anthology *Semovientes*, and Jesús David Curbelo's *Las quebradas oscuras (antología personal, 1984–2002)* [*The Dark Ravines (Personal Anthology, 1984–2002)*].[22] Some titles in the collection are published with Japanese-style *Kangxi* hand-stitched book-bindings, while other titles are published as press-produced paperbacks. Rodríguez likely turned to the *Kangxi* style for practical reasons, in a bid to avert the production delays often associated with press-produced titles in Cuba. Nonetheless, as Rodríguez's collaborators on the *Kangxi* books thread bits of yarn through paper to make loose pieces cohere into a larger whole, they once more recall birds building their aerial abodes, forging nest-like habitats fit for words and the worlds they create.

In hosting gatherings in an archipelagic constellation of nest-like spaces located simultaneously in and above Havana, and in publishing, translating, and promoting the work of a transnational cohort of authors, Rodríguez implicitly called into question longstanding power structures in Cuban letters.[23] Within Cuba, Rodríguez's gatherings in the 1990s and early 2000s not only challenged distinctions between public and private spaces, but also offered participants the opportunity to stage "a strangely visible resistance to the revolutionary embrace of local culture."[24] In their work, those who gathered in the *azotea* often focused on topics other than the most vaunted aspects of Cuban identity, and at times even openly challenged the status accorded such national heroes as José Martí. This was considered wildly transgressive and resulted in visits from undercover agents who sought to unmask participants' potential subversion.

Rodríguez's archipelagic gatherings also contested longstanding hierarchies privileging the work of writers from the nominal centers of power and prestige over that of writers from the so-called peripheries.[25] As part of this contestation, Rodríguez has long promoted the work of relatively unknown authors alongside that of the so-called greats of the literary canon. In so doing, she points to ongoing changes in literature, and to the dangers implicit in assuming that the renowned authors of the past will be those of the future as well. Additionally, the coordinates of the gatherings that Rodríguez has hosted in (and above) Havana have shifted once and again over time, first from *azotea* to Torre, and then from one Torre (on the Plaza de Armas) to another (on the Calle Obispo). Signaling the evolution and ephemerality of all mappings of space and time, each of these aerial perches itself also calls attention to the changes that occur from the (colonial) past to the (Revolutionary) present, as the crumbling facades visible from the windows—or over the walls—of both spaces serve as reminders of the vicissitudes of time. Each space, moreover, is itself characterized by its precariousness. Rodríguez built the *azotea* herself, along with her then-partner, Jorge Miralles, from scraps of building materials that she found and repurposed, much as a bird might build a nest. Like many of the buildings in Old Havana,

Figure 3. The view from poet Reina María Rodríguez's Azotea. Photo by author.

furthermore, the building that housed the Torre on the Plaza de Armas desperately needed substantial work. (See Figure 3.)

Nests and Islands in . . . *te daré de comer como a los pájaros* . . .

In her poetry, Rodríguez creates a metaphoric space that expands upon—even as it exists in tandem with—the material perches of the *azotea* and the Torre. In her prose poem . . . *te daré de comer como a los pájaros* . . . [*I Will Feed You as the Birds*] (2000) and her anthology *Bosque negro* [*Black Forest*] (2013), Rodríguez calls into existence an alternative space of identity for all interested individuals in the far-flung, transnational Cuban archipelago that she invokes: a space that spans land and sea, and that is open to all those who wish to enter.

The book . . . *te daré de comer como a los pájaros* . . . is a slim, sixty-one-page volume written in the 1990s but published in 2000.[26] Rodríguez states that the working title served as a reference to *For the Birds* [*Para los pájaros*] (1981), a collection of interviews with musician and composer John Cage, but that the final title is a verbatim phrase uttered by writer and artist Djuna Barnes.[27] Rodríguez wrote ... *te daré de comer* ... at the same time that she and Miralles constructed the *azotea*, and the text contains multiple references to the difficulties of obtaining the necessary materials to finish the project. Much as the *azotea* was built from scraps and repurposed materials, moreover, the text is composed of fragments of material from a variety of genres: dated journal entries are accompanied by undated comments on everyday happenings, excerpts from the poet's own previous work, and references to the work of others.

The heterogeneous compilation of material in ... *te daré de comer* ... is presented to readers in two side-by-side columns of text, both of which are printed in green (rather than black) ink. This innovative format resulted in the book being known as "el libro verde" [the green book], at the same time that it caused formatting difficulties and print delays.[28] In the introduction to a new edition of the text, forthcoming from the Virginia-based press Casa Vacía, Rodríguez writes that the difficulties in bringing the book to press were exacerbated by the scarcities of the Special Period:

> Después de pasarlo muchas veces [...] en una máquina portátil japonesa— una banda primero, la otra después—[...] al entregarlo [...] a la editorial Unión me dijeron que era muy difícil o imposible de imprimir por su formato, hasta que con la aparición de un programa de computación y la habilidad de un amigo fotógrafo (Adalberto Roque) pude armarlo en un disquete y traerlo a LC [la editorial Letras Cubanas], donde un grupo de diseñadores y editores lo acogieron.
>
> [After passing it many times through a portable Japanese typewriter [...] —first one column, then the other—[...] upon submitting it [...] to the Unión Press they told me that it would be very difficult, or impossible, to print because of its format; until, with the appearance of a computer program and the ability of a photographer friend (Adalberto Roque), I could put it all together on a disk and bring it to LC [the press Cuban Letters], where a group of designers and editors took it up.][29]

The right-hand column, which is slimmer and printed in a smaller typeface, is more focused on the details of the poet's everyday life: less "poetic" and more mundane. The left-hand column, which occupies more space and is printed in a slightly larger and bolder typeface, is somewhat more abstract and "poetic" in its content. Hence the right-hand column begins, "dice que me vaya de la casa el primer día del año y maldice" [he says that I should leave the house the first of the year, and he swears]; the left-hand column, in contrast, begins by evoking " . . . la muerte de Katherine Mansfield entre las vacas, en el espacio dispuesto por aquel hombre, el olor de la leche fresca" [. . . the death of Katherine Mansfield amongst the cows, in the space left by that man, the smell of fresh milk].[30]

Even as Rodríguez's use of two columns in . . . *te daré de comer* . . . suggests a distinction between the "poetic" and the "mundane," the divide between the two is far from absolute. In both columns, for instance, the poet scatters the names of important literary and critical figures. She refers to New Zealand–born modernist writer Katherine Mansfield, U.S. poet Adrienne Rich (13), Cuban author José Lezama Lima (19), French writer Marguerite Duras (10, 26), Portuguese poet Fernando Pessoa (30, 32, 33, 44, 54), U.S. composer and writer John Cage (20, 35, 36, 37), and the aforementioned French philosopher Gaston Bachelard (12, 42, 54, 55), among others.[31] Also in both columns, the poet references, and at times includes excerpts from, her own previously published work, such as *Para un cordero blanco* (47), *En la arena de Padua* (18, 22–23), *Travelling* (18, 30), and *Páramos* (41).[32]

On one level, the references to literary and critical figures scattered throughout the two columns may be seen as an attempt to highlight the artificiality of any potential division between the poet's work and her private life. This division was especially stark during the years of the Special Period, when Rodríguez suffered from illness, experienced difficulties with her partner, and endured extreme scarcities, as did so many of her compatriots.[33] Rodríguez writes, "Este libro puede ser leído desde cualquier ángulo, empezar por cualquier columna, porque 'todas las cosas en él, son la misma cosa'" [This book can be read from any angle, starting with any column, because 'all things in it, are the same thing'].[34] The poet's repeated references to food (11, 26, 34, 50), illness (17), and menstruation (13, 15, 30, 35, 52) certainly bespeak the prominence of the physical body in a time in which basic needs were often difficult to meet, and such references undeniably signal as well the resulting difficulties in living a life of the mind.

On another level, the divide between the columns of text in . . . *te daré de comer* . . . might also be considered a symbolic reference to the lines of division that separate Rodríguez's readers—the geographic boundaries separating those individuals living on the island from those living elsewhere, or the socioeconomic boundaries separating those with empty bellies from those with full stomachs. In line with this interpretation, the references to critical and literary figures that appear in both columns read as an attempt to dialogue with sympathetic readers, regardless of locale or socioeconomic status, who similarly belong to the larger transnational archipelago that the poet invokes. Considered from this vantage point, . . . *te daré de comer* . . . can be construed as an appeal to what Michael Warner terms a "public," or a group of people who do not know each other, but who come together through their common perusal of shared texts.[35] Publics are by definition multiple rather than singular in nature, and through her inclusion of literary and critical references in her printed work, Rodríguez simultaneously maps and dialogues with a wider public composed of individuals who may not know the poet personally or attend the gatherings that she hosts in Havana.

Chronicling and appealing to a like-minded public in . . . *te daré de comer* . . . , Rodríguez also inaugurates an archipelagic space in the text in which her readers might gather: a space that expands upon the *azotea* and the Torre, that supersedes the space of the island(s), and in which time is suspended. Rodríguez's references to the book—*el libro*—in . . . *te daré de comer* . . . are suggestive in this regard. In one instance, Rodríguez characterizes the book as "intemporal" [timeless];[36] in another, she states that individuals are books: "cada uno en sí, es un libro" [each person is, indeed, a book].[37] In a parenthetical comment in the closing pages of . . . *te daré de comer* . . . , furthermore, Rodríguez writes of a "holographic-literary space" in which, paradoxically, language no longer "signposts":

(con este libro, esta rara recopilación intemporal, mi deseo ha sido producir una estructuración diferente, combinatoria (la estructuración de una estructura) acercándome a los textos fuera del tiempo, o del espacio en que son concebidos, mezclándolos hacia un discurso continuo-discontinuo y una revisión crítica de los ángulos desde donde los acechamos, provocando un espacio literario-holográfico, abierto a la propia confusión y límites de una voz interrumpida por aquel desplazamiento del lenguaje hacia lo cotidiano y real (hasta lo doméstico) y el deseo de trascender hacia otra realización, en la cual, el lenguaje no señaliza, no es preciso, no acompaña y se queda siempre por debajo de la pretensión . . .)

[(with this book, this strange non-temporal recompilation, my desire has been to produce a different structure, combinatory (the structuring of a structure) approaching texts outside of time, or the space in which they are conceived, mixing them toward a continuous-discontinuous discourse and a critical revision of the angles from which we watch them, provoking a literary-holographic space, open to the confusion and limits of a voice interrupted by that displacement of language toward the everyday and the real (even the domestic) and the desire to transcend toward another realization, in which language does not signpost, is not precise, does not accompany, and remains forever beneath pretension . . .)][38]

For Rodríguez, the creation of "una estructuración diferente, combinatoria" [a different structure, combinatory] in . . . *te daré de comer* . . . allows texts to coexist outside the bounds of time. This recalls philosopher Michel Foucault's description of a heterotopia, which is located both within and outside a society's physical space. As Foucault writes, a heterotopia exists as:

> . . . a kind of effectively enacted utopia in which the real sites, all the other real sites that can be found within the culture, are simultaneously represented, contested, and inverted. Places of this kind are outside of all places, even though it may be possible to indicate their location in reality.[39]

For Foucault, museums and libraries represent "the idea of accumulating everything, of establishing a sort of general archive, the will to enclose in one place all times, all epochs, all forms, all tastes, the idea of constituting a place of all times that is itself outside of time and inaccessible to its ravages."[40] Similar to the museum or the library referenced by Foucault, the heterotopic space that Rodríguez inaugurates "do[es] exist" at the same time that it is located outside of time. As such, in conjunction with the *azotea*, or the Torre, Rodríguez's "rara recopilación intemporal" [strange non-temporal recompilation] may be described not only as archipelagic, but also as resembling a heterotopia.

The literary and critical references that are scattered through both columns of . . . *te daré de comer* . . . thus function on two levels. On the one hand, they serve as a lingua franca of sorts for a like-minded "public." As such, the references form part of Rodríguez's efforts to bridge the gap between intellectuals on the island(s) and their peers elsewhere in the *arcubiélago*, as well as between readers of different backgrounds. On the other hand, the references signal the poet's attempts to inaugurate a space that—similar to a heterotopia, as described by Foucault—surpasses the spatial and temporal limitations of the *azotea* and the Torre. Rodríguez's inclusion of her own prior work in . . . *te daré de comer* . . . forms part of this attempt. For José Prats Sariol, this decision represents a certain *picardía*:

la picardía de burlarse a sí misma y de sus 'experiencias' en . . . *te daré de comer como a los pájaros* . . . Sus propios poemas anteriores son ensamblados bajo *otra* concomitancia, bajo una nueva vecindad que los transforma.

[the *picaradía* of making fun of herself and her 'experiences' in . . . *te daré de comer como a los pájaros* . . . Her own prior poems are assembled under *another* concomitance, under a new proximity that transforms them.][41]

Rather than constituting solely a *picardía*, however, Rodríguez's references to her prior work form part of her larger attempt to craft a space large enough for all to gather: a space open to readers in Havana and elsewhere, and capacious enough to encompass both her own writings and those of others.

At the same time that Rodríguez constructs an archipelagic "espacio literario-holográfico" [literary-holographic space][42] in her poetry, she repeatedly reminds readers that this space is of necessity ephemeral, much as are the nests built by birds, as the limitations of the present are only momentarily transcended despite what Foucault describes as the "will" to do otherwise.[43] The evanescence of all spaces, and all times, is underscored from the opening lines of the left-hand column that evoke " . . . la muerte de Katherine Mansfield entre las vacas" [. . . the death of Katherine Mansfield amongst the cows].[44] Calling to mind the famous writer's untimely death from tuberculosis at the age of 34, Rodríguez signals the inevitable coexistence of life and death, and suggests that even beginnings contain their own endings. The message of the opening lines of the left-hand column is reinforced in the corresponding lines of the right-hand column, which allude to the end of a relationship, as well as in Rodríguez's repeated references throughout the text to her own bodily limitations and the difficulties of everyday life.

Seas and Trees in *Bosque negro*

Throughout . . . *te daré de comer como a los pájaros* . . . , Rodríguez simultaneously chronicles her everyday life and crafts an archipelagic, ephemeral space of identity. Metaphoric and nest-like, this space expands on that of the *azotea* and the Torre. Here time is suspended, albeit fleetingly, and longstanding dichotomies between public and private, center and margins, are once more rendered obsolete, allowing all "birds of a feather" to gather, irrespective of island(s) identity or provenance. In *Bosque negro* [*Black Forest*], Rodríguez's 2013 "antología personal" [personal anthology], the poet engages specifically with the questions of island spaces that are intrinsic to the material archipelago.[45] Seeking to "sea" the forest for the trees and contributing to the ongoing dialogue on the time and space of the island(s), Rodríguez here imagines a wider, archipelagic space of sea and salt, word and world.

As a collection of seemingly disparate parts that, together, nonetheless form a whole, the form of the anthology to some extent mirrors that of the archipelago.[46] In both, moreover, the framing of individual parts as a whole—or as "'such and such an assemblage,'" to return to Elaine Stratford et al.'s apt description of the archipelago—calls attention to how representations take shape more broadly.[47] In the preface to *Bosque negro*, Rodríguez underscores the convergences between anthologies and assemblages:

> Porque no me gustan las antologías, he querido que esta conforme un nuevo libro, por eso las referencias a los títulos de los poemarios particulares solo aparecen ligeramente marcadas debajo de la página de inicio, como parte de los fragmentos escogidos del libro donde se encontraban originalmente [. . .]

> [Because I don't like anthologies, it is my hope that this will be a new book, thus the references to the titles of specific poetry collections appear only lightly marked at the bottom of the first page [on which poems from a given collection appear], as part of the fragments chosen from the book where they were originally found [. . .]][48]

Rodríguez then continues:

> respeté las letras minúsculas con las que escribí durante una época [. . .] pero he hecho cambios considerables en muchos poemas [. . .] Hay textos que no se han publicado en Cuba [. . .] hay otros de los que no quedan ejemplares ya. Por eso, agradezco a mis editores el permitirme hacer una antología que no es una antología, sino un cúmulo de textos [. . .]

> [I respected the lower-case letters with which I wrote during a time [. . .] but I have made considerable changes in many poems [. . .] There are texts that have not been published in Cuba [. . .] there are others of which no copies remain. For this reason, I thank my editors for allowing me to make an anthology that is not an anthology, but a series of texts [. . .]][49]

Rodríguez's open acceptance of her poetry's shifting contours, along with her description of the anthology as "cúmulo" in the preface, is echoed in her descriptions of islands and seas in *Bosque negro*. Variously translated as "load, pile, heap," and "series, host, string," *cúmulo* evokes the interconnections intrinsic to the archipelago.[50] In much the same way as the word *cúmulo* signals the connections between poems in the anthology, Rodríguez underscores the ties between land and sea in *Bosque negro*, turning repeatedly to images of water, coastlines, and islands. In "El arca" ["The Ark"], for instance, Rodríguez explicitly references what she describes as "la frontera ficticia / de un mar" [the fictitious frontier / of a sea];[51] in "Mar de leva" ["Choppy Sea"], she similarly alludes to the fictitious boundary between the earthly and the aqueous. Here she writes: "El niño mira al mar que se levanta y salpica / toda la calle" [The small boy looks at the sea that rises and splashes / the entire street].[52] Describing in this instance a small boy who watches the sea splash on the street, Rodríguez again blurs the boundaries between sea and land.

Rodríguez further highlights the archipelagic connections between individuals, sea, and shore in the three poems in *Bosque negro* that mention "island(s)" in their titles: "las islas" ["the islands"], "Violet Island," and "la isla de Wight" ["the Isle of Wight"]. With their titles intimating the ongoing importance of the trope of the island in her work, Rodríguez here limns the archipelagic interconnections between spaces and seas, writing islands that, together, form part of the larger *arcubiélago*.

"las islas" first appeared in *En la arena de Padua*, published in 1991. In the opening lines of the poem, Rodríguez urges the reader to "mira" [look]:[53] islands are plural, existing simultaneously as "mundos aparentes" [apparent worlds], "tierras sin raíz" [rootless lands], and "mancha[s]" [stain(s)]. To some extent, the poet continues, islands are characterized by the "soledad" [solitude] that results from being "cortadas en el mar" [cut off in the sea]; this solitude, however, is undone by the fact that the islands are, as Rodríguez states later in the poem, "manchas de sal" [salt stains].[54] Mobile and multiple, islands are thus not foreign to the sea but of it: composed of residual salt, they move through the water that creates them.

Islands also represent spaces of freedom for Rodríguez, who notes that she begins to experience what it means to be "libre" [free] in a space that exists between limits. Upending once again the normal confines of time and space, for Rodríguez the islands offer an "intervalo entre dos tiempos" [interval between two kinds of time].[55] Following Kristin Dykstra, this characterization not only "destabilizes certainties," but also "contributes to dialogues about the meaning of 'insularity,' a repeating issue in Cuba's literary history."[56] By portraying a plurality of islands (rather than a single *isla*), and by identifying them as "mundos aparentes" [apparent worlds], Rodríguez appeals to a more open, archipelagic space and again calls into question the hierarchies that often privilege the so-called center over the periphery.

A similar archipelagic dynamic is apparent in the poem "Violet Island," which first appeared in Rodríguez's *Páramos*, published in 1993. The poem establishes a connection between a lighthouse-keeper and a woman who falls asleep, dreaming of finding more time. The island invoked in this poem is singular and specific, as opposed to "las islas" [the islands] portrayed in the aforementioned poem of this name. Yet the focus in "Violet Island" on the communication between land and sea, here enabled by lighthouses and ports, once more contributes to Rodríguez's characterization of Cuban space as multiple and interconnected—as archipelagic. Thus Rodríguez begins the poem by referencing the beams of light that guide ships safely through the sea, then describes a lighthouse-keeper's search for "another" light:

> [. . .] allí, en su isla
> él intercambiaba con su faro las sensaciones
> esperando cada día, cada noche, esa otra luz
> [. . .]
> y el ojo que mira volver, por encima y transparente,
> la ilusión provisional que se eterniza.

> [. . .] there, on his island,
> he exchanged sensations with his lighthouse,
> waiting every day, every night for another light
> [. . .]
> and the eye, overhead and transparent, that watches the return
> of temporary illusion that becomes eternal.][57]

The search for this light (and the connection that Rodríguez subsequently establishes between the lighthouse-keeper and the woman who falls asleep) is explained in part by the origins of the poem. As Rodríguez explains, "Violet Island" was inspired by the story of a lighthouse-keeper who fell asleep on duty, and consequently caused ships to run aground: "The woman [in 'Violet Island'], just like that lighthouse-keeper, wants to experience spiritual enlightenment; she wants to understand many things; but she falls asleep, she stays asleep, and she loses that possibility."[58]

In addition to foregrounding the importance of maintaining archipelagic ties between island and sea, as well as the individuals who move between them, Rodríguez once more questions the strictures of time in "Violet Island," as "la ilusión provisional se eterniza" [temporary illusion becomes eternal]. Upending time and space in suggesting that the temporary might in fact be the eternal, Rodríguez undercuts the idea of fixed boundaries in her description of what was once a port city in the poem's final lines. Characterizing what "bien antes fue un límite" [a long time ago [. . .] was a boundary] as now "solo la apariencia de un límite" [just the appearance of a boundary], Rodríguez again signals the ever-shifting borders and impossible bounds of time and space.[59] The inability to clearly and definitively delineate these borders and bounds is reinforced in the poem's concluding series of questions about where key elements of the port—including ships and sailors—have gone. Ending with interrogatives rather than answers, the poet leaves open a multitude of possibilities for her readers.

As do "las islas" and "Violet Island," "la isla de Wight" again evidences the archipelagic space that extends rhizomatically through Rodríguez's poetry. In this poem, which first appeared in *La foto del invernadero* (1998), Rodríguez establishes a connection between the poetic "yo" [I] and "aquella chica de la isla de Wight" [that girl from the Isle of Wight].[60] In establishing this connection, Rodríguez points to the ties that join islands across the transnational Cuban archipelago, extending from Europe, where the Isle of Wight lies just south of England, to the Caribbean.

As Rodríguez makes clear in "la isla de Wight," the poetry that makes this transnational, archipelagic space possible is, much like the space itself, unfinished and inherently ephemeral.[61] As is true of the space that Rodríguez evokes in "Violet Island," communication is fraught and at times unsuccessful in "la isla de Wight." Echoing the questions at the end of "Violet Island" about the location of the port, ships, and lighthouses, Rodríguez here suggests that not all searches yield results and that not all questions have answers. With the poet acknowledging "esa indiferencia de la materia / a su necesidad" [matter's indifference / to her need], a girl's "desperate" search for "ese indicio" [some sign] offers, in lieu of answers, a loss of even the questions that had likely prompted her search.[62] Even so, Rodríguez states that it is nonetheless the poem that is to some degree able to organize the chaos of the world:

(un poema es lo justo, lo exacto, lo irrepetible,
dentro del caos que uno intenta ordenar y ser,
y lo ha ordenado para que el poema no sea
necesario).

[(a poem is the precise thing, the accurate thing, the unrepeatable thing
within the chaos that one tries to arrange and be
and she has arranged it so the poem won't be necessary.)][63]

If "aquella chica de la isla de Wight" [that girl from the Isle of Wight][64] attempts to "arrange" the chaos so that the poem is no longer "necessary," the poet herself recognizes the ongoing need for "lo justo, lo exacto, lo irrepetible" [the precise thing, the accurate thing, the unrepeatable thing] that the poem affords.

Much as Rodríguez characterizes islands as *of*, as well as *in*, the sea in "las islas," in "la isla de Wight" she portrays how salty seawaters run through her poems. For the space of the "espera" [waiting] exists "materialmente" [materially] on the page, at the same time that it is traversed by the waters of the sea:

—también aquí se trata del paso del tiempo,
de la travesía del mar por el poema—.

[—here too it deals with the passage of time,
with the ocean travelling through the poem—][65]

Serving as an archipelagic constellation of their own, Rodríguez's poems thus bridge the spaces of Europe and the Caribbean and offer a series of archipelagic spaces for a far-flung public.

.   .   .

In *Travelling*, a collection of prose poems composed in the 1980s and published in 1995, Rodríguez writes of the need to remain afloat even when not immersed in water: "hay que saber flotar como flotan las palabras, sin raíces y sin agua. hay que saber navegar sin latitudes ni longitudes, sin motor. [. . .] la cuerda tiene que ser de arena, el ancla de aurora boreal" [one has to know how to float like words, without roots and without water. one has to know how to navigate without latitudes nor longitudes, without a motor. [. . .] the cord has to be made of sand, the anchor, of the northern lights].[66] As I have suggested here, Rodríguez's efforts to remain afloat "without roots" are evident in the poems collected in *Bosque negro* and . . . *te daré de comer como a los pájaros* . . . , as well as in the gatherings the poet long hosted in Havana. Inviting readers, writers, and artists to join her in the pages of her poetry and the perches of the *azotea* and the Torre, Rodríguez crafts an archipelagic space that allows her publics to gather under even the most difficult of circumstances, and to more adroitly navigate the changing currents of time and space. In so doing, Rodríguez consistently eschews the roots of nation and diaspora and employs instead the rhizomatic poetics of Relation that Glissant associates with the archipelago.

Also in *Travelling*, Rodríguez references her early sojourns in Miami, Chicago, and Moscow, invoking the capacious contours of the *arcubiélago* and emphasizing once again the need to recognize the connections—rather than the disjunctions—between spaces.[67] In "la memoria del agua" ["memory of water"], for instance, the poet details her corporeal connection to the sea in recalling the Malecón in September:

> el Malecón, en ese tiempo, está lleno de peces y de anzuelos perdidos contra el muro que está salado y pegajoso. me gusta pasar la lengua por la sal [. . .] y en ese momento el resto de la ciudad puede perderse, sólo estamos ese mar y yo [. . .] entonces me desnudo y entro, sé que voy a encontrar algo y que los barcos—que están como suspendidos en el horizonte y han perdido sus límites, quietos y pintados allí—también son míos . . .

> [the salty, sticky wall of the Malecón is covered with fish and forgotten hooks. i like to lick its sheen of salt [. . .] in that moment the rest of the city can vanish, it's just that sea and me [. . .] then i undress and enter, knowing i'll find something, and that the boats—which seem suspended on the horizon, seem to have slipped their limits, motionless and painted there—are also mine . . .][68]

Eschewing, if only momentarily, the city for the sea, the poet invokes the archipelagic ties between *terra firma* and *mar* and calls attention to the limitless boats that enable her to see past the horizon to appreciate the fullness of the archipelago.

The poet reiterates the importance of retaining the archipelagic ties between land and sea in *Travelling* in "primera vez" ["first time"], in which she recounts the otherworldly experience of walking into a grocery store in Miami for the first time. Shocked by the variety of goods for sale—mandarin oranges from Morocco, eggs painted different colors to indicate their "best-by" dates—Rodríguez is drawn to the seafood. Here, she writes:

rocé las conchas con la punta de los dedos, eran suaves, delicadísimas, pero, comprobé que las conchas donde se ponen los mariscos son falsas, se usan y se botan, [. . .] no han visto ningún mar.

[i brushed the shells with my fingertips, they were smooth and delicate, but obviously artificial, made to be used once and thrown away [. . .] they've never even seen any sea.][69]

In contradistinction to her characterization of the interconnectedness of individual and sea in "la memoria del agua," in "primera vez" Rodríguez offers a pointed critique of the lack of such connectivity in the U.S. *grocery*, signaling the need for a greater archipelagic consciousness.

As these poems evince, Rodríguez did of course *travel* during the 1990s. Yet the poet long resisted spending long periods of time outside Cuba, even as her growing international prominence led her to accept invitations to speak and teach abroad. In the 2000s, however, the world of U.S. *groceries* became a more familiar one for Rodríguez, as she increasingly spent more time in Miami, where her daughter lives, and less time in Havana.

As of this writing, Rodríguez continues to produce books under the rubric Colección Torre de las Letras, but the gatherings held in the Torre appear to have ended. With these changes, the *azotea* has become not only Rodríguez's Havana home, but a storied site of past encounters. In *Otras mitologías* [*Other Mythologies*] (2012), Rodríguez reflects on the gatherings she hosted in the *azotea*, implicitly relegating—even then—the vaunted space to the realm of the "mitologías" [mythologies] that she invokes in her title. In the collection as a whole, Rodríguez reminisces about what the book jacket describes as the "mundo ruso" [Russian world] of her youth and the "*quereres* perdidos" [lost loved ones] who frequented the gatherings she held on her rooftop patio. In this regard, the poet reminds her readers that the *azotea* served as a safe, mobile harbor for the poets, writers, and artists who gathered there:

Viento en popa subimos los huérfanos (los náufragos), a la averiada azotea que se mueve por el zarandeo de unos años tras otros sin destino, como *La nave va* de Fellini. De cartón piedra la casa-barco surcando el deseo de triunfar y de ser reconocidos, pero sobre todo, de ser queridos. [. . .] Los amigos de mi hija, cuando vienen, preguntan: '¿Y esto fue un barco?'

[Wind in our sails, we climb aboard, the orphans (the shipwrecked), to the damaged *azotea* that moves through the tossing of years following years without a destination, like Fellini's *And the Ship Sails On.* Made of papier-mâché the house-ship traversing the desire to triumph and be recognized, but above all, to be loved. [. . .] My daughter's friends, when they come, ask: 'And this was a boat?']⁷⁰

Characterizing her rooftop patio as a "barco" [boat] afloat in the larger *arcubié-lago* that the poet both envisions and creates, the poet offers a nod toward her characterization of her home as a "nest" in . . . *te daré de comer como a los pája-ros* . . . At the same time, the question posed by her daughter's friends—"'¿Y esto fue un barco?'"⁷¹—tellingly inserts the *azotea* into the past through its use of the preterit: the *azotea was* a boat and is now a mythical, storied space.

Although Rodríguez no longer holds gatherings in the *azotea*, she continues to generate an archipelagic, interconnected space. Wherever she is, she socializes almost daily with other writers and creates a space for others to join her. Continuing to create a rhizomatic, archipelagic space of identity, Rodríguez recognizes the difficulties as well as the importance of her endeavor. In an interview I conducted with her over email in May 2019, Rodríguez underscored the "pain" of U.S.-Cuban relations:

Sobre las relaciones entre los dos lugares (el aquí o el allá) creo que todo permanece inamovible sin el deseo de abrir verdaderos canales de comunicación! Como si todo retrocediera sin cesar bajo la conveniencia de mantener un precio político obsoleto! Quisiera estar muy lejos de todo esto! Lejos de la metástasis! Porque la isla no es una isla ni un archipiélago, sino un dolor! Lamento parecer patética pero así lo siento: una punzada terrible en el pecho.

[On the relations between the two spaces (the here or the there) I think that everything remains immovable without the desire to open real communication channels! As though everything were to move backward without stopping in the interest of maintaining an obsolete political price! I would like to be far away from all this! Far from the metastasis! Because the island is not an island nor an archipelago, but pain! I'm sorry to seem pathetic but that is how I feel it: a terrible stab of pain in my chest.]⁷²

Writing from her daughter's house in Miami, Rodríguez highlighted the ongoing difficulties of retaining open channels of communication. Tying space and time to "dolor"—which can be translated as both pain and sorrow, and which the poet also evokes in "Resaca" ["Undertow"], the poem that serves as this chapter's epigraph—the poet poignantly references the difficulties, as well as the importance, of crafting alternate, archipelagic spaces of identity that resist what she describes as the "metastasis" of geopolitics.

Be it on the Malecón or in Miami, Rodríguez thus continues to work toward writing islands in which one might float free, without roots. Even as she traverses the "dolor" [pain, sorrow] that accompanies the lack of what she describes as "verdaderos canales de comunicación" [real communication channels], the poet beckons to others to join her.

3

Artistic Collaborations from Jaruco to Habana

In the years that followed the 1990s heyday of the gatherings held by poet Reina María Rodríguez in her Azotea, many longtime attendees opted to leave Cuba for outcroppings of the *arcubiélago* in Europe, Latin America, and the United States. Those who remained confronted a rapidly changing society in which it sometimes seemed that literary culture was asked to take a back seat to consumerism as tourism increased. At the same time that literary gatherings faltered, colonial-era mansions across Havana were renovated to house tourists as the Castro regime implemented policies designed to relieve a struggling economy, and 1950s-era cars were meticulously restored to cater to visitors' every (transportation) need. While these changes benefited some, they did not benefit all. Writers, artists, and intellectuals who did not profit from the influx of cash that accompanied the uptick in tourism often felt obligated to trace new itineraries through cityscapes that were, in some instances, changing seemingly overnight.

The work of poets Ricardo Alberto Pérez and Ramón Hondal illuminates this change. Pérez and Hondal are longtime friends and collaborators of Rodríguez who remained in Cuba when many others left. With social stratification increasing in Cuba in the 1990s and 2000s, Pérez and Hondal offer a critique of the status quo in their work and contribute to the formation of an alternate, archipelagic imaginary. In their collaborations with visual artists, in particular, the poets trace what might be described, following Michel de Certeau, as "'indirect' or 'errant' trajectories"[1] and insinuate the possibility of alternative itineraries through the landscape of contemporary Cuban culture. In so doing, the poets bemoan the loss of the itinerant archipelago envisaged by Rodríguez and signal the possibilities of remixing media through artistic collaborations to create new outcroppings of the *arcubiélago*.

Ricardo Alberto Pérez: Poetic Collaborations and Porcine Performances

Ricardo Alberto Pérez (known to friends as "Richard"; 1963–present) is a well-known poet in Cuba, and he has received awards and honors from *La Gaceta de Cuba* (2003), Nosside Caribe (2005), Nicolás Guillén (2007), and La Pupila Insomne (2007).[2] His published collections of poetry include *Geanot (el otro ruido de la noche)* [*Geanot: The Other Sound of the Night*] (1993), *Nietzsche dibuja a Cósima Wagner* [*Nietzsche Draws Cósima Wagner*] (1996), *Trillos urbanos* [*Urban Threshers*] (2003), *Vibraciones del buey* [*Vibrations of the Ox*] (2003), *Oral B* (2007), *Los tuberculosos y otros poemas* [*Tuberculosis Patients and Other Poems*] (2008), and *¿Para qué el cine?* [*For What Cinema?*] (2010).[3] Pérez lived in Brazil for four years and has published two anthologies of his translations into Spanish of Brazilian poets: *Catorce poetas brasileños* [*Fourteen Brazilian Poets*] (2006) and *Perhappenis: Antología poética de Paulo Leminski* [*Perhappenis: Poetic Anthology of Paulo Leminski*] (2007). Pérez also frequently publishes essays on art on the British website Cuba Absolutely.[4]

Pérez, who has short hair and eyes creased from laughter, is voluble and enthusiastic, especially when discussing his work. For many years, Pérez traveled to Havana from his home in Jaruco, a small town some 30 miles from the capital, to attend Rodríguez's salons.[5] As the poet states in an interview, the departure of many of those who attended the gatherings during the Special Period resulted in a concomitant loss of the space they had created together: "Pero es un espacio que no existe ya. La Azotea, Paideia, Reina; [. . .] había ocasiones en que lo mismo nos encontramos amigos en cafés . . . que en la Plaza Vieja, en un parque. Pero es que esta gente [ya] no existe. Los espacios, tampoco" [But it is a space that no longer exists. The Azotea, Paideia, Reina; [. . .] there were occasions in which we met up in cafés . . . in the Plaza Vieja, in a park. But it is that this group no longer exists. And neither do the spaces].[6] Characterizing the gatherings held in Havana as mobile and multiple, Pérez suggests the shifting contours of the alternate, archipelagic space called into existence by the writers who came together, albeit briefly, to forge and inhabit it. At the same time, he echoes Rodríguez in describing this space as inherently ephemeral. Shifting for many years between the Azotea and the Torre, as well as the park and the plaza, the space created through the gatherings of Rodríguez and her collaborators no longer exists.

For Pérez, the loss of the space emblematized in the Azotea and those who gathered there was accompanied by a concurrent, pernicious loss of literary culture. In light of what he perceived as the disappearance of the space once afforded literature in Cuba, Pérez began to pursue collaborations with artists, rather than writers, in the 2000s: "Llamo a Ramón [Hondal], y voy bastante a la ciudad; pero [. . .] Tengo más encuentro con los artistas, con muchos artistas" [I call Ramón [Hondal], and I go frequently to the city; but [. . .] I have more contact with artists, with many artists].[7] Mixing media through his poetic collaborations with visual artists, as well as through his performances of his own work, Pérez critiques what he considers to be the diminished state of Cuban letters and invokes a new, archipelagic space in which a transnational group of like-minded *letrados* and artists might gather. This space is both materially anchored (through Pérez's performative work) and metaphoric (through the space he constructs in his poetry).

¿Para qué el cine?, published by the Cuban press Ediciones Unión in 2010, reflects Pérez's growing interest in the visual arts. As the poet states in an interview:

Y llegó un momento, en que ya las influencias, que han sido, quizás la última década, no son tantas literarias, son influencias de imágenes. [. . .] ahora cuando veo la realidad, y la proceso [. . .] casi siempre [. . .] pasa por estos recuerdos tremendos que tengo de las imágenes del cine.

[And there came a moment, perhaps in the last decade, in which the influences are no longer as literary, but are visual influences. [. . .] now when I look at reality, and I process it [. . .] almost always [it] passes through these tremendous memories that I have of the cinema.][8]

Composed of eighty-two pages and fifty-three poems, *¿Para qué el cine?* offers readers two texts in one, with underlined words in each poem offering a second possible reading.[9] Pérez frequently collaborates with artists, and *¿Para qué el cine?* is a joint undertaking with visual artist Ezequiel Suárez:[10] Pérez wrote the poems, and Suárez underlined the words that he thought were most important to create a poem within a poem.[11] Suárez includes an oblique reference to this process in a poem titled *La digestión a mi manera* [*My Way of Digestion*] that serves as a prologue to the text.[12] Here he writes:

Yo metía en mi cuerpo un sapo / entero y lo maltrataba: / ácidos jugos y dientes se encargaban de todo. / Luego al terminar la digestión, / ¡La digestión a mi manera! / [. . .] / Yo me acostaba contigo a vaciarme

[I put a whole toad in my body / and I mistreated it: / acid juices and teeth took care of it all. / After finishing the digestion, / My way of digestion! / [...] / I lay down with you to empty myself out]

In English, of course, "digest" also refers to the process of reducing a whole to a more manageable part: "Arrange in a systematic or convenient order, especially by reduction."[13] In *¿Para qué el cine?*, to extend the artist's metaphor, Suárez first consumes the poems written by Pérez, then digests them for the reader, with the underlined words in each poem tracing the path he has taken through the poetry to arrange them in his own "manera" [way].

In *¿Para qué el cine?* Suárez and Pérez reference the possibility of alternate "trajectories" such as those described by Michel de Certeau in *The Practice of Everyday Life*, underlining the point through their innovative collaboration. Here de Certeau writes on the ways in which space is negotiated, differentiating between the "strategies" employed by those who wield power (such as institutions or governing bodies) and the "tactics" employed by those "everyday" people who do not. For de Certeau, while those in power impose an organizing logic onto spaces, individuals who live in a society but do not make its rules or determine its city grids nonetheless assert agency in the spaces they carve out and the ways in which they move between them. Departing from the paths plotted on maps, for instance, de Certeau writes that individuals forge everyday "trajectories [that] form unforeseeable sentences, partly unreadable paths across a space. [...] the trajectories trace out the ruses of other interests and desires that are neither determined nor captured by the systems in which they develop."[14] Tracing lines to connect the dots for readers in *¿Para qué el cine?*, Pérez and Suárez suggest, more broadly, the possibilities of everyday "tactics" that can be employed to negotiate the cityscapes and culture of a society in flux.

Signaling the possibility of alternate itineraries through the space of the city and the poem alike, in *¿Para qué el cine?* it is thus possible to read a given poem as it is written, or the poem-within-a-poem as it is underlined.[15] In the latter (digested) case, the lines serve as a seam of sorts that connects words; in each case, the poems also offer readers an alternate space of identity. For example, the poem "tipología de un espacio" ["typology of a space"] explicitly references the rendering of such a space.

| tipología de un espacio | [typology of a space |
| colmado | filled |

de espacio,	with space
<u>la ciudad desaparece</u>	<u>the city disappears</u>
y tiene coyunturas.	and has articulations.

ojo	the eye of the needle
de esta **singer** puntando	of this **singer** stitching
una secreta relación	a secret relationship
<u>entre paredes</u>	<u>between walls</u>
huecos,	empty spaces,
un rastro contenido	a trace contained
en lente	in lens
o lengua.	or tongue.

<u>así fluctúa</u>	<u>and so fluctuates</u>
el fondo natural	the natural background
que frecuento	that I frequent
<u>son parcelas</u>	<u>they are parcels</u>
que vienen	that come
<u>escenarios</u>	<u>scenes</u>
con	with
pájaros que cagan	birds that crap on
<u>los escombros.</u>	<u>the ruins.</u>

reordeno	I reorder
este derrame	this leakage
de vidas pasadas,	of past lives,
signos que fecundan	signs that fertilize
en lo raso,	in the satin,
breve	brief
de lo inerte	from the inert
brotan.	they flow.][16]

With poetry functioning as architecture, and words creating space for alternate "escenarios" [scenes], the references to the city that disappears "entre paredes" [between walls] remind readers of the multiple spaces that exist within cityscapes, and of the myriad readings that are contained within collections of poetry, whether or not they are characterized as "duplo" [double]. For in the poem within a poem, the "tipología de un espacio / colmado / de espacio" [typology of a space / filled / with space] falls away, leaving, as a result, room for an alternate arrangement of "parcelas / escenarios / los escombros" [parcels / scenes / the ruins].

The poem "desmontar las cosas" ["to dismantle the things"] also explicitly references the dismantling of one set of "things" to make space for another, as readers are asked to engage in multiple and simultaneous readings.

desmontar <u>las cosas</u>	[to dismantle <u>the things</u>
de su eje	from their axes
para ver el paisaje	to see the landscape
<u>que las cosas</u>	<u>that things</u>
<u>ocultan</u>	<u>hide</u>
al rayo	the lightning
y al hongo	and the mushroom
situarlas en extremos	situate them in
radicales,	radical extremes,
forcejeo	I struggle
para tachar <u>la frase:</u>	to cross out <u>*the phrase:*</u>
"el hongo nace del	"the mushroom is born from
relámpago,"	lightning,"
dioses	gods
sin una digestión	without a
definida.	defined digestion.
desmontar,	to dismount,
<u>ya quedas cerca.</u>	<u>you're almost there.</u>][17]

Dismantling—"desmonta[ndo]"—one set of "cosas" [things], readers are promised that they will see another: "las cosas / que las cosas / ocultan" [the things / that things / hide]. Be it on the page or on the street, readers are thus reminded of their ability to envision and inhabit new, archipelagic spaces of identity that are simultaneously multiple and singular, as are the poems in this innovative collection.

In a society replete with Revolutionary rhetoric, the need for the act of dismantling (or, following Suárez, of digesting) is highlighted in Pérez's references to "rayo" [lightning] and "hongo" [mushroom] in "desmontar las cosas"—a seemingly nonsensical combination of words that might nonetheless serve as a reference to the Castro regime's warnings of "lightning" attacks by enemies of the state, "mushroom" clouds, and nuclear doom.[18] With public discourse in post-1959 Cuba often marked by such rhetoric, the poet signals the need to *tachar* [cross out] to achieve a greater clarity of vision: "tachar la frase: / 'el hongo nace del relámpago'" [cross out the phrase / "the mushroom is born from lightning"]. This act of crossing out once more reveals the poem within a poem:

las cosas	[the things
que las cosas	that things
ocultan	hide
la frase:	the phrase:
ya quedas cerca.	you're almost there.]

The decision to *tachar* (and to <u>underline</u>) lays bare the *cosas* [things] that might otherwise remain hidden: *cosas* that are tied—or perhaps sewn—to *la frase* [the phrase]. These words, stitched together in verse, as might a "**singer** puntando" [**singer** (sewing machine) stitching],[19] are part and parcel of the literary language of the transnational Cuban archipelago. This language is often hidden in a proliferation of Revolutionary rhetoric but is potentially accessible to those willing to *desmontar* [dismantle, dismount] to reach a destination close by: "desmontar/ya quedas cerca" [to dismount/you're almost there].

The need for alternate spaces, and for alternate trajectories through extant spaces, is also manifest in Pérez's 2010 "Recital porcino" [Porcine Reading]: the poet's performative reading of his poetry to some two hundred pigs in Jaruco.[20] In an unpublished piece titled "Los cerdos: retorno a la virtud" ["Pigs: Return to Virtue"], Pérez explains the importance of the porcine.[21] Pigs are often a symbol of the abject in Western culture, at the same time that they are also an important food source. In evoking a "return to virtue" in the title of this unpublished essay, Pérez would seem to underscore the positive connotations of the porcine, along with the value of the agrarian in Cuban culture. The poet echoes, in this regard, the Revolutionary rhetoric that long upheld the benefits (and virtues) of the *campo* [countryside] and the *campesino* [country person].

If Pérez invokes the positive attributes of pigs in the title of his unpublished essay, however, he offers a full-throated critique of what he characterizes as the impoverished state of Cuban culture in his "Recital porcino." On the hot August day of the 2010 performance, Pérez read selections of his then-unpublished *Miedo a las ranas* [Fear of Frogs] to his porcine public.[22] (See Figure 4.) In an interview, Pérez states that he chose to stage the Recital on the same day as an annual cultural event for Cuban youth, organized by the group La Juventud Comunista [Communist Youth], to highlight what he considered to be the cultural degeneration of the event:

> la política [del recital porcino] era, hacer una lectura a cerdos, en el día en que se reúnen miles de jóvenes para bailar reggaetón [. . .] es como una especie de guiño, o sonrisita, a la ideología, que es atroz. Que la ideología siempre es una mueca. [. . .] Una mueca fea que puede ser muy grotesca. Y que puede ser muy peligrosa también, en ciertas circunstancias.

> [the politics [of the porcine reading] were, to do a reading for pigs, on the same day that thousands of young people gather to dance to reggaeton [. . .] it is a sort of wink, or little smile, at the ideology, which is atrocious. The ideology is always a mocking grimace. [. . .] An ugly grimace that can be grotesque. And that can also be very dangerous, in certain circumstances.][23]

Reading his poetry to pigs at the same time that young Cubans across the country danced to reggaeton, Pérez offers a wink and a nod to like-minded literati.

Figure 4. "Recital porcino" (Porcine Recital). Photo provided courtesy of Ricardo Alberto Pérez. Photo by Omar Miranda Jr.

Pointing to the limits of a literary culture that, in his view, now represents a "mueca," or mocking grimace, Pérez appeals to those in the know across the transnational Cuban archipelago. In so doing, he gestures once again to the need for readers to employ a variety of tactics to create both alternate spaces and new paths through extant spaces, be it in Havana, Jaruco, or elsewhere in the *arcubiélago*.

Ramón Hondal: Scratch-ed Records and Books in the Weeds

Poet Ramón Hondal (1974–present) published his first book, *Diálogos* [*Dialogues*], with the Cuban press Ediciones Extramuros in 2014, after winning the Premio Luis Rogelio Nogueras for that collection in 2013.[24] In 2018, *Scratch* followed, from the Netherlands-based press Bokeh; and in 2019, a third title, *Prótesis* [*Prosthesis*], was published by the U.S.-based press Casa Vacía. Hondal frequently publishes his poems and essays as well on websites such as Diario de Cuba and Rialta;[25] he has also edited books with Rodríguez's Torre de Letras imprint, including a new edition of Polish writer Witold Gombrowicz's 1937 novel *Ferdydurke* (2015), which the author famously translated into Spanish with Cuban writer Virgilio Piñera in 1947.[26]

Hondal, who lives in downtown Havana, is tall, thin, and quiet; he wears his dark hair pulled back in a ponytail, and almost always sports a baseball cap. Born some ten years after Pérez, and publishing his first works in the early years of the new millennium, Hondal forms part of what Javier L. Mora and Ángel Pérez term the "Generación Cero" [Generation of the Zero Years].[27] Originally coined by Orlando Luis Pardo Lazo to describe writers who began to publish in the early 2000s,[28] the use of the term to describe Cuban poets such as Hondal has, on the one hand, strictly chronological underpinnings:

> En la práctica, esa clasificación devino un comodín retórico para advertir, simplemente, la aparición de un conjunto de escritores que comienzan a publicar en la década inicial del siglo en curso.

> [In practice, this classification became a generalized rhetorical tool to announce, simply put, the appearance of a group of writers who began to publish in the first decade of the present century.][29]

More broadly, the term serves to signal the shared approaches and characteristics of the writers of this generation. The nation and the Revolution are no longer the all-encompassing markers of identity that they once were for "Zero Years" writers like Hondal, who came of age during the Special Period; and the remixing of media that is evident in Hondal's poetry is more broadly characteristic of writers of his generation, who often foreground references to cinema, pop culture, and mass media in their work.[30]

Hondal began to attend the gatherings that Rodríguez organized in the Torre in 2001 and met Pérez soon thereafter.[31] In an interview, Hondal underscores the importance that Rodríguez and the Torre gatherings had for him:

> En la Torre conocí a [. . .] muchos o varios autores que para mí fueron importantes porque, sobre todo Reina, ¿no?, me abrieron a un mundo de literatura que no conocía. [. . .] Y creo que sigue siendo importante para mí. [. . .] Lamentablemente eso cambió y ya la Torre no es lo que era antes.

> [In the Torre I met [. . .] many or various authors who were important to me [. . .], above all Reina, no?, because they opened me up to a world of literature that I didn't know. [. . .] And I think that this continues to be important for me. [. . .] Unfortunately, this changed and the Torre is no longer what it used to be.][32]

Crediting the Torre gatherings with opening up a new "world of literature" for him, Hondal subsequently sought to make the same experience possible for others. During the final years of the Torre gatherings, Hondal helped to organize events and film screenings for participants. As of this writing, he continues to work as an editor and copyeditor for Rodríguez's Torre de Letras imprint.

In an interview, Hondal stated that he sees his editorial work with the Torre de Letras as helping to fill what would otherwise be a cultural "void" in Cuba. He explained:

> También es una locura nuestra, ¿no?, creer que estos libros, en este país, donde . . . quiero decir donde casi nadie tiene interés, hacer estos libros, y que tengan alguna importancia, publicar eso, ¿para quiénes? Pero bueno, es nuestra . . . qué sé yo, idea, utopía, pensar que aunque sea una persona se interese por eso, que pueda leerlos, que existan. En el gran vacío cultural y editorial que es este país . . . que eso exista . . .

> [This is also our insanity, no? Believing that these books, in this country, where . . . I mean, where almost no one is interested, making these books, and that they have some importance, publishing this, for whom? But, well,

this is our . . . how do I put it, our idea, our utopia, to think that even if it is one person who is interested, that he can read them, that they exist. In the great cultural and editorial void that is this country . . . that this exists . . .][33]

Like Pérez in his characterization of a culturally impoverished landscape, for Hondal the "insanity" of publishing a wide-ranging list of otherwise unavailable titles in Cuba—such as the aforementioned *Ferdydurke*—remains important. In practical terms, for Cubans unable to make purchases from online vendors such as Amazon, the publication of Torre books allows a greater degree of access to out-of-print or unpublished titles. The very existence of the titles published through the Torre de Letras imprint, moreover, is a way for Hondal to continue to foment the connections that linked him, if only momentarily, to the transnational Cuban archipelago through the gatherings he attended in the Torre.

Hondal's efforts to write islands in the *arcubiélago* are also evident in *Diálogos* and *Scratch*, as well as in the poet's collaborations with visual artists on projects related to these texts. Hondal characterizes *Diálogos* and *Scratch* as the first two books in a poetic trilogy, which is completed by *Prótesis*. In an interview with writer and cultural critic Carlos Aguilera, Hondal expands on the characteristics of the trilogy:

A los tres libros les une la progresión de una voz que en *Diálogos* es personal, íntima, delirante pero casi cálida, obsesionada por una compañía (Beckett) que busca aun cuando sabe imposible, y que se mueve por una ciudad que mantiene al margen, como si estuviera desierta. Ya esto no sucede en *Scratch*, donde la voz se mezcla en el drama social que le distorsiona y lacera. Finalmente, en *Prótesis* la voz va hacia adentro, no queda nada afuera, es pura esquizofrenia, delirio, sabe que no hay posibilidad de compartir nada ni lo quiere, es solo ella misma.

[The three books are linked by the progression of a voice that in *Dialogues* is personal, intimate, delirious but almost warm, obsessed with a company (Beckett) that it looks for even though it knows it is impossible, and that moves around a city that remains at the margins, as though it were deserted. This no longer occurs in *Scratch*, where the voice mixes with the social drama that distorts and damages it. Finally, in *Prosthesis* the voice goes within, nothing remains outside, it is absolute schizophrenia, delirium, it knows that it is not possible to share anything nor does it want to, it is only itself.][34]

Foregrounding silences and omissions in *Diálogos*, and calling attention to the "scratches" that mar the surface of Cuban culture in *Scratch*, Hondal points in both instances to the difficulties of communication in an era of sweeping societal change. At the same time, the poet echoes Pérez in hammering home the need for a new, archipelagic space for Cuban letters. To this end, he traces alternate itineraries through the metaphorical and literal landscape of Havana in his work and collaborates with visual artists Luis Enrique López-Chávez Pollán (on *Diálogos*) and Léster Álvarez (on *Scratch*).

In *Diálogos*, Hondal offers readers a series of conversations between a couple that sets off on a walk around the city of Havana. Readers are asked to watch and listen as a guide offers knowing commentary on the couple, who talk as they move together from the interior space of an apartment to a series of exterior spaces including a street and a park. The desire for dialogue is manifest throughout the collection, as is the impossibility of true communication: drawing on Samuel Beckett's *Company* and pushing language to its limits, Hondal points in *Diálogos* to the need for new itineraries through city and text alike, at the same time that he ultimately signals the inability of speech to communicate truth or meaning.

Titles interspersed between poems in *Diálogos* (most of which are themselves untitled) serve to orient readers, who might otherwise get lost along the way. Following the opening poems "*Las voces dialogan*" ["*The Voices Dialogue*"] and "Uno" ["One"], poems are divided among sections titled "Despertar" [Awakening], "La calle" [The Street], "Parque" [Park], "Encuentro" [Encounter], "Noche" [Night], "Mesas" [Tables], "Encuentro" [Encounter], and "Habitación" [Room]. The collection concludes with "Decir . . ." ["To Say . . ."] and "Uno" ["One"]. The first poem in the section "Despertar" [Awakening] explains to readers that they must look and listen closely:

Mire. Abren los ojos. Despiertan.
Comience a seguir gestos. Siga el primero del día.
Pequeño enredo de palabras. El primero del día. Cada gesto cuenta para luego. Cuéntelos. Desde que abran los ojos cuente. Con cuidado. Siempre de lejos.
Usted escuchará la voz, la callada, y nunca la suya. Ciérrese y dele lugar solo a ellos.
Entre. Ojos abiertos.

[Look. They open their eyes. They awaken.
Begin to follow their gestures. Follow the first of the day.

A small tangling of words. The first of the day. Each gesture counts for later.
Count them. From the moment they open their eyes, count. Carefully.
Always from afar.
You will hear the voice, the hushed voice, and never your own. Close your-
self off and make room only for them.
Enter. Eyes open.][35]

The third poem in the section asks readers to not only look and listen, but also to
follow the couple, first as they get out of bed, and, later, as they leave their home
to walk through the city: "Pero sígalos. [. . .] Sígalos desde el primer paso en el
suelo" [But follow them. [. . .] Follow them, from their first step on the floor].[36]
Readers willing to tag along are thus promised that they will see and hear the
city from the couple's standpoint.

The couple's decision to set out on foot might be considered a sign of their
limited economic means—they are not, after all, getting into a rented 1950s
Buick (or a Russian Lada of their own) or flagging down a *colectivo* [ride-share],
as they might do on a hot day if they had money to spare—and the exhortation
to "follow" might be considered an appeal to readers to put themselves in someone else's shoes. The couple's ambling walk from "street" to "park," and from
"night" to "tables," however, also points to the possibility of forging new itineraries through established cityscapes; what de Certeau describes as "walkers."
Following de Certeau, the walkers are "practitioners [who] make use of spaces
that cannot be seen; their knowledge of them is as blind as that of lovers in each
other's arms."[37] Wandering through the city (or the text), the couple in *Diálogos*
is able to assume agency in the face of seemingly immutable city grids.

Highlighting individuals' ability to assert agency as "poets of their own acts"[38]
by treading along previously unforeseen routes, Hondal also foregrounds individuals' ability to forge new paths through language. For de Certeau, walking
and talking are both ways to assume tactical agency. He writes: "The act of walking is to the urban system what the speech act is to language or to the statements
uttered."[39] Individuals' paths through language, de Certeau reminds us, are created with the words and patterns of existing discourses and grammatical forms,
much as the paths we tread are related to the city grid. As with walking, though,
these paths through language can nonetheless represent the possibility of different routes that, in turn, might contribute to the formulation of different spaces.

In *Diálogos*, at the same time that the couple plots a novel course through
the city in their meandering walk, they also plot an innovative course through

language. The dialogue that is included in the second half of the first poem in the section "Despertar" serves as an example of how Hondal plays with language in the conversations he includes between the couple.

—Empezar.
—¿Acerca de qué esto?
—¿Quisiera esto?
—Y el paso.
—¿Sin lengua? ¿Sin voz? ¿Cómo?
—La luz. El mismo gesto.
—Se enreda todo. Nunca todo.
—Un deseo. Otro.
—Y la presión del cuerpo en la cama.
—¿Acerca de qué?

[—To begin.
—What is this about?
—Would you want this?
—And the passage.
—Without language? Without voice? How?
—The light. The same gesture.
—It all gets entangled. Never all.
—A desire. Another.
—And the pressure of the body on the bed.
—About what?]⁴⁰

In the first part of the poem, the poetic voice addresses the reader, telling him or her to "Mire" [Look]; this command is followed by the imperative to "Comience a seguir" [Begin to follow] and to "Cuéntelos" [Count them], as well as by the promise that you—"Usted"—will hear ("escuchará"). What "you" will "hear," however, might not be the same as what you will understand: as new paths are forged through language in *Diálogos*, meaning often seems to become inextricably "entangled," as wordplay clouds easy comprehension. In the example above, this wordplay is evident in the multiple potential meanings of many of the words in the terse dialogue. I have translated "paso" as "passage," for instance, but it might also be translated as "pace"; similarly, I have translated "lengua" as "language," but it might also be translated as "tongue."

As manifest in *Diálogos*, writers of the "Generación Cero" [Generation of the Zero Years] such as Hondal often reject readily comprehensible images in favor of more esoteric formulations, taking "an interest in how resistance could operate in language itself, sometimes by way of a refusal to offer 'clarity.'"[41] In this regard, although *Diálogos* in some ways lives up to the implicit promise of its title, offering a series of conversations such as that included above, it is ultimately the *lack* of possible understanding that is repeatedly underscored in the text—and, by extension, the closing of space and possibility, even in the *arcubiélago*.

While this is evident to some degree in the aforementioned example, in which the poetic voice reminds readers that they will never be able to hear or understand completely, it is particularly manifest in the opening poem, *Las voces dialogan* [*The Voices Dialogue*]. Here the poet insinuates that the possibility of dialogue invoked in the title represents an impossible dream rather than a reality:

> *Las voces dialogan.*
> *Los silencios espían, dividen.*
>
> *Uno de ellos, el guía, arrastra al otro que no resuena y es solo escucha.*
>
> *Van hacia esas voces que se mueven de un lugar a otro de la ciudad, de una casa, de un cuarto. Hacen un mapa de las voces, hablan y se descubre la palabra del guía.*
>
> *El arrastrado es silencio.*
>
> *Al final un mismo diálogo. La palabra silenciada y la palabra dicha ocupan el mismo lugar.*
>
> [*The voices talk.*
> *The silences spy, divide.*
>
> *One of them, the guide, drags the other that does not reverberate and is only listening.*
>
> *They go toward those voices that move from one place to another in the city, in a house, in a room. They make a map of the voices, they speak and the voice of the guide is discovered.*

Silence is the one dragged.

At the end one dialogue. The silenced word and the spoken word occupy the same place.]⁴²

The possibility of a plurality of dialogues that is foregrounded in the book's title is thus belied in the opening poem, which points to the pernicious role of silence(s), as well as to the silencing of one voice (or voices) by another. With the "silenced word" and the "spoken word" occupying the same space, the possibility of a plurality of dialogues that is held out in the title is replaced by the reality of "one dialogue."

The mapping of space that is implicit in the couple's walk through the city, moreover, would initially seem to offer the possibility of finding—and potentially inhabiting—new spaces throughout the *arcubiélago*; but ultimately results instead in a closing down (rather than an opening up) of possibility, as the guide imposes his or her own map. In this way, the brief possibility of what might be characterized, following de Certeau, as "'indirect' or 'errant' trajectories obeying their own logic,"⁴³ is forestalled, with the guide serving as a reminder that those in power are able to employ "strategies" rather than "tactics" to influence cityscapes and the paths that crisscross them.

In 2018's *Scratch*, Hondal again signals the difficulties of engaging in true dialogue—and of forging alternate spaces of identity—in the face of the material and cultural scarcities of the present. For Hondal, *Diálogos* and *Scratch* each communicate what the poet considers to be "La misma sensación, pero con diferentes matices" [The same sensation, but with different nuances].⁴⁴ More specifically, Hondal states that *Scratch* was motivated by the idea of a scratch on a long-playing (LP) record:

Y pensaba en el sonido que se ha convertido en algo insalvable, de lo que hace falta, [. . .] en el *scratch*. [. . .] detrás del sonido, que debería ser limpio pero nunca lo es.

[And I thought of the sound that has become an insurmountable part of that which is needed, [. . .] the *scratch*. [. . .] behind the sound, which should be clean but never is.]⁴⁵

In line with its title, *Scratch* offers readers a collection of poems whose organization mimics the form of an LP record: the opening section, "Cara A" [A-Side], is followed by "Cara B" [B-Side], which, in turn, is followed by "Se levanta el brazo" [The Arm Lifts].[46] *Scratch* was inspired in part by what Hondal describes as the disjuncture between his everyday life and the music, films, and books he enjoyed, and in part by his search for vinyl records in Havana with a close friend.[47] When this friend left to return to Europe, she took their record player with her, leaving Hondal without a means of listening to his collection. Nostalgia for the past thus permeates the poems, which often foreground memories of spaces past.

In some of the poems in *Scratch*, Hondal again signals the artistic opening up of space and time, highlighting in this instance the ability of poets and musicians alike to construct an alternate, archipelagic space in which all might gather through the recording of music and poetry and the soaring of sound and language.[48] This is apparent in section V of a poem titled "El mismo violonchelo, diferente sonido" ["The Same Cello, Different Sound"], which tells of a Stradivarius cello once owned by British cellist Jacqueline du Pré, and now used by Chinese-American cellist Yo-Yo Ma:

> Esto no ocurre en la palabra
> Esta palabra que se tira a esta acera, sobre el sol.
>
> No hay intérpretes para esta lengua
> No hay forma de agarrar lo escrito y lo dicho
> Cambiar su tiempo
> Su palabra
> Ni hacer que se arrastre la lentitud
> Y entre por los pies hasta la cabeza.
>
> Las palabras, una vez dichas, se entierran en su cárcel.
>
> El sonido vuela de un tiempo en otro
> Cambia, salta y suma notas.
>
> Una nueva palabra a Celan se cae Celan
> Y no entra por los pies hasta la cabeza. Este sol.
>
> Si se quita sigue igual.
>
> [This does not occur in the word
> This word that is thrown on this sidewalk, on the sun.

There are not vocalists for this language
There is no way to grasp the written and the spoken
Change its tempo
Its word
Nor to make the slowness drag on
And enter from head to toes.

Words, once spoken, are buried in their prison.

Sound flies from one time to another
Changes, jumps, and sums up notes.

A new word to Celan, Celan falls.
And does not enter from head to toe. This sun.

If it is taken away, it continues the same.][49]

As the poet proclaims, sound—music—is endowed with a power that words alone do not have. Words, once spoken, are buried in their "cárcel" [prison]; sound, in contrast, "vuela de un tiempo en otro / Cambia, salta y suma notas" [flies from one time to another / Changes, jumps, and sums up notes]. Sound, then, is capable of moving from one time to another, staging an alternate time for an alternate space that is simultaneously one and many.

In *Scratch*, Hondal also highlights the necessarily fleeting existence of any alternate space of identity, emphasizing, as he does in *Diálogos*, that it will flicker in and out of existence. The dual thrust of Hondal's collection of poems, in which he simultaneously creates and contests an alternate space of identity, is clear in the references to poet Paul Celan in "El mismo violonchelo, diferente sonido," and, by extension, to Celan's firsthand experience of the Holocaust. It is also evident in "La Casa Haneke" ["Haneke House"], which includes Hondal's meditations on the film *Caché* [*Hidden*],[50] along with his recounting of the experience of viewing a filmed version of a Queen concert in Havana's Charles Chaplin cinema. As the concert, filmed in 1982, is projected to spectators in present-day Havana, Hondal writes that time and space become confused:

[. . .] Se entra a ver un concierto, y ni siquiera a uno con músicos de carne y hueso, sino un concierto grabado. No es un concierto reciente para colmo, es un viejo concierto de 1982.

¿Y qué diferencia habría entre un concierto y otro? ¿La muerte, tal vez?

Queen toca para los pocos que hay en la sala. [...] Se viene más que a ver a Queen, a encontrarse con lo que no pudo ser.

[One enters to see a concert, and not even a concert with flesh-and-blood musicians, but a recorded concert. To top it off it's not a recent concert, it's an old concert from 1982.

And what would the difference be between one concert and another? Death, perhaps?

Queen plays for the few who are in the room. [...] More than to see Queen, one comes to be with that which could not be.][51]

Through his references to British rock band Queen and Austrian film director Michael Haneke, Hondal again signals the possibility of a transnational space out of time. In this space, now constructed through music and song, lyric and tone, like-minded readers may gather to listen to old records and catch a glimpse of international cultural icons. At the same time, Hondal implies that this alternate space is ephemeral. It is likely not only to shift in time and space (as occurs with Rodríguez's Azotea and Torre), but also to disappear, as suggested in the poem's mention of "muerte" [death] and "lo que no pudo ser" [that which could not be]: references to Freddie Mercury's early death from AIDS complications at age 45.[52]

In describing the "scratch" that gives the collection its title in a poem on "Cara A" [A-Side] titled "Cuatro" ["Four"] (a reference to a record's track number), Hondal again offers a cautionary reminder of the limitations of creating an alternate space out of time, in this instance through music and media. As he writes:

Está el Scratch. El Scratch, ¿qué es?

Se limpia el disco para eliminar el Scratch. No. Se mantiene el Scratch. El Scratch es parte de la música, y tanto se quiere la música, rememorar, como ese Scratch que se cuela desde el surco hasta el oído y hace saltar la aguja que marcha y marcha.

El Scratch es el ruido, lo que interfiere, lo que debería sobrar. Pero no sobra. El Scratch no sobra. Uno. Dos. Uno tras otro. Tres. Cuatro. No sobra.

[There is the Scratch. The Scratch, what is it?

The record is cleaned to eliminate the Scratch. No. The Scratch is maintained. The Scratch is part of the music, and as much as the music is loved, to remember how that Scratch that passes from the groove to the ear and causes the needle that goes and goes to jump.

The scratch is the noise, that which interferes, that which should be superfluous. But it is not superfluous. The Scratch is not superfluous. One. Two. One after another. Three. Four. It is not superfluous.][53]

Over time, the scratches that cut across the vinyl become intrinsic to the music, offering an alternate rendition from that which has been recorded. At the same time, the scratches continue to interfere. The "ruido" [noise], or "lo que interfiere" [that which interferes], is so ingrained that it does not "sobra" [is not superfluous]. But, by virtue of this very fact, neither does the "scratch" allow listeners to leave the space and time of the present for more than a brief moment, even as it serves, materially, as a record of a moment in time that is accidentally preserved.

This portrayal of the possibilities, as well as the limitations, of creating alternate trajectories through established cityscapes is underscored in Hondal's collaborations with visual artists. For *Diálogos*, Hondal partnered with visual artist and friend Luis Enrique López-Chávez Pollán. Hondal included various images from López-Chávez's photograph series "Fuera de campo" ["Out of Sight"] in the original manuscript, and asked that they be included in the printed edition as well.[54] The press was unable to accommodate this request, but featured a reproduction of the photograph "Escena #2" ["Scene #2"] on the cover. (See Figure 5.)

In "Escena #2," López-Chávez offers a close-up shot of the ceramic tiles that are often found in Havana's grand colonial homes. Havana is one of the most photographed cities in the world and is known for its ruinous mansions. Yet while López-Chávez foregrounds a detail of the architecture for which the city is well known throughout the *arcubiélago* in "Escena #2," he departs from stock photographs that romanticize Havana's dilapidated ruins. Disturbing the neat order of the geometric patterns that often lie underfoot, he shoots the tiles at a slant and overlays them with the shadows of two figures that stretch down from the top of the image. Thereby resisting the easy pleasure that would accompany a straight shot, the artist suggests by showing the shadows, rather than the bodies that cast them, that viewers of necessity apprehend only part of the whole. In much the same way that viewers of "Escena #2" will never see the image in its totality, readers will hear only part of the book's "dialogues," despite their best attempts to listen closely.

Figure 5. Jacket cover of Ramón Hondal's *Diálogos* (*Dialogues*), published in 2014 by Ediciones Extramuros. Cover image, "Escena #2" (Scene #2), from Luis Enrique López-Chávez Pollán's photograph series "Fuera de campo" (Out of Sight). Photo by author.

For *Scratch*, Hondal collaborated with visual artist Léster Álvarez on his project "La Maleza" ["The Weed"]. As professor Rachel Price writes of "La Maleza": "The title—meaning weed, a subjective rather than a scientific category—suggests an unwanted growth, but also resilience and energy bursting forth in the most inhospitable of circumstances [. . .]."[55] In the "La Maleza" project, which he began in 2015, Álvarez uses repurposed wood that he finds on Havana streets to create a series of book covers for works not published in Cuba, including *Scratch*.[56] (See Figure 6.) In forging the book covers from the

Figure 6. In his "La Maleza" project, visual artist Léster Álvarez creates book covers from salvaged wood to draw attention to titles not published in Cuba. Photo provided courtesy of Léster Alvarez.

remnants of construction projects that began as tourism in Havana increased in the 2000s, leading to a rush of renovation and the creation of a *nouveau riche*, Álvarez highlights the economic disparities between those able to afford new construction materials to renovate their homes, and those who must rummage through discarded waste—or weeds—to find the materials they need for work or sheer sustenance.[57] At the same time, he gestures toward the materiality of the book as a physical object, and underscores once again that the books in the "La Maleza" series cannot be read.[58] In this way, he draws attention to the limitations and difficulties of book publishing and distribution in Cuba, where it is easier to produce books as art for display in galleries than to publish and distribute them through bookstores and libraries.

Remixing media through his collaborations with visual artists López-Chávez and Álvarez, as well as through his inclusion of multiple references to music, cinema, and culture in his poetry, Hondal points to the need for a new space for Cuban culture. Releasing his own work throughout the *arcubiélago*, and publishing otherwise inaccessible books in Cuba through his editorial work with the Torre de Letras imprint, Hondal joins Pérez in seeking to amplify the alternate space of identity envisaged by Rodríguez. At the same time, he too recognizes the inherent evanescence of any such space. With dialogues blocked by miscommunications and sound marred by scratches, any space in which like-minded literati might gather is, of necessity, fleeting.

Remixing the Archipelago

On one of my final trips to Cuba to research this book, I picked up Hondal in a restored 1950s-era Buick I had rented for the day for a road trip to visit Pérez in Jaruco. Visual artist Álvarez, who had agreed to accompany us, rode shotgun. Windows down, we cruised along as stretches of undeveloped space opened up along the highway, with fields—often dotted with grazing cows or horses—in stark contrast to the busy and crowded streets of the capital.

En route to Jaruco, we decided to make a short detour to visit the nearby town of Hershey, known for its "jardines," or gardens, with Pérez. Hershey, Cuba, is named for the U.S. conglomerate headquartered in Hershey, Pennsylvania. Prior to the 1959 Revolution, the town processed sugar for the company known for its chocolate bars (and iconic kisses), with executives and their families living in a bustling town that replicated the layout of its U.S. counterpart. Today, the skeletal ruins of the sugar mill and the dilapidated buildings that once offered company housing serve as a reminder of a capitalist, neo-colonialist past that is no more. The "jardines" are lush and overgrown, with palm trees rising through dense vegetation. Once dedicated to exclusive parties and gatherings, the now-public gardens recall the Revolutionary government's commitment to making spaces and opportunities open to all, even as the overgrowth signals the difficulties of maintaining vast tracts of manicured gardens with limited economic resources. (See Figure 7.)

Walking through the Hershey Gardens with Hondal and Álvarez, I wondered aloud how space and social stratification were negotiated in contemporary

Figure 7. *From left*, Ricardo Alberto Pérez, Léster Álvarez, and Ramón Hondal in the Jardines de Hershey (Hershey Gardens). Photo by author.

Cuba. The gardens, after all, represented a decolonizing project: an attempt to plant the new seeds of a future in which all Cubans enjoyed the sweet deal once reserved for the employees and associates of U.S. conglomerates. Yet despite the opening of once-private spaces such as the Hershey Gardens to the public, the poets and artists' projects demonstrated that access was limited in new ways in the years following the Special Period. Responding to my query, Álvarez stated that social divisions are evident both in the spaces that Cubans inhabit and in the ways in which they move through these spaces. To reach a destination in the city, for instance, some people can afford to take a *taxi colectivo* (a sort of Cuban ride-share costing 10 pesos, or approximately one U.S. half-dollar); some are privileged enough to own their own cars; and some must rely on often-crowded and comparatively slow—but eminently affordable—buses for transportation. (A bus ride in Havana cost 40 cents in *moneda nacional* in 2018, less than one U.S. nickel at that year's exchange rates.)[59] To reach a town such as Jaruco without access to a private car was even more of an undertaking, requiring a long wait for a public bus operating on an unpredictable schedule.

Álvarez's comments served as a reminder of the need to continue to tread innovative paths through cities and cultural productions alike. For as de Certeau writes, consumers, as well as poets, can forge alternate paths through existing spaces: "As unrecognized producers, poets of their own acts, [...] consumers produce through their signifying practices [...] 'indirect' or 'errant' trajectories obeying their own logic."[60] Underscoring the need to write and walk new paths through islands and cities, streets and gardens, the poets and visual artists whose projects I have described in this chapter work collaboratively to discover and inspire novel trajectories. Charting new routes through what they perceive as the cultural and material detritus of life in the twenty-first-century capital and its environs, Pérez and Hondal remix media and point to the need for new archipelagic formations in a time of sea change.

4

Blogging on (and Beyond) the Palenque

On a warm February night in 2017, I clambered into a Havana taxi and gave the driver the address of Afro-Cuban poet Julio Moracen.[1] I had returned to Cuba for the Feria del Libro [Book Fair], and I had been invited to a party to celebrate the birthdays of Moracen and his longtime friends (and fellow poets) Caridad Atencio and Roberto Zurbano. Moracen now lives in Brazil, but he is often in Havana for the Feria, and, coincidentally, the three birthdays. Moracen told me, "Siempre lo celebramos así" [We always celebrate like this].

After a few wrong turns, the taxi driver deposited me at Moracen's house, where I found people and music spilling out into the street as the party expanded beyond the walls of the poet's modest family home. When I gave Moracen the bottle of rum I had brought as a gift, he promptly offered it to his *orishas*. His mother approached me with a plate heaping with food (*maduros, arroz con frijoles, carne*), and I sat down to eat with Atencio and her partner, poet Rito Ramón Aroche. We were soon joined by a couple from Holland who, I learned, had just brought Aroche copies of his most recent book, *Límites de Alcanía* [*Limits of Alcanía*]; the book had been published in the Netherlands by Bokeh Press and sent to him via a mutual friend. Aroche gave me a copy and asked if I would bring it to his translator, Kristin Dykstra, when I returned to the United States. I was happy to oblige: "¡Por supuesto!" [Of course!].

Sharing drinks and dinner, the aforementioned poets—who are known, along with some of their friends, as the "Grupo del Palenque" [Palenque Group]— swapped books and shared stories.[2] Circulating texts not widely available in Havana, the poets forged an alternate distribution circuit that connected the nation's capital to the wider transnational Cuban archipelago, much as occurred in the case of poet Reina María Rodríguez and her collaborators when they gathered in the Azotea or the Torre. These exchanges of books are one example of how goods flow across national borders in Cuba; the well-known "paquete semanal" [weekly packet], which allows Cubans to download digital media to their devices for a modest fee, is another.[3]

Crafting an alternate space of identity *in situ* through their gatherings, the Palenque poets expanded the parameters of the space they created in Havana through their blog, "Del Palenque . . . y para . . ." ["From the Palenque . . . and for/toward . . ." ; 2007–2014].[4] Regardless of whether they found themselves in Brazil or Barcelona, Havana or Holland, the blog allowed the Palenque poets to maintain their ties with each other, and to reach a wider public. The blog also allowed the Palenque poets to gesture "toward," or *para*, a metaphoric, archipelagic space in which (trans)national diversity is celebrated.[5] This space departs "from," or *del*, the overly simplistic notion of race manifest in their very name, and signals the need for an ongoing conversation on the negotiation of race and identity in nominally post-racial Cuba.

The Grupo del Palenque

Slavery in Cuba was officially abolished in 1886, marking, at least on paper, an end to the chattel bondage that dated from the sixteenth century. Racial discrimination and prejudice continued to flourish in the ensuing decades, however, as the long history of enslavement continued to reverberate through time and space.[6] In a bid to right this historic wrong, Fidel Castro declared race-based discrimination illegal in Cuba shortly after assuming power in 1959, implementing policies designed to desegregate public spaces and the workforce, as well as to ensure equal access to housing, education, and medical care.[7] Although there were limits to Castro's push for equality, public discussion of discrimination was nonetheless prohibited as the Revolutionary government declared success.[8] By 1962, Fidel Castro even went so far as to state that it had "not cost the revolution much effort to resolve that problem."[9] If the government declared that the end of discrimination had been an easy win, though, this did not mean that the subject was closed. Conversations on race continued unchecked in the private sphere, and "notions of race continued to affect social relations in a myriad of ways."[10]

The ongoing effects of race on Cuban society—as well as Cuban economics— became particularly salient some three decades after the Revolutionary regime's declaration of the end of race-based discrimination, during the Special Period of the 1990s. Events such as the 1980 Mariel Boat Lift had drawn attention to the still-vexed intersection of race and national identity in Cuba, as many of the *marielitos* were Black or *mulato*. In turn, these issues were exacerbated following the 1989 collapse of the Soviet Union, when Cuba experienced extreme scarcities due to the loss of the aid it had long received from its key ally. To combat widespread hunger and destitution, the government then turned to the tourist sector to increase revenue; it also opened the economy to private ventures and began to depend more significantly on remittances from abroad.

As writer and Palenque Group member Roberto Zurbano details in an influential 2013 *New York Times* op-ed, "For Blacks in Cuba, the Revolution Hasn't Begun," it soon became clear that light-skinned Cubans were best positioned to benefit from these changes in governmental policy. Light-skinned Cubans were hired disproportionately for jobs in the tourist sector that paid in highly desirable dollars (rather than the *peso*, the national albeit significantly less valuable currency); were more likely to receive funds from relatives abroad; and were more likely to own the types of homes that lent themselves to use as *casas particulares* [in-home inns]—such as the one I stayed in when I traveled to Havana to research this book—or *paladares* [in-home restaurants].[11] As Zurbano notes in his essay "Soy un negro más" ["I Am One More Black Person"], furthermore, dark-skinned Cubans were also more likely to face discrimination in the 1990s: they were more routinely stopped by the police and were more often incarcerated for minor infractions.

Like Zurbano's essays, the history of the Palenque poets' name points to the ongoing reverberations of race in Cuba in the 1990s and early 2000s. According to Zurbano, the Palenque Group was officially baptized in 2004 at a gathering of the Unión Nacional de Escritores y Artistas Cubanos (UNEAC) [Union of Cuban Writers and Artists] held in the southwestern Cuban city of Pinar del Río:

En ese evento, Basilia Papastamatiu, crítica cubano-argentina, bautizó al Grupo del Palenque, integrado por Ismael González Castañer, Caridad Atencio, Julio Mitjans, Antonio Armenteros y otros pocos autores negros.

[At that event, Cuban-Argentine critic Basilia Papastamatiu baptized the Palenque Group, composed of Ismael González Castañer, Caridad Atencio, Julio Mitjans, Antonio Armenteros, and a few other Black authors.][12]

Choosing to baptize the group with a term used to describe Cuba's runaway slave settlements of the nineteenth century, Papastamatiu foregrounded the importance of race as a criterion for Palenque group membership.[13]

In linking the Palenque Group's identity to race, Papastamatiu hewed to a larger trend identified by writer and critic Alberto Abreu in an interview with poet Rito Ramón Aroche. Abreu states, "Allá por los años noventa me llamó mucho la atención que ciertos escritores dentro de la ciudad letrada se refer- ían a ustedes como 'los negros'. Y eso en verdad me causaba cierta confusión" [Sometime in the 1990s it caught my attention that certain writers within the lettered city referred to you as "the Blacks." And this honestly caused me some confusion].[14] In his response, Aroche notes that Abreu's "confusion" was shared by "los negros" [the Blacks] themselves:

> Nunca oí decir tal de un grupo de amigos preocupados más por escribir y escribir bien. [. . .] No tenemos programa ni mucho menos anexos se- cretos. No tenemos revistas donde pronunciarnos, tampoco manifiestos. [. . .] La amistad es otra cosa [. . .] eso de "los negros" *otra cosa*. ¿O de verdad tú puedes pensar que la amistad es un asunto de raza y color?

> [I never heard that said of a group of friends who were concerned primar- ily with writing, and writing well. [. . .] We don't have a program, and much less secret annexes. We don't have journals in which we make dec- larations, neither do we have manifestos. [. . .] Friendship is something else [. . .] that of "the Blacks" *something else*. Or do you really think that friendship is a matter of race and color?][15]

The Palenque poets' lack of manifesto stands in contradistinction to those of other groups, such as the well-known Grupo Diásporas.[16] It also stands in con- trast, historically, to the manifestos that well-known Afro-Cuban poet Nicolás Guillén (1902–1989) co-authored with anthropologist and essayist Fernando Or- tiz (1881–1969), such as "Contra los racismos" ["Against Racisms"].

In contradistinction to groups such as Diásporas, the Palenque poets self- identified as friends united by a love of writing, rather than as members of a literary movement joined by common principles or social goals (much less—as Papastamatiu implied—by race). As such, they initially objected to Papastama- tiu's facile categorization. Subsequently, however, they assumed the name as their own. Zurbano recalls in tongue-in-cheek humor: "Primero me desagradó el término [. . .] Luego, se agradece que sea el Palenque y no el Barracón" [At first I didn't like the term [. . .] Later, it was appreciated that it was the Palenque and not the Slave Quarters].[17]

While the terms *palenque* and *barracón* both point to the long history—and ongoing repercussions—of slavery in Cuba, the former represents a space of resistance, while the latter denotes a space of bondage. This is true throughout the Caribbean, where, as scholar Antonio Benítez Rojo writes, "the model of the transgressive community is the *palenque*—also called *quilombo, mocambo, ladeira, cumbe, mambí*, etc. [. . .] The word *palenque* refers to the stockade that usually surrounded a village of runaways, but, in reality, the palenque was much more than runaway slaves' huts inside a stockade; it was an entire defensive system."[18] Although the space of the palenque was associated with the runaway slaves, or *cimarrones,* who lived there, Indians and some Whites also inhabited palenques in nineteenth-century Cuba, according to writer Pedro Marqués de Armas, and the space was generally considered to be an oasis of freedom for those subjugated by society.[19]

In 2007, some three years after their "baptism," the Palenque poets launched the blog "Del Palenque . . . y para . . ." Members of the group lived in Brazil and Spain as well as Cuba, and they sought to remain in touch and share information about what they were reading. Signaling this intent, the blog's full name (which appears in truncated form on the site) is "Del Palenque . . . y para . . . *los amigos*" ["From the Palenque . . . and for . . . *friends*"].[20] Over the seven years of its active existence, from 2007 to 2014, a total of 821 posts were made to the blog, with between one and thirty-one posts made each month (excluding those months when no posts were made). Posts featured work by Palenque poets, as well as poems, essays, short stories, interviews, and artwork by a transnational, multiracial group of writers and artists. Those featured on the blog from April 3, 2007 (the date of the first post) to September 27, 2014 (the date of the last) represented more than 40 countries, and were born between 429 A.C. (Plato, featured in August 2008) and 1981 (F. Salem Daie, featured in June 2010).

Although Internet pages are increasingly recognized as evanescent, as of this writing, the blog "Del Palenque . . . y para . . ." is still available online.[21] On the main webpage, the blog's title, "DEL PALENQUE . . . Y PARA . . . ," is written in all white capital letters that stand out against a black background. Under the title, to the left, there is a small photograph of some of the Palenque poets sitting around a coffee table, a visual reminder of the times that the group gathered together in person. Beneath this photograph is a button for Google Translate that allows visitors to instantaneously translate the entire site into one (or all) of the 104 languages available in the drop-down menu, be it English (listed first), Afrikaans (listed second), or Zulu (listed last). Underneath the Google Translate button is the "archivo del blog" [blog archive], organized by month; and on the other side of the page, also under the title but to the right, are the current

Figure 8. *From left,* Caridad Atencio, Julio Moracen, Elena Lahr-Vivaz, and Rito Ramón Aroche in Havana in 2017. Photo provided courtesy of author.

month's entries. The most recent, from September 2014, appears first and is titled "Tres poemas de Leonardo Sinisgalli" ["Three poems by Leonardo Sinisgalli"]. Scrolling down, this post, featuring poems by Italian poet Sinisgalli, is followed by 13 additional posts featuring the work of, respectively, Spanish writer Cristina Garcia Rodés, Russian writer Daniil Kharms, Korean writer Kim Ki-taek, Canadian poet and essayist Anne Carson, Polish poet Wisława Szymborska, Cuban poet Nelson Simón, U.S. poet Robert Frost, Russian writer Varlam Shalámov, Cuban poet Regino Boti, Argentine poet Juan Gelman, U.S. poet Adrienne Rich, and Cuban poet Caridad Atencio. (The final post features the cover of a 2014 issue of Potemkin ediciones.) As is often the case on the blog, most posts for this month are accompanied by photographs of the authors whose work is featured; as is also often the case, all posts are credited as "publicado por D.L." [published by D.L. (Dolores Labarcena)].[22]

While there is, to my knowledge, no published criticism to date on the blog

"Del Palenque ... y para ... ," a nascent body of scholarship on Cuban blogs has emerged. This scholarship forms part of a larger body of work on "digital humanities," an interdisciplinary field that might be defined as "using information technology to illuminate the human record, and bringing an understanding of the human record to bear on the development and use of information technology."[23] The specificities of blogging in Cuba add another dimension to scholarship in digital humanities more generally. In particular, what André Brock terms "critical technoculture discourse analysis (CTDA)," which "applies critical race and technoculture theories to IT artifacts and accompanying online conversations to analyze technology's cultural and discursive construction,"[24] allows an approach to digital humanities scholarship that avoids what Miriam Posner and Kim Gallon, among others, argue is a prevalent tendency to reduce race and gender identities to overly reductive categories in data analysis. Considering the posts to the blog "Del Palenque ... y para ... ." along with the comments that these posts elicited sheds light on the ways in which technology and culture are together used to create and negotiate alternative, transnational spaces of identity.

Since 2007, recent scholarship suggests, blogs in Cuba have proliferated,[25] even as Internet access has remained limited. According to Cristina Venegas, for example, in 2009, just over one in eleven Cubans (or approximately 1.4 million individuals) had Internet access, most of whom were academics, cultural producers, or professionals. Security clearance was required to browse online, and 56K dial-up connections were often the norm, making it difficult to post (or view) blogs and other media-rich content.[26] Despite these impediments, however, the early 2000s saw an increase in the number of blogs in Cuba, both by those officially on state rolls as Internet users and by those who resorted to clandestine connections to make their posts. This uptick is particularly noteworthy given governmental denigration of many bloggers' work as "'ciberchancleteo,'" or, in the words of professor Paloma Duong, "the virtual equivalent of the sound made by flip-flops, which in Cuban slang refers to the mannerisms of the uneducated and the poor, the marginal sectors of society."[27] Yoani Sánchez's "Generación Y" ["Generation Y"], launched the same year as "Del Palenque ... y para ... ," is perhaps Cuba's best-known blog. Sánchez's blog differs significantly from that of the Palenque poets in its content, which is overtly political (and highly critical of the Castro regimes); posts to the blog, however, are similarly made by individuals outside Cuba.[28]

Given the restrictions on Internet access in Cuba, and the official rhetoric of blogging as low-class "ciberchancleteo," print remains an important—and prestigious—means of disseminating work in Cuba. Indeed, perhaps for this reason, "Del Palenque . . . y para . . ." blog posts frequently include references to print editions of work, as well as to the literary prizes that writers have received. For instance, the first post to the blog, on April 3, 2007, introduces aforementioned Cuban poet Rito Ramón Aroche as follows:

> Ha publicado los poemarios "Puerta Siguiente" Premio Luis Rogelio Nogueras 1993. "Material entrañable," Premio Abril 1994. "Cuasi II," Premio Pinos Nuevos 1997 y "Cuasi I" (2001) "Libro de los Colegios Reales" y "Andamios" (2005) "Del río que durando se destruye" (2005).

> [He has published the poetry collections "The Next Door," Luis Rogelio Nogueras Prize 1993. "Endearing Material," April Prize 1994. "Quasi II," Pinos Nuevos Prize 1997 and "Quasi I" (2001) "Book of the Royal Colleges" and "Scaffolds" (2005) "From the River that Lasting Is Destroyed" (2005).][29]

While stock in Cuban bookstores varies tremendously from one moment to the next, Aroche's work—as well as that of other Palenque poets—is generally available for purchase in Havana. The blog, however, allowed the Palenque Group to more adroitly reach a wider readership: a readership that extended beyond the confines of the island(s), and into the spaces that together comprise the transnational Cuban archipelago, or the *arcubiélago*. In an interview, Aroche explains how the Palenque poets in Cuba worked together with their *amigos* in Barcelona, as well as Brazil, to create their blog as a transnational project:

> Enviamos la información, por correo, a amigos, y ellos también agregaban información; Dolores Labarcena [en Barcelona] y Julio Moracen [en Brasil], [. . .]; y ellos montan [. . .] el blog. [. . .] es muy interesante lo que Julio Moracen nos dice a nosotros. [. . .] nos dice, Uds. los cubanos, no, nosotros los cubanos, los que quedamos, es que no tenemos Internet. Pero sí tenemos, Uds. sí tienen una cosa buena. [. . .] Y es que todos están en red. Eso sí. Porque en un Pen Drive, una memoria flash, pasábamos el blog, eso sí, cuando ellos tenían el blog montado, lo enviaban a nosotros. [. . .] nosotros lo circulábamos. Siempre con etiqueta, no?, que decía Palenque.
>
> Esto íbamos andando a crecer; y súmale, tres por tres. Uno se lo dice a tres, y cada uno de estos tres, se lo dice a otros tres, cuando viene, todo el mundo oye. Así se ha enterado el país. La ciudad letrada, no? Así el país se enteraba, que había un grupo, que se llame el Palenque.

Figure 9. Dolores Labarcena in Barcelona in May 2018, with her partner, Pedro Marqués de Armas. Photo by author.

[We emailed the information to friends, and they also added information; Dolores Labarcena [in Barcelona] and Julio Moracen [in Brazil], [. . .]; and they put up [. . .] the blog. [. . .] it is very interesting what Julio Moracen tells us. [. . .] he tells us, you Cubans, no, we Cubans, we who have stayed, it is that we do not have Internet. But we do have, you do have a good thing. [. . .] And it is that everybody is on the network. That is true. Because we passed around the blog on a Pen Drive, a flash memory stick, when they had the blog up, they sent it to us. [. . .] and we circulated it. Always with a tag, no?, that said Palenque.

And we went on growing; and adding, three at a time. One says it to three, and each of those three says it to another three, when they come; everyone hears. Thus the country has learned. The lettered city, no? Thus the country learned, that there was a group, may it be called the Palenque.][30]

In creating their blog as a collaborative venture, the Palenque Group worked to share their own work, as well as that of others, more widely. (See Figure 9.)

Table 1. Visitors to the blog "Del Palenque . . . y para . . ." as of
November 2018 (information provided courtesy of Dolores Labarcena)

United States	17,002
Spain	13,291
Germany	6,400
Russia	5,679
Mexico	4,800
Argentina	3,971
Colombia	2,512
France	1,824
Cuba	1,431
China	1,410

Promoting the blog by word of mouth, moreover, the poets conjoined digital circuits and personal networks, foregrounding the transnational, archipelagic ties that connected them and asserting their identity as "un grupo, que se llame el Palenque" [a group, may it be called the Palenque].[31]

The available quantitative data suggest that the blog had received almost 60,000 visitors online as of November 2018.[32] (See Table 1.) This data suggests that visitors to the blog were primarily from Europe (46.6%), the United States (29.2%), and Latin America and the Caribbean (21.8%), with a small number from China (2.4%). With texts traveling an alternate circuit of routes between friends, however—from screen to printout to *amigo*, or from hard drive to USB to *amiga*—the total reach of the "Del Palenque . . . y para . . ." blog is difficult to ascertain. For instance, it is unavoidable that the number of visitors from Latin America and the Caribbean is artificially low given the blog's alternate circulation in Cuba; and the same might be true in other cases as well.

Much as the available quantitative data is unable to paint a complete picture of the blog's traffic, the comments posted to the blog do not reveal the full contours of the conversation that occurs between blog participants. This is because, as Aroche explains in an interview, "no teníamos retroalimentación con los comentarios. Porque estos comentarios los recibe Julio [Moracen], y luego los comparte con [nosotros]" [we didn't have feedback with the comments. Because Julio [Moracen] receives these comments, and then he shares them with (us)].[33] Those comments that do exist, however, signal the transnational, archipelagic ties that exist between visitors to the blog who, as a far-flung group of participants, nonetheless self-identify as a public. In one instance, for example, JAAD posts a comment to "Dolores Labarcena" to wish the blog administrator and Palenque poet a happy Saint's Day:

JAAD dijo . . .
Besos para Dolores, que ayer viernes fue su santo . . .
Buenos poemas y bella en la foto . . .

[JAAD said . . .
Kisses for Dolores, since yesterday, Friday, was her Saint's Day . . .
Good poems and pretty in the photo . . .][34]

Writing to Labarcena to send her "besos" [kisses] and compliments, JAAD's knowledge of Labarcena's "santo" [Saint's Day]—information that is not included on the blog itself—intimates that he also knows her offline, or IRL (In Real Life).

Similarly suggesting the potential contours of the wider conversation that occurs across the *arcubiélago*, visitors to "Del Palenque . . . y para . . ." at times request that comments be shared. While JAAD addresses Labarcena directly, for instance, those who respond to the blog also sometimes ask that their remarks be passed on to others. This occurs in the case of a comment posted to "Jesusa Espino":

Anónimo dijo . . .
    Me ha sorprendido gratamente recibir la foto de Jesusa. Y también que esté metida en un taller literario, una inquietud que ahora ella tiene la ocasión de desarrollar, hacer crecer hasta llegar a un arbol de copa bien tupida, con ramas robustas y llena de hojas de brillante verde que son sus textos y poemas.
    La felicito. Reenvíale este comentario.
    La extrañamos todos.
    Un abrazo
    Carlos Mochini

[Anonymous said . . .
    It has pleasantly surprised me to receive the photo of Jesusa. And also that she is involved in a literary salon, an interest that she will now have the occasion to develop, to make it grow until arriving at a tree with a well-pruned top, with robust branches and the brilliant green leaves that are her texts and poems. I congratulate her. Re-send her this comment.

We all miss her.
A hug,
Carlos Mochini][35]

The request that comments be passed on to Jesusa, the author whose work is featured in the post, suggests that blog administrator Labarcena is in contact with Jesusa outside the space of the "Del Palenque . . . y para . . ." blog. In much the same way, Ophir Alviárez requests that Labarcena give "Domingo" a hug, recalling their time spent together in Medellín in a comment posted to "En los 75 años de Domingo Alfonso" [On Domingo Alfonso's 75th]:

Ophir Alviárez dijo . . .
Leyendo un libro de Norberto Codina y me tropecé con un epígrafe que me revolvió las entrañas y quise indagar sobre el poeta Virgilio Piñera, así llegué hasta acá y qué sorpresa. Por favor, dele un abrazo de mi parte a Domingo y dígale que se le recuerda. Fue un gusto inmenso compartir con él poesía y charlas en Medellín.
Saludos venezolanos!
Ophir

[Ophir Alviárez said . . .
I ran into an epigraph that tied me up in knots reading one of Norberto Codina's books, and I wanted to investigate the poet Virgilio Piñera; thus I arrived here and what a surprise. Please give Domingo a hug for me and tell him that he is remembered. It was an immense pleasure to share poetry and chats with him in Medellín.
Venezuelan greetings!
Ophir][36]

As is true as well in the case of Mochini, Alviárez's comment suggests that Labarcena is in touch with Alfonso and that she will be able to convey the writer's message without the need for him to access the blog (and its comments) online.

Although limited in number, a digital humanities analysis of the comments posted to the blog thus suggests the ways in which the blog "Del Palenque . . . y para . . ." allows the Palenque poets to forge a space for a wider conversation between a like-minded public (following Michael Warner's use of the term) not always able to gather in one place, or at one time. The comments also intimate the expansiveness of the transnational, archipelagic space that this public inhabits: Alviárez self-identifies as Venezuelan ("Saludos venezolanos!" [Venezuelan greetings!]), and states that she enjoyed the time shared with Cuban poet Domingo Alfonso in Colombia; JAAD writes to Labarcena, who lives in Barcelona, from an undisclosed locale.[37] With "Del Palenque . . . y para . . ." created as a space distinctly " . . . *para los amigos*" [for friends],[38] the online space of the blog thus not only allows participants to share readings and information of interest, but also to forge and retain ties across (and beyond) the Palenque.

Archipelagos Online

In working collaboratively to create and maintain their blog, as well as in posting the work of a transnational cohort of writers and artists from across time and space, the Palenque poets manifest their desire to transcend the borders and boundaries inherent in the notion of the singular island and to forge instead a more open, archipelagic space. Through the blog, for instance, Palenque poets Rito Ramón Aroche, Ismael González Castañer, Caridad Atencio, and Julio Mitjans are able to rub elbows with U.S. writer Gwendolyn Brooks, Argentine poet Alejandra Pizarnik, and Russian writer Vladimir Nabokov, among others, in July 2007 postings. Similarly, Mitjans and Atencio are able to share space with Peruvian poet Antonio Cisneros, Argentine poet Fabián Casas, and U.S. writers Kurt Vonnegut, Robert Frost, and Billy Collins in March 2012 postings; and Labarcena is able to share the page with Cuban poets Filiberto González and Rafael Alcides, Finnish author Peter Sandelin, Polish author Krystyna Rodowska, U.S. poet Carl Sandburg, and Argentine author Ricardo Piglia in July 2014 postings.

In serving as a transnational, archipelagic space, the poets' virtual palenque retains characteristics of its nineteenth-century material antecedents. To return to Benítez-Rojo, the palenques to which slaves fled in pre-emancipation Caribbean societies formed part of a wider constellation of spaces:

> The maroon's flight carries him far beyond the linear geography that we studied at school: maroons from Jamaica were transported to Nova Scotia and to Sierra Leone; maroons from the three Guianas (Surinam, Cayenne, Guyana) fled to the forest, mixed with the indigenous people, invented languages and beliefs, and penetrated deeply into the South American interior, how deeply no one knows; slaves from Cuba captured the schooner *Amistad* and sailed to New England, where they were tried, acquitted, and returned to Africa [. . .] the runaway slave's flight to "freedom" has no frontiers, unless they are those of the meta-archipelago.[39]

Indeed, the repetition of the ellipses in the title of the blog "Del Palenque . . . y para . . ." might be taken as an implicit reference to the rich, archipelagic history of the palenque in (and beyond) Cuba. Following Elaine Stratford et al., just as constellations such as Orion take form only when the stars align, archipelagos emerge only when a scattering of islands, keys, and inlets is seen as comprising a larger whole:

> Deleuze & Guattari (1986) use the example of constellations: assemblages of heavenly bodies that, like Orion the Hunter, take on one (or more) recognizable forms only when their wholeness arises out of a process of articulating multiple elements by establishing connections amongst them. An archipelago is similar: its framing as "such and such an assemblage" draws our attention to the ways in which "practices, representations, experiences, and affects articulate to take a particular dynamic form" (Slack & Wise, 2005: 129).[40]

Here, in much the same way, each of the small dots on the screen must of necessity be considered in conjunction with the others for its full meaning to be clear. With the blog's use of white typeface running across a black screen, furthermore, posts themselves might be considered to form part of a larger, archipelagic constellation: indents call to mind inlets, keystrokes prove reminiscent of keys, and textual bodies float by in a sea of black.

Crafting a commodious, archipelagic space in which words written in the distant corners of the transnational Cuban archipelago exist virtually in a shared time and space, the Palenque poets participate in—and help to sustain—a space that is both national and transnational. As suggested in journalism professor Milena Recio's comments included in Claudio Peláez Sordo's documentary short *BlogBang Cuba* (2014), the space of "Del Palenque . . . y para . . ." is in this sense typical of Cuban blogs of the early 2000s:

> ¿Por qué hacer blogs, con tan poca gente conectada al Internet en Cuba? En primer lugar, porque cada vez más, hay más personas conectadas en Cuba. Y se cubaniza la relación de comunicación. Los temas, cada vez son más para Cuba, con Cuba, desde Cuba. En segundo lugar, porque hay una parte de la nación cubana que no esté en Cuba, y tiene conexión al Internet. Y que está, la diáspora. Y que también forma parte inequívoca de este espacio de diálogo. [. . .] Y en tercer lugar, porque, en definitiva, bloguear, es decir, hacer pública una voz privada [. . .] es un acto de derecho contemporáneo.

[Why make blogs, with so few people connected to the Internet in Cuba? In the first place, because there are ever more people connected [to the Internet] in Cuba. And the way of communicating becomes Cuban. The topics are increasingly for Cuba, with Cuba, from Cuba. In the second place, because there is a part of the Cuban nation that is not in Cuba, and that has an Internet connection. And there is, the diaspora. And that also forms an unequivocal part of this space of dialogue. [...] And in the third place, because blogging, which is to say, making a private voice public [...] is definitively a contemporary right.][41]

While Castro declared in his 1961 "Palabras a los intelectuales" ["Words to the Intellectuals"] that "todo" [or "all"] was to be permitted "within" the Revolution (with "nothing" allowed "against," or outside, it), Recio highlights the fact that the blogosphere exists as an alternate space that is neither exclusively "within" nor entirely "without." Rather, for Recio, as for many Cuban bloggers in the early 2000s, the blogosphere serves as an alternative space that allows individuals to share their "private" voices publicly in and beyond Cuba.

Creating an alternate, transnational space of identity online and off, the Palenque poets use their blog to assert what Julio Moracen describes in an interview as the "universality" of their identities. Referencing the longstanding debate about what it means to be a "Black" (or Afro-) Cuban writer, Moracen explains:

Existe una grande discusión [...] sobre si los escritores negros cubanos hacen un tipo de literatura negra. Hay quien cobra eso, de un escritor negro. Hay quien se pregunta, por qué los escritores negros, no hacemos literatura negra. Si la sociedad cubana de por sí, que dice que todos somos iguales, ¿no es así?, y nosotros somos negros. Ya el hecho, de ser escritores, pienso que es una identidad de negra. Pero no necesariamente estamos obligados, a escribir, como piensan las personas que escribiría un negro, porque eso también es un estereotipo. Nosotros somos parte de un *universe* universal.

[There exists a great discussion [...] about whether Black Cuban writers make a type of Black literature. There are those who demand this, of a Black writer. There are those who ask themselves, why don't we Black writers make Black literature? If Cuban society says that we are all equal, is it not so?, and we are Black. I think that the fact of being writers, is already a Black identity. But we are not necessarily obligated to write the way that people think that a Black person would write, because that too is a stereotype. We are part of a universal universe.][42]

Rejecting the need to "escribir, como piensan las personas que escribiría un negro" [write the way that people think that a Black person would write], the Palenque poets assert both the universality and the equality of their identities through their blog.[43]

At the same time that the Palenque poets use their blog to create a transnational, archipelagic space in which diversity is celebrated, they also call attention to the fallacy of what Ada Ferrer describes as Cuba's long-held "conception (dominant to this day) of a raceless nationality," and hint at the fact that the nation continues to need to engage in decolonizing work to address what Ivan César Martínez terms a "skin color caste" that privileges "those with a lighter skin color and White physical features."[44] The blog's name—and, of course, the group's—foregrounds these issues from the start.[45] In addition, some of the writers and artists whose work is posted to the "Del Palenque . . . y para . . ." blog employ a tongue-in-cheek tone to call attention to the ongoing issues related to race in nominally post-racial Cuba.

Visual artist Elio Rodríguez's print "Gone with the Macho" (1996), posted in April 2007, serves as one example.[46] Here the artist reworks the tropes of the U.S. film *Gone with the Wind* (Victor Fleming, 1939) to humorously send up stereotypes about race and national identity. Recasting well-worn images of tropical island desire into the sphere of U.S. cinema, Rodríguez offers viewers a mock movie poster with the title "Gone with the Macho" written in large letters across the top. Just beneath the title, the words "She comes looking for . . ." and "and he was around waiting . . ." float in the air to either side of an image of a Black man holding a light-skinned woman. Wearing a revealing red dress, the blonde-haired woman is identified in the credits at the bottom of the poster as "Any Tourist as the Tourist"; the man is identified as "Elio Rodríguez as el Macho."

As Moracen notes in a comment glossing the piece on the blog, "Gone with the Macho" represents a larger trend in Rodríguez's work: to utilize irony to represent emblems of Cuban identity. Moracen explains:

En sus obras ironiza la cubanidad conectada a mitos sexuales con infinitas alucinaciones y una sociedad de monomanías que crea queloides del pasado / presente.

[In his works, he ironizes the *cubanidad* connected to sexual myths with infinite hallucinations and a society of obsessions that creates keloids of the past / present.][47]

In so doing, Rodríguez references prevalent stereotypes surrounding race and national identity, at the same time that he invokes an archipelagic space that includes (even as it also surpasses) the "island" of Cuba, the "continent" of North America, and the waterways that connect them. In "Gone with the Macho," that is, the "Tourist" and "El Macho" are accompanied by emblems of Cuban identity, including a box of cigars and a 1950s car, even as the title of the piece calls to mind a classic (and highly contested) U.S. film about this nation's Civil War (1861–1865).

In Rodríguez's "LA GRAN CORRIDA," also posted in April 2007, the recasting of well-worn images of tropical island desire into the Spanish bullfighting ring again invokes ongoing stereotypes at the same time that it once more bespeaks a desire to forge a transnational, archipelagic space. Here a Black man characterized as an angry bull towers over a light-skinned woman dressed as a *toreadora* who is lounging on the ground at his feet, looking out at the viewer. The threat (or, conversely, the promise) of Black male sexuality implicit in the image is underscored in the title that runs underneath: "LA GRAN CORRIDA." The *doble entendre* of "corrida," which refers both to bullfights and to sex, is in turn doubled in the series title, "Corridas y venidas," which "translates as a word play on 'jumping from one place to another,' but can also refer to explicit sexual ecstasy."[48] Here, as an announcement for Rodríguez's 2014 show in London proclaims, "Bombastic tropical environments overflow with exaggerated sexual scenes between the mulatta and the tourist, lightly veiling the realities of sex tourism that has profited from the Western view of a Cuban paradise."[49] At the same time, "'jumping from one place to another'"—island-hopping, as it were—one tourist's gaze in effect overlaps with another's, with the images of desire associated with the Caribbean accompanied by images of the keepsakes visitors to Spain might purchase at the Corte Inglés in Madrid or Barcelona: the *toreadora* is dressed in the garb of the typical Spanish bullfighter, holds a fan in her hand, and lies on a festive, multi-colored Spanish shawl.

The inclusion of a poem from Yansy Sánchez's *Maldita sea* [*Damn It*], posted in August 2007, similarly highlights the prejudices of the present. Sánchez refers to the ways in which tourists see Black Cubans. Referring to "Primo Golomón" as a "negro elemental" [elemental Black] who is located at the center of the periphery, Sánchez establishes the ongoing marginality of Black bodies and subjects in Revolutionary Cuba in his poem. At the same time, he suggests the prejudice inherent in tourists' interest in the Black body for precisely its marginality, now re-coded in the language of privilege as exotic, as the tourists "lo exhiben en las plazas con orgullo" [exhibit him in the plazas with pride].[50] As such, the poet calls attention to the problematic nature of the Revolutionary regime's claim that it has successfully eradicated discrimination—and, implicitly, the racism that accompanies it—and critiques the opening of the market that has increased the number of tourists who come to Cuba to take pictures of exoticized Black bodies. In so doing, Sánchez underscores the complexities of navigating race in an era of increasingly transnational encounters.

The ongoing repercussions of race on (and beyond) the *palenque* are further highlighted in an interview, posted in October 2009, that Caridad Atencio conducts with fellow Palenque poet Ismael González Castañer. Here, González Castañer signals that Afro-Cubans continue to face significant hurdles to success. When asked to explain a line from one of his poems that reads "un negro no halla el árbol si no va corriendo en la noche" [a Black doesn't find the tree if he doesn't run in the dark], González Castañer states that Blacks must work twice as hard as Whites to achieve success:[51]

> Esa imagen del poema "El de las Amigas," en *Mercados verdaderos*, resume la magnitud del trabajo que pasamos para conseguir un sueño o la más nimia mundanidad: atravesando el oscuro . . . ¡y a toda velocidad!
>
> Como aseveraba el célebre cineasta afronorteamericano Spike Lee aquí mismo en *La Gaceta*: "se nos exige ser diez veces mejores."

> [This image from the poem "He of the Friends," in *True Markets*, sums up the magnitude of the work that we do to achieve a dream or the most trivial commonplace: making our way through the dark . . . and at top speed!
>
> As the famous Afro-American director Spike Lee affirmed right here in *La Gaceta* [a publication of UNEAC]: "they demand that we be ten times better."][52]

Even as he points to the fact that darker-skinned Cubans must work harder to achieve the same goals and status as lighter-skinned Cubans, González Castañer recognizes that the issues of race that he identifies in Cuba are common to the Americas more broadly. Including a reference to U.S. director Spike Lee in the segment above, González Castañer subsequently refers to the U.S. pop star Lionel Ritchie, the U.S. television series *Roots*, the aboriginal population in colonial Mexico, and the work of West Indian philosopher Frantz Fanon. In so doing, the poet reflects on his own lived experiences at the same time that he establishes a series of transnational, archipelagic connections with a wider group of writers and artists.

For González Castañer, as for the Palenque poets more generally, the transnational, multiracial group of writers and artists whose work is included on the blog thus points to the wide-open parameters of the Palenque poets' self-imagined identities, and to the capacious nature of what they consider to exist "dentro de" [within] the transnational, archipelagic space of "Del Palenque . . . y para . . .": a space that exceeds both the physical space of the island(s) and the metaphoric space of the nation. Considered from this perspective, it is noteworthy that, in his concluding remarks in his interview with Atencio, González Castañer states that his primary focus in the present is "el país" [the country]: "Pero mi verdadera preocupación es el país, su economopolítica y futuro. Realmente, como dice la canción de don César Portillo de la Luz, ese es mi delirio" [But my real concern is the country, its economics and politics and its future. Truly, as don César Portillo de la Luz's song says, that is my delirium].[53] With the "país" [country] existing as both a "preocupación" [concern] and a "delirio" [delirium], the poet joins the other members of the Palenque Group in affirming his existence as an Afro-Cuban at the same time that he contests attempts to limit him to race-based identities.

Del Palenque . . . y para . . . *The New York Times*

At the same time that the Palenque poets drew attention to the ongoing importance of race and race-based discrimination in Cuba through their blog, a number of other bloggers joined the incipient conversation on the vexed intersection of race and identity in Cuba. Calling attention to the role of gender and sexuality as well as race, for instance, Sandra Abd'Allah-Álvarez Ramírez launched her blog, "Negra cubana tenía que ser" ["I Had to Be a Black Cuban Woman"],[54] in 2006; and Yasmín S. Portales Machado launched her blog, "En 2310 y 8225" ["In 2310 and 8225"],[55] in 2007. A forerunner of these blogs, the website AfroCubaWeb was launched in 1997 to foreground the contributions of Afro-Cubans.[56]

In this way, the blogosphere helped to enable a conversation on a topic that, following Zuleica Romay, had long been taboo:

> Apalancado por el dogmatismo—con su tendencia a confundir igualdad política e igualdad social—, y por una obsesiva búsqueda de la unidad ante el enorme desafío de garantizar la sobrevivencia del proyecto revolucionario; el espejismo de igualdad racial se convirtió en barrera, al considerarse su cuestionamiento como una amenaza a "la unidad de la nación."

[Leveraged by dogmatism—with its tendency to confuse political equality and social equality—, and by an obsessive search for unity before the enormous challenge of guaranteeing the survival of the revolutionary project; the mirage of racial equality became a barrier, on considering its questioning to be a threat to the "unity of the nation."][57]

In her comments in the documentary *BlogBang Cuba*, journalism professor Recio underscores blogs' productive ability to address precisely the long-taboo topic of racism:[58]

De toda la diversidad que hoy se está manifestando en la blogosfera y en las redes sociales; a mí me interesaría más si fuéramos a hablar de la interacción política y del debate político me interesa más todo el resto de otras voces, cuyas agendas son muchísimo más diversas; cuyas agendas son muchísimo más conflictivas finalmente, porque están atravesando los problemas radicales de la sociedad cubana. Por ejemplo: el racismo.

[Of all the diversity that is manifesting itself today in the blogosphere and the social networks; I would be more interested if we were to talk about the political interaction, and of the political debate, I am most interested in all the other voices, whose agendas are much more diverse; whose agendas are finally much more conflictive, because they are going through the radical problems of Cuban society. For example: racism.][59]

It bears noting, however, that while the Palenque poets used their blog to draw attention to the vexed intersection of race and identity in Cuba, the critique they leveraged was more opaque than overt. To some degree, as Duong notes, this was typical of Cuban bloggers in the early 2000s, who tread carefully when entering the public sphere online: "Blog writing in Cuba [. . .] involves at this particular juncture a search for a new kind of discourse on citizenship that denounces and subverts the power dynamics of the public sphere—though not directly the political order."[60]

In addition, the Palenque poets did not, as a group, self-identify as what Caridad Atencio describes in an interview as "militante" [militant]:

Y esa es una cosa que, [. . .] es quizás lo que nos salva, en gran medida, es algo que ha hecho que la gente del gremio, que los creadores negros, que los militantes negros, no nos miren bien. Que nosotros no somos militantes negros. Somos negros, estamos orgullosos de ser lo que somos, [. . .] pero no somos militantes. [. . .] somos seres humanos.

[And this is something that, [. . .] is perhaps what saves us, to a large extent, it's something that has made the people of the guild, the Black creators, the militant Blacks, not think much of us. That we are not Black militants. We are Blacks, we are proud of what we are, [. . .] but we are not militants. [. . .] we are human beings.][61]

Having created a transnational, archipelagic space online through their blog, the poets devoted part of that space to engaging with and healing from the ongoing, damaging effects of racism and discrimination. At the same time, they asserted their pride in their identities as both "negros" [Blacks] and "seres humanos" [human beings]; and, in so doing, self-identified as part of what might be described, following Moracen, as a "*universe* universal" [universal universe].

As the Palenque poets moved from, or *del*, the blog "Del Palenque . . . y para . . ." to the pages of *The New York Times*, the need for a space such as that they envisioned in their blog over its seven years of active existence—with all its complications and consequences—became even more apparent. For while the nascent discussion on race in Cuba was tolerated and to some degree even celebrated in the Cuban blogosphere, the publication of Zurbano's aforementioned *New York Times* op-ed, "For Blacks in Cuba, the Revolution Hasn't Begun," provoked an immediate outcry in Cuba in 2013. Although Zurbano addressed many of the same issues in the op-ed as in his previous works (including posts to the blog "Del Palenque . . . y para . . ."), the op-ed—complete with its provocative title—essentially aired racial grievances in a forum that many in Cuba associated with the capitalist enemy. For this, Zurbano was seen as treacherous.[62] While Zurbano claimed that the controversy stemmed from the mistranslation of his original title, "El país que viene: ¿y mi Cuba negra?" ["The Country to Come: And My Black Cuba?"],[63] he nonetheless lost his prestigious post as the director of the publishing house for the Casa de las Américas (the nation's preeminent cultural institution) in the fallout from what would become known as the "Caso Zurbano" [Zurbano Case].[64]

"For Blacks in Cuba, the Revolution Hasn't Begun" was published in the digital edition of *The New York Times* on March 23, 2013, and appeared in the paper's print edition the following day. On the website, Zurbano's name appears just below the title, and beneath this is a photograph captioned "Havana, 2013."[65] The photo shows a young Black man looking out from behind what seems to be a wall, his brow slightly furrowed and his smile somewhat fixed. A flip-flop is visible atop the wall and in the background the sea and the Malecón beckon from just across the road that encircles the capital city, separating land from water. To the left of the man in the foreground, a light-skinned woman is visible walking along the sidewalk, and to this woman's left is a sign that reads "Ceda el paso" [yield].

While "Havana, 2013" to some degree offers a stock image of Cuba as it might be seen in tourist brochures, the photograph also offers an apt pictorial summary of "For Blacks in Cuba," in which Zurbano argues that darker-skinned Cubans have repeatedly, if implicitly, been asked to "ceda el paso" [yield] to their lighter-skinned counterparts. Zurbano begins his piece by listing the recent, much-vaunted, changes in Cuba—the ability to purchase a cell phone, for instance, or to spend the night in a hotel—and by suggesting that these changes are not for all: "the reality is that in Cuba, your experience of these changes depends on your skin color."[66] This colorism, the author asserts, is due to the nation's long history of slavery, racism, and discrimination, which results in darker-skinned Cubans inhabiting a world that is strikingly different from (and significantly less advantaged than) that of lighter-skinned Cubans, despite the gains of the Revolution.

The publication of "For Blacks in Cuba" caused an immediate uproar, as information about *The New York Times* op-ed—but not the op-ed itself—began to appear on various Cuban websites in the days following its publication. In their published comments on the op-ed, many Cuban critics objected to Zurbano's piece on the basis of its title alone. For instance, Esteban Morales's "La Revolución Cubana comenzó en 1959" ["The Cuban Revolution Began in 1959"] is representative in this regard:

> Bajo un título carente de rigor histórico y objetividad, Roberto Zurbano trata de caracterizar la situación de los negros en la Cuba de hoy. [. . .] Afirmar que "para los negros cubanos la Revolución no ha comenzado," no se sostiene, ni aun dentro de la compleja realidad cubana de hoy.

> [Beneath a title lacking historical rigor and objectivity, Roberto Zurbano tries to characterize the situation of Blacks in Cuba today. [. . .] To affirm that "for Black Cubans the Revolution has not begun" is not sustainable, not even within the complex Cuban reality today.][67]

To some degree, given Cubans' limited access to the Internet in the early 2000s, critics' focus on the op-ed's eight-word title made sense: the title, after all, served as a capsule summary that was more easily circulated than the op-ed itself (much less the photograph that accompanied it). Yet the debate over the title was also curious, for, according to Cuban writer Victor Fowler, no one attempted to contact Zurbano to confirm that the title was his own, and, furthermore, when Zurbano attempted to explain that the title was the result of a gross mistranslation, no one seemed to pay attention.[68]

Considered in conjunction with the dialogue on race on the blog "Del Palenque . . . y para . . . ," the firestorm set off by Zurbano's op-ed reveals the difficulties of translating not only words, but also concepts, in a transnational sphere. For while the title proved a lightning rod in the debate, this focus to some degree distracted from the more salient question of how to translate what it means to be Afro-Cuban—much less Afro-Cuban and Revolutionary—into a *lingua franca* understood throughout (and beyond) the *arcubiélago*. For, as Zurbano noted in his op-ed, "Black" does not always translate clearly into *New York Times* English, nor is it always clear in *cubano*:

> The Black population in Cuba is far larger than the spurious numbers of the most recent censuses. The number of Blacks on the street undermines, in the most obvious way, the numerical fraud that puts us at less than one-fifth of the population. Many people forget that in Cuba, a drop of white blood can—if only on paper—make a mestizo, or white person, out of someone who in social reality falls into neither of those categories.[69]

As one indication of the difficulties of translating race, while Zurbano refers to "Blacks" and "Whites" in his op-ed, including a passing reference to "mestizos," there are in fact over twenty terms used to describe Blackness in Cuba[70]—a list far longer than that commonly used in the United States or Europe, and with terms that are understood differently.[71] The term "mulato," for instance, is widely used in Cuba to refer to an individual of mixed African and European origin; the same term in the United States, however, is generally considered to be pejorative.

In choosing to publish his op-ed in *The New York Times*—the paper of record for the United States, and a publication with a global reach and reputation online—Zurbano thus inadvertently foregrounded the fractures inherent in translations. In an era of machine translation, after all, it is increasingly recognized that words written in one language will necessarily slip and slide as they are translated into another, as stories of mishaps with Google Translate abound. It is perhaps less understood, however, that race is read differently in one context and another, as the meanings of *negro* and *blanco*—not to mention *mulato, blanconazo*, or *moreno*—are far from Black and White; and, too, that titles shift and morph as they move from draft to publication, be it online or off.

Although Wikipedia lays bare the fact that online content is constantly changing as it is edited, adapted, and (at times) redacted, it is also perhaps less well known that newspapers generally retain the right to run op-eds and articles under titles of their choosing, and in fact frequently publish one piece online with two different headings, to see which of these "A/B" titles gets more clicks. This is true not only for mainstream publications, but for academic publications as well. In his introduction to the issue of the *Afro-Hispanic Review* focused on the "Caso Zurbano," for instance, editor William Luis notes that he opted to change the title of an essay that Zurbano contributed to the volume, without noting the similarities to what had occurred with *The New York Times*. Zurbano submitted the essay to Luis with one title ("Moviendo los caracoles: informe personal de una batalla" ["Moving the Shells: Personal Report of a Battle"]), but Luis—as journal editor—opted to change it ("'Soy un negro más: Zurbano *par lui-même*'" ["'I Am One More Black: Zurbano *par lui-même*'"]).[72]

Considered from this vantage point, both the blog "Del Palenque . . . y para . . ." and the "Caso Zurbano" foreground the fact that race both is and is not a fiction—and that there exists, in both cases, an acute need to pay attention to not only the (mis)translated, but also to the "untranslatable." For, as Barbara Cassin aptly reminds us, there are words that cannot be translated.[73] As the blog "Del Palenque . . . y para . . ." and the "Caso Zurbano" both demonstrate, moreover, "untranslatable" words—and, I would add, "untranslatable" concepts such as race—exist not only between languages, but within languages as well. Following Cassin, with words as with race(s), "The perspectives constitute the thing; each language is a vision of the world that catches another world in its net, that performs a world; and the shared world is less a point of departure than a regulatory principle."[74]

More broadly, the untranslatability of words and concepts highlighted in the "Caso Zurbano" forms part of what Édouard Glissant theorizes as opacity: the lack of transparency that is part and parcel of the poetics of Relation, as well as multicultural communication. For Glissant, opacity is particularly noticeable in translation, which "strive[s] to bridge two series of opacities."[75] Yet the inevitability of opacity—even with the scandals that might ensue—is to be celebrated rather than bemoaned. Following Glissant, "What is here is open, as much as this there. [. . .] This-here is the weave, and it weaves no boundaries. The right to opacity would not establish autism; it would be the real foundation of Relation, in freedoms."[76]

Somewhat paradoxically, the publication of "For Blacks in Cuba, the Revolution Hasn't Begun" thus cast new light on precisely the issues that the Palenque Group sought to address through their blog, at the same time that it signaled the limits of the project they proposed. For although the Palenque poets asserted their right to a "universal" identity, and through their blog sought to create a space open to all across the *arcubiélago*, the Zurbano Case ultimately demonstrated that any such space is necessarily fleeting. And indeed, the publication of Zurbano's op-ed may have inadvertently presaged the end of the blog as an active publication. While posts to the blog continued until 2014, somewhat surprisingly, the blog includes no mention of the scandal caused by "For Blacks in Cuba, the Revolution Hasn't Begun." When asked why the poets decided to stop posting to the blog, furthermore, blog administrator Labarcena indicated that the submissions she was receiving from Cuba had become too "political."[77] While Labarcena did not elaborate, her comments once again point to the ongoing need for a transnational, archipelagic conversation on race and for decolonizing work on space and identity: a necessarily opaque conversation both on and beyond the Palenque, and in *cubano* as well as in translation.

5

Rankling José Martí

José Martí es una termoeléctrica y una biblioteca enorme.
Es la más alta orden gubernamental y una radio que ataca al
gobierno que entrega esa orden. Es un aeropuerto y un montón
de avenidas. Es el centro del parque en pueblos y ciudades. Es la
dispersión de frases suyas que se repiten incesantemente. Es el
dinero que circula con su efigie.

[José Martí is a thermoelectric plant and an enormous library.
He is the highest government order and a radio that attacks the
government that bestows that order. He is an airport and a ton of
avenues. He is the center of the park in towns and cities. He is the
dispersion of his sentences that are incessantly repeated. He is the
money that circulates with his effigy.][1]

Antonio José Ponte, "Martí: historia de una bofetada" ["Martí: the History of a Slap"]

In April 2018, I traveled to Philadelphia to meet Cuban writer Antonio José
Ponte for coffee. I had met Ponte more than ten years earlier, during my first
trip to Havana, and he had agreed to have coffee with me in Philadelphia before
the keynote address he was to deliver at a conference held at Temple University.[2]
(See Figure 10.)

I interviewed Ponte about his work on nineteenth-century writer José Martí,
the larger-than-life figure who, as Ponte notes in the quotation that serves as this
chapter's epigraph, has been used by the authorities to name airport and avenue,
library and park, radio station and thermoelectric plant. Ponte is known for his
lucid essays as well as his short stories and novels, and his work on Martí is key to

Figure 10. The author with Antonio José Ponte in Philadelphia in April 2018. Photo provided courtesy of author.

the *arcubiélago*. To date, Ponte has written three essays on Martí and the scholars who study him: "El abrigo de aire" ["The Coat of Air"] (2000), "Martí: historia de una bofetada" ["Martí: the History of a Slap"] (2007), and "Martí: los libros de una secta criminal" ["Martí: the Books of a Criminal Sect"] (2017).[3] Ponte's essays on Martí are generally considered polemic manifestos on the need for a (productive) destruction of a key Revolutionary figure whose name graces everyday life through infrastructure and media, not to mention visual mementos of Cuba's past.

While there is a significant bibliography on Ponte's *oeuvre*, and, in particular, on his short stories, there is a relative paucity of scholarship on his essays on Martí, in spite of the fact that "El abrigo de aire" is frequently reprinted and widely read. An archipelagic lens reveals that the essays, considered in conjunction with Ponte's writings on Cuban culture and ruins, can be read as indicative of a desire to create a wider space that transcends the bounds of any one island or nation. This space encompasses Madrid (Ponte's home since 2006), Matanzas (Ponte's birthplace), and the *mar* between them, and forms part of the transnational Cuban *arcubiélago*.

Antonio José Ponte and "El abrigo de aire"

Born in the northwestern Cuban city of Matanzas, Ponte (1964–present) serves as Vice Director of the online publication *Diario de Cuba*, which seeks to offer an alternative perspective on Cuban news and culture. Ponte frequently foregrounds ruins in his work, and is known as "el ruinólogo de La Habana del 'Período Especial,' [. . .] uno de los escritores cubanos contemporáneos que más ha trabajado el tema de las ruinas" [the ruinologist of 'Special Period' Havana, [. . .] one of the Cuban writers who has most written on the topic of ruins].[4] Ponte lived in Havana for many years and frequently participated in the gatherings held in the Azotea of his close friend Reina María Rodríguez. Ponte relocated to Madrid in 2006, after his membership in the Unión Nacional de Escritores y Artistas Cubanos (UNEAC) [National Union of Cuban Writers and Artists] was rescinded in 2003 for his collaboration on what was considered to be the dissident publication *Encuentro de la Cultura Cubana*.[5]

Ponte's essay collections include *La lengua de Virgilio* [*The Language of Virgilio*] (1993), *Un seguidor de Montaigne mira La Habana* [*A follower of Montaigne Looks at Havana*] (1995), *Las comidas profundas* [*Profound Foods*] (1997), *El abrigo de aire: ensayos sobre la literatura cubana* [*The Coat of Air: Essays on Cuban Literature*] (2001), *El libro perdido de los origenistas* [*The Lost Book of the Origenistas*] (2002), and *Villa Marista en plata. Arte, política, nuevas tecnologías* [*Villa Marista in Silver: Art, Politics, New Technologies*] (2010). His fiction includes the short story collections *Cuentos de todas partes del Imperio* [*Tales from the Cuban Empire*] (2000) and *Un arte de hacer ruinas y otros cuentos* [*An Art of Making Ruins and Other Stories*] (2005), as well as the semi-autobiographical novel *La fiesta vigilada* [*The Supervised Party*] (2007). Ponte is also the author of several volumes of poetry, including *Naufragios* [*Shipwrecks*] (1992) and *Asiento en las ruinas* [*A Seat in the Ruins*] (1997). In addition to his work on ruins, Ponte is known for his innovative remappings of what he refers to, tongue in cheek, as the "Cuban Empire."

Ponte wrote his first essay on José Martí, "El abrigo de aire" ["The Coat of Air"], in 1995, when he still lived in Havana, to commemorate the centennial

Figure 11. Books by José Martí for sale in a bookstore in Havana. Photo by author.

of Martí's death. Martí (1853–1895) is widely recognized as an iconic figure throughout the *arcubiélago*, where he is referred to as Apóstol [Apostle], Maestro [Teacher], and Héroe Nacional [National Hero] in recognition of his historic stature. Martí is the author of numerous essays, including the well-known "Nuestra América" ["Our America"] (1891); he also wrote poems, plays, and the novel *Lucía Jérez: Amistad funesta* [*Lucía Jérez: Ill-Fated Friendship*] (1885).[6] In addition to his prolific literary production, Martí was a central figure in Cuba's struggle for independence from Spain. The emblematic visage and well-known words of Martí are seemingly omnipresent in Cuba and throughout the *arcubiélago*: Martí and his writings are featured on street murals, monuments, and souvenir t-shirts as well as in essays, speeches, and books.[7] (See Figure 11.)

In "El abrigo de aire," Ponte contends that it is precisely Martí's status as an omnipresent Revolutionary icon that necessitates a change of course. The long-venerated Revolutionary figure, Ponte states, must be resignified—and even sullied—to remain relevant. To set up this controversial argument, Ponte begins his essay by recounting the tale of Martí's last coat, which traveled extensively after its owner's death. Martí spent many years in exile, living in Spain, France, Mexico, and Guatemala before moving to New York City, where he lived from 1881 until shortly before his death in 1895. In Ponte's retelling, the story of Martí's last coat begins just before the nineteenth-century author leaves New York for the Cuban battlefields. One chilly morning, Ponte tells his readers, Martí visited the home of the Baralt family, with whom he had a close relationship. When he departed, he accidentally left behind his coat:

> Aquella misma tarde Martí salía de Nueva York hacia Santo Domingo para encontrarse con Máximo Gómez. Los Baralt y él, en efecto, no pudieron verse más. Unos días después de su partida, [. . .] alguien de la casa notó aquel sobretodo marrón abandonado en el mueble de la entrada. [. . .] se decidieron al fin a vaciar sus bolsillos y registraron hasta encontrar cartas y papeles dirigidos a Martí.

> [That same afternoon Martí was leaving New York for Santo Domingo to meet up with Máximo Gómez. He and the Baralt family, indeed, would not be able to see each other again. Some days after his departure, [. . .] someone from the house noticed that brown overcoat abandoned in the entryway. [. . .] they decided at last to empty its pockets and looked until they found letters and papers addressed to Martí.][8]

After being found by the Baralts in New York, Ponte continues, Martí's coat later resurfaced in Madrid, in the home of Mexican writer Alfonso Reyes. The coat had arrived in Madrid on the back of Dominican writer Pedro Henríquez Ureña, who (on break from his teaching duties in Minnesota) had traveled to Havana, where some relatives of Martí had lent him the coat. Henríquez Ureña had then traveled to Madrid, visited Reyes, and (like Martí before him) left the coat behind upon his departure.

For Ponte, the tale of Martí's *abrigo de aire* is emblematic both of how Martí *is* treated and of how he *should* be treated. On the one hand, Ponte contends, the coat serves as an emblem of how Martí now represents an ethereal, airy figure without real substance. As Ponte states, "Martí es elemental, es uno de los elementos, es aire imprescindible. [. . .] Es aire y todo el resto es literatura, autores, y el aire está por encima de estos, está más allá, no pueden compararse una cosa y la otra" [Martí is elemental, he is one of the elements, he is indispensable air. [. . .] He is air and all the rest is literature, authors, and the air is above these, it is beyond these, one thing and another cannot be compared].[9] Omnipresent and immaterial, Ponte argues, Martí is "uno de los elementos" [one of the elements], both "aire" [air] and "naturaleza" [nature]:[10] he is necessary for life, but often taken for granted. At the same time, Ponte asserts, the coat's final fate suggests that Martí should be reintroduced into the realm of the material, even with the possibility of a destructive "desgarrón" [tear].

According to Ponte, after being found in Madrid, Martí's coat subsequently went missing in Toledo after Reyes lent it to Artemio del Valle Arizpe, a fellow Cuban en route to Toledo on a chilly day. Here the coat disappeared forever after a dramatic *desgarrón* [tear] and a mysterious encounter with an unidentified woman:

> Un día, mientras [Artemio del Valle Arizpe] cruza un puente [en Toledo], en medio de una pelea de perros, el abrigo recibe tremendo desgarrón. Sin tardar un minuto, como si se tratara de una herida en el cuerpo propio, quien lo viste corre hacia su hotel y lo entrega a zurcir a quien toma por una de las camareras. [. . .] la camarera del hotel no es la camarera del hotel y el abrigo desaparece o, mejor, entra a la historia de gente sin historia.

> [One day, as he [Artemio del Valle Arizpe] crosses a bridge [in Toledo], in the middle of a dogfight, the coat receives a tremendous tear. Without waiting even a minute, as though it were a wound in his own body, Del Valle Arizpe runs toward his hotel and gives it to someone he takes to be a chambermaid to mend. [. . .] the chambermaid is not the chambermaid and the coat disappears or, better said, enters the history of people without history.][11]

Despite the coat's unknown fate, Ponte contends that the *abrigo*'s onetime owner and his writing—like the element of clothing with which Ponte associates him—must be subjected to the edifying desanctification of the streets. Just as Henríquez Ureña and Reyes continue to use the coat rather than place it behind glass in a museum, writes Ponte, "lo escrito por Martí debería arriesgarse a la rotura, a la pérdida, a la pelea de perros de la crítica, para seguir fluyendo" [that written by Martí should risk fracture, loss, the critics' dogfight, to continue flowing].[12] Martí and his writings—like his coat—must be put to good use and, as such, exposed to the change and risk intrinsic to archipelagic constellations, rather than enshrined for perpetuity.

While Martí is a larger-than-life figure throughout the *arcubiélago*, in Cuba

Martí is largely considered synonymous with Cuba's nineteenth-century struggle for independence from Spain; and this struggle, in turn, is largely considered synonymous with the 1959 Revolution. Establishing this connection in an oft-quoted 1968 speech, Fidel Castro states, "[en] Cuba solo ha habido una Revolución: la que se había iniciado, en 1868, en contra de la esclavitud y en favor de la independencia de España, y que se había continuado en 1959, en contra del imperialismo norteamericano y a favor del socialismo" [in Cuba there has only been one Revolution: that which had begun, in 1868, against slavery and in favor of independence from Spain; and that which had continued in 1959 against U.S. imperialism and in favor of socialism].[13] For Castro, the Revolution is thus singular and all-encompassing.

Not surprisingly, given this historic tie between Martí and the Cuban Revolution, Ponte's polemic retelling of the story of the "coat of air" was considered scandalous even before its publication. The essay had been commissioned by Bladimir Zamora for an international edition of the cultural publication *El Caimán Barbudo*, and Ponte had pieced together the story of the *abrigo* from various sources that had not previously been considered together.[14] When Ponte submitted the piece for publication, however, only a truncated version was deemed acceptable for print. As Ponte writes of the editor's response, "Biografía sí, de acuerdo, pero nada de crítica" [Biography, yes, okay; but nothing of criticism].[15] With his essay initially published only in a truncated form (and primarily for a readership abroad, rather than in Cuba), Ponte opted, as an alternative, to read the complete text of "El abrigo de aire" aloud at a gathering held in Rodríguez's Azotea. Given Martí's larger-than-life stature, it was a radical move to read the fully uncensored text. In an indication of the concern over the potential fallout of what was widely considered to be an attack on a national hero, the government sent undercover agents to attend the reading.[16] Ponte and other attendees feared that violence might break out, but the gathering ended peacefully.

"El abrigo de aire" was only published in its entirety some five years after it was written, appearing in the Spanish publication *Encuentro de la Cultura Cubana* in 2000; in the Cuban publication *Temas* in 2002; and in the online journal *La Habana Elegante*, where it was published with the addition of an epilogue, in 2003. Widely read and discussed throughout the *arcubiélago*, the essay was excoriated by Fidel Díaz, director of the Cuban edition of the aforementioned publication *El Caimán Barbudo*, after its publication in *Temas*. Underscoring Martí's bona fides as Cuba's founding father, Díaz accused Ponte of seeking to minimize the contributions of a national hero: "Ponte intenta rebajar la condición de escritor de Martí, [. . .] [e] igualarlo a un conjunto indistinto de autores; achacarle una enfermiza pasión estilística, y convertir en algo negativo el concepto del deber que sostiene su vida y su obra" [Ponte tries to reduce Martí's status as a writer, [. . .] [and] to equate him to an indistinct group of authors; to attribute to him a sick passion for style, and to make something negative out of the concept of duty that sustains his life and work].[17] Intimating that Ponte would like the larger-than-life Martí to vanish into thin air, Díaz concluded his essay by under-scoring once again the importance of Martí's contributions to the patrimony: "Contar con un legado tan rico y vigente como el de la vida y la obra de Martí es en realidad un privilegio [. . .] Martí es, en efecto, aire que respiramos, luz en un mundo sembrado de trampas" [To count on such a rich and vibrant legacy as the life and work of Martí is, in truth, a privilege [. . .] Martí is, in effect, the air that we breathe, light in a world full of traps].[18] Paradoxically reinforcing Ponte's point, Díaz thus claimed Martí's airiness as a virtue—and even a "privilege"—rather than a problem.

At the same time that "El abrigo de aire" sparked vehement criticism such as this for its treatment of a national icon, it also, if more subtly, pointed to the need to rethink the space of Cuba itself and to recognize the space as both transna-tional and archipelagic. The circuitous path that the coat travels before crossing into uncharted terrain with the "camarera del hotel [que] no es la camarera del hotel" [the chambermaid [who] is not the chambermaid][19] is indicative in this regard. This path not only intimates that Martí's coat continues to live in the realm of the material after the death of its original owner, but also offers a first indication of how Ponte limns Cuba's transnational, archipelagic contours in his essay. The coat is left in an apartment in New York City; travels south to Havana, and then to Mexico City; and, finally, crosses the Atlantic to make its way to Madrid and Toledo.

It is worth noting that many of the stops on this far-ranging journey are themselves archipelagic. Cuba is a nation that comprises some 1,600 islands, inlets, and keys; likewise, New York City and Mexico City are metropolises that include islands among their boroughs or mayoralties.[20] It is also noteworthy that it is not only the coat that moves between and among these island spaces. Martí himself travels throughout Europe and the Americas before arriving in New York City, where he lives for many years before his departure for Cuba; Ponte, more than a century later, also travels through Europe and the Americas before (and after) taking up residence in Madrid. Much as do their authors, moreover, the essays penned by Martí and Ponte also travel widely via cultural diffusion.

With its publication in the international edition of *El Caiman Barbudo*, "El abrigo de aire" reached readers throughout Latin America, and, in particular, in Colombia, where the international edition was published.[21] With its publication in *La Habana Elegante*, the essay reached a transnational readership, available to anyone with relatively unfettered Internet access (or the ability to use a USB drive to access a downloaded copy).

As he chronicles the travels of papers and protagonists throughout the *arcubiélago*, Ponte foregrounds what might be described as the *errantry* of Glissant's poetics of Relation. Glissant writes: "Whereas exile may erode one's sense of identity, the thought of errantry—the thought of that which relates—usually reinforces this sense of identity. [. . .] Errant, he challenges and discards the universal [. . .] He plunges into the opacities of that part of the world to which he has access."[22] Foregrounding the errantry of Martí, Ponte makes no claims to universality as he focuses instead on the "opacities" of the *arcubiélago*. Traveling and publishing his own work widely, furthermore, he goes without what Glissant describes as the "arrowlike nomadism" of conquest to embrace instead what the Martinican writer characterizes as "a dialectics of rerouting."[23]

Signaling Cuba's transnational, trans-oceanic ties—ties that contribute to the formulation of an archipelagic space that is simultaneously one and many, and that is characterized by errantry—Ponte describes Cuba as plural rather than singular in "El abrigo de aire." In the same paragraph in which he argues that Martí and his writings should "arriesgarse a la rotura, a la pérdida" [risk fracture, loss][24]—like the coat that is first found, then lost—Ponte states that Martí's deconstruction is necessary for what he describes as the myriad of Cubas that exist in the present: "Todas las Cubas existen no solo gracias a José Martí, sino a pesar de él. Por eso se desvían de él cubriéndolo de citas, borrándolo de tanta cita" [All Cubas exist not only thanks to José Martí, but in spite of him. That's why they stray from him covering him with quotes, erasing him with so many quotes].[25] The "Cubas" that Ponte references, and that he himself traverses, might be found in the same places as Martí's coat: in New York City, in Mexico, and in Madrid. Forming a whole that is larger than the sum of its parts, this constellation of "Cubas" together comprises an *arcubiélago* that challenges both the idea of the nation as "island" and the idea of that nation as a singular, bounded entity yoked to a singular, bounded Martí.

Ponte limns Cuba's archipelagic contours not only in his reference to a multiplicity of "Cubas," but also in his allusion to the comments that Argentine author Jorge Luis Borges made about Martí. Borges is well-known for advocating for a "universal" literature, suggesting in his 1932 essay "El escritor argentino y la tradición" ["The Argentine Writer and Tradition"] that the confines of the nation were too limited for the literature to which he aspired. Perhaps because Martí is often closely associated with the "tradition" of a national literature, Borges reputedly spoke little of Martí. As Ponte writes, in one instance Borges claimed not to know who Martí was; when he subsequently admitted that he did know just a bit about him, he notably tied him not to the space of the island, but to the wider space of the Caribbean.

> Alguien lo mencionó [a Martí] en [. . .] [una entrevista] y el argentino [Borges] despachó su nombre con este comentario rápido: "Ah, sí, Martí, esa superstición antillana." Reseñando un libro, le menciona iguales: "La gloria de Romain Rolland parece muy firme. En la República Argentina lo suelen admirar los admiradores de Joaquín V. González; en el mar Caribe, los de Martí [. . .]"

> [Someone mentioned him [Martí] in [. . .] [an interview] and the Argentine [Borges] dismissed his name with this quick comment: "Ah, yes, Martí, that Antillean superstition." Reviewing a book, he mentions him in the same way: "The glory of Romain Rolland seems very firm. In the Republic of Argentina the admirers of Joaquín V. González tend to admire him; in the Caribbean Sea, those of Martí [. . .]"][26]

In neither of the instances referenced by Ponte does Borges establish a connection between Martí and Cuba, or between Martí and the island. Rather, both of the spaces with which Borges associates the nineteenth-century writer are part and parcel of transnational archipelagos: the Caribbean is home to a number of different archipelagos, of which Cuba is one and the Antilles is another. Martí, furthermore, is described by Borges not as a reality, but as a "superstición" [superstition]. In much the same way, the idea of Cuba as (singular) island might be considered a convenient fiction rather than an inconvenient truth; or, following Borges's penchant for *ficciones* that mix fiction and truth, a Borgesian combination of both.

Ponte again suggests Cuba's status as a transnational archipelago in "El abrigo de aire" in referring to a map of the island that, in his telling, takes flight.

> En el año 1872, [. . .] un Martí muy joven, que no ha llegado a cumplir sus veinte años, habla en público. Han colgado en la pared detrás suyo, un mapa de la isla. Como están en Madrid el mapa es todo un símbolo.

Martí habla, se enciende y en el momento en que pronuncia <<Cuba llora, hermanos . . . >>, se desprende el mapa de Cuba y se pliega sobre la cabeza del orador.

[In 1872, [. . .] a very young Martí, who has not yet turned twenty, speaks in public. They have hung a map of the island on the wall behind him. As they are in Madrid, the map is very symbolic. Martí speaks, he becomes heated, and in the moment in which he pronounces the words <<Cuba cries, brothers . . . >>, the map comes off and falls on the speaker's head.][27]

For Ponte, the nickname of "Cuba llora" [Cuba cries] that Martí receives as a result of this episode is indicative of the need to engage with the mythical figure of Martí in any number of ways, rather than to venerate him. Yet at the same time, the incident signals the movement intrinsic to Cuba as island(s). Much as is true of Martí, traditional renderings of Cuba as a singular island nation have become so ubiquitous that they are all too often taken for granted: the prevailing notion of Cuba as an insular "isla" [island], that is, has become "elemental, [. . .] uno de los elementos, [. . .] aire imprescindible" [elemental, [. . .] one of the elements, [. . .] indispensable air],[28] just as is true of Martí. In Madrid in 1872, however, the cartography of the island literally takes flight as it jumps off the wall. Borne aloft by the same air that fills Martí's coat decades later, the map displaces time and space and signals the contours of a more open, aerial space that surpasses the fixed coordinates implicit in the sketching of lines on a page consigned to a table or wall.

In portraying Cuba as an archipelagic constellation in these ways, Ponte insinuates that Martí and the "island" have a shared characteristic: both have become so commonplace that it is impossible to escape them. These touchstones of culture and identity are so "elemental" that they are ultimately filled with nothing but air. As such, Ponte's hopes for Martí as an iconic figure in need of sullying might also signal his hopes for the nation: as is true of the individual and his writing, in Ponte's telling, the nation, too, should "arriesgarse a la rotura, a la pérdida, a la pelea de perros de la crítica, para seguir fluyendo" [risk fracture, loss, the critics' dogfight, to continue flowing].[29] Considering the airborne island portrayed on the map as one of a multiplicity of spaces that, together, comprise the *arcubiélago* would therefore contribute to allowing both Martí and the nation to achieve the goals that Ponte establishes for Martí in his essay: "[que] fluyera, que no disminuyera en vida y continuara en su corriente vida propia" [[that] he flows, that he is not diminished in life and that he continues his own life in his current].[30] Intimating that Martí and his writings might flow across nominal boundaries as do the seawaters that crash over the Malecón, Ponte proposes a revisionist reading of Martí in "El abrigo de aire" that would allow him and his readers to navigate the currents anew.

Slaps and Sects

After meeting with Ponte in Philadelphia in 2018, I attended his talk at a conference held at Temple University. Here Yale professor Roberto González Echevarría asked the author to explain why he had been cast out of UNEAC. In his response, Ponte clarified that he was never thrown out: rather, he stated, "me desactivaron" [they deactivated me]. This "deactivation," he explained, was due to a change in policy: during a certain time, there were politics of "encuentro" [encounter] among "escritores de las muchas orillas de la cultura cubana" [writers of the many shores of Cuban culture]. When this politics of "encuentro" ended, Ponte was asked to terminate his contract with the journal *Encuentro de la Cultura Cubana*, which was published in Madrid. He refused, he stated, and continued as well to cite exiled authors such as Reinaldo Arenas in his work; to have contact with those who had left Cuba, either voluntarily or under duress; and to criticize Fidel Castro, as well as authors belonging to the foundational Orígenes Group, such as Cintio Vitier and Fina García Marruz. (Ponte did not mention his essay on Martí as one of the reasons for the decision to rescind his UNEAC membership, but the controversy it sparked likely did not help his case.) As a result of his transgressive writing, his membership in UNEAC was rescinded.

In *La fiesta vigilada* [*The Supervised Party*], Ponte writes of a "deactivation" similar to his own. Composed as a semi-autobiographical novel, or as a novelized essay, *La fiesta vigilada* defies the expectations of genre, resisting categorization. Following professor Anke Birkenmaier in this regard, "The genre of *La fiesta* is a hybrid, with the carefully stylized narrative perspective and framing of the novel and the focus, typical of the essay, on the subject's interpretation, as opposed to objective scientific knowledge."[31] Near the end of the text, Ponte's narrator describes learning that he has been "'Desactivado'" ['Deactivated'] from UNEAC, much as occurred to the author himself.[32] The narrator then goes on to note that his appeal of the decision must be submitted in writing, in contradistinction to the authorities, who are not so constrained: "Las instancias gubernamentales podían darse el lujo de la oralidad [. . .]. Los individuos, en cambio, debíamos medir muy bien nuestras palabras, ponerlas en papel" [Governmental requests could allow themselves the luxury of orality [. . .]. Individuals, in contrast, had to measure our words carefully, put them on paper].[33]

A subsequent encounter with a writer identified as G reveals that the words as written by Ponte's narrator (as well as the author himself) likely go on to form part of a secret archive created by the state. Sitting in G's apartment in Berlin during one of his frequent stays abroad, the narrator is handed "dos gruesas carpetas" [two thick folders] from the now-public archives of East Germany's secret police. Full of correspondence, transcriptions of phone conversations, and reports on G's activities penned by neighbors, the folders represent "todo el jugo que las autoridades consiguieran sacar de la vida de G" [all the juice that the authorities could wring out of G's life].[34] Speaking of East Germany, but with implications for Cuba, writ large, the narrator makes clear that all *fiestas*—and all "deactivations"—are ultimately *vigiladas* [monitored], and that all words—written or floating in the air—are subject to inclusion in state archives.

In continuing to work with journals such as *Encuentro de la Cultura Cubana* (published in print and online) in the late 1990s and early 2000s, and in publishing his work online in digital journals such as *La Habana Elegante*, Ponte sought to create an alternate archive and contribute to the formation of an alternate space of identity. On one level, this space forms part of what Francisco Morán describes as "Cuba.com." Writing of the journals published outside Cuba (such as *La Habana Elegante*, which he directs, and where Ponte published "El abrigo de aire"), Morán states:

Las revistas que se hacen fuera de Cuba no miran hacia Cuba—es decir, hacia el espacio físico de la Nación—o, cuando menos, no de manera exclusiva. La Cuba que interpelan no tiene punto de anclaje en ningún lugar geográfico específico. Los lectores [. . .] pueden estar—y están—en cualquier parte del mundo.

[The journals that are made outside Cuba don't look toward Cuba—that is to say, toward the physical space of the Nation—or at least not exclusively. The Cuba that they interpolate doesn't have an anchor in any specific geographic place. Readers [. . .] can be—and are—in any part of the world.][35]

As long as they have a reliable Internet connection (or the means to access documents shared on a USB), readers can move beyond an anchored Cuba to surf the Web and access the broader Cuba.com.

More broadly, the space that Ponte crafts forms part of the *arcubiélago*, as readers and writers congregate on (and off) a constellation of sites to form a rhizomatic assemblage of communication across a range of media. In *Villa Marista en plata: Arte, política, nuevas tecnologías* [*Villa Marista in Silver: Art, Politics, New Technologies*], Ponte chronicles some of the less formal ways in which Cuba. com expands beyond the sites described by Morán. Here he writes:

> Para escribir estas páginas me he valido de mensajes electrónicos que otros se cruzaron, de imágenes captadas *in situ* por teléfonos móviles ajenos, de grabaciones de audio, y hasta de un expediente de seguimiento policial. Entradas de blogs, frases de Twitter, videos en YouTube, archivos digitalizados . . . He transcripto diálogos sostenidos por gente a las que ni siquiera conozco, como si mi trabajo fuera el de un escucha secreto. No en vano el título de este libro alude al cuartel general de la policía política cubana.

> [To write these pages I have made use of electronic messages exchanged by others, images captured *in situ* by others' cell phones, audio recordings, and even a political dossier. Blog entries, Twitter phrases, YouTube videos, digital archives . . . I have transcribed dialogues between people who I don't even know, as though my job were that of a secret eavesdropper. It is not for nothing that the title of this book alludes to the headquarters of the Cuban political police.][36]

Analyzing digital communications across a variety of platforms, Ponte signals the existence of an alternate archive and points to the rhizomatic interconnections of the *arcubiélago*.

After relocating to Madrid in 2006, Ponte continued to craft an alternate space of identity by publishing his work—and that of others—in online journals. From Madrid, Ponte penned two more essays on Martí: "Martí: historia de una bofetada" ["Martí: History of a Slap"] (2007), first published in the online journal *La Habana Elegante*; and "Martí: los libros de una secta criminal" ["Martí: The Books of a Criminal Sect"] (2017), first published in the Spanish journal *Sibila* under the title "José Martí leído fuera y según qué ediciones" ["José Martí Read Outside and According to What Editions"].[37] At the same time that Ponte again argues for the need to deconstruct Martí in these essays, he also signals once more the wide-open contours of the space that he envisions for the *arcubiélago*: a space that contests the limitations imposed by dogmatic Martí scholars, or *martianos*, who belong to what Ponte characterizes as a pernicious "secta criminal" [criminal sect], as well as those *anti-martianos* who, he contends, are similarly restrictive in their imaginings of Martí and the space he might inaugurate.

In "Martí: historia de una bofetada," Ponte builds on the argument that he makes in "El abrigo de aire" to contend that Martí—or, at least, the vision of Martí as Revolutionary icon—must be *soslayado* [circumvented] to allow him to achieve his full, multifaceted potential.[38] Ponte here establishes the need for such a stance by telling of the "bofetada" [slap] referenced in the essay's title. This, Ponte reveals, is an allusion to Cuban revolutionary Julio Antonio Mella's 1926 essay "Glosas al pensamiento de José Martí. Un libro que debe escribirse" ["Comments on the Thought of José Martí. A Book that Should Be Written"], and, more specifically, to Mella's contention that those who oppose an idealized vision of Martí deserve a bracing "bofetón" [hard slap]. As Martí was increasingly venerated in Cuba in the years following the Revolution, critics and scholars began to amplify Mella's call to "slap" those who questioned the nineteenth-century writer's privileged status. Indeed, some even went so far as to claim that there was no place in Cuba for those who had opposed Martí and, by extension, the Revolution that he had come to symbolize. As writer and politician Juan Marinello summarily argued in this regard in 1974, for instance, "'Los martianos antimartianos no tiene cabida en la Cuba de ahora'" ['there is no room in the Cuba of today for the *martianos* who are *anti-martianos*'].[39]

While for Marinello (as for Mella before him) a *bofetada* was needed to knock sense into the problematic *martianos antimartianos*,[40] Ponte argues in "Martí: historia de una bofetada" that it is the ethereal Martí himself who is most in need of a bracing *bofetón*. For, Ponte suggests, it is only by moving beyond the vision of Martí that has been created by *martianos* and *antimartianos* alike that productive change is possible: "Me pregunto si no habrá que prescindir, entre otros autoritarismos, del autoritarismo de Martí. Y pienso que, de cualquier modo que se presente el futuro para la cultura cubana, en ella ha de caber la posibilidad de soslayarlo" [I ask myself if it won't be necessary to do without, among other authoritarianisms, the authoritarianism of Martí. And I think that, in whatever way the future presents itself for Cuban culture, there has to be the possibility of circumventing him].[41] Be it through the decision to slap or to *soslayar* [circumvent], for Ponte, it is necessary to refigure Martí to allow the inhabitants of the *arcubiélago* to venture into more uncertain yet also more productive realms, in which Martí is decoupled from the singular (island) nation.

In this regard, Ponte writes that he sometimes plays with the idea of traveling through time to reach a moment when Martí is not yet the all-encompassing figure that he will become:

> Y llego al punto en que Domingo Faustino Sarmiento, en carta a Paul Groussac de junio de 1887 celebraba la crónica martiana a propósito de la inauguración de la Estatua de la Libertad y, refiriéndose a un autor poco conocido por entonces, lo menciona de esta manera: "Martí, un cubano, creo."
>
> Me abismo ante esta insegura correspondencia entre Cuba y Martí como ante esos nudos del tiempo donde las cosas que son, podrían haber resultado diferentes.

> [And I arrive at the point at which Domingo Faustino Sarmiento, in a June 1887 letter to Paul Groussac, celebrated Martí's chronicle on the inauguration of the Statue of Liberty and, referring to a then little-known author, mentions him in this way: "Martí, a Cuban, I believe."
>
> I am engrossed by this uncertain correspondence between Cuba and Martí, as when facing those knots of time where the things that are, could have turned out differently.][42]

Proposing an upending of time that would allow him to enter a space in which Martí is not yet a revered figure equated with the nation, Ponte signals once again the transnational contours of the *arcubiélago* in his reference to the chronicle that Martí is writing on the inauguration of the Statue of Liberty. The Statue of Liberty—a gift from France emblematizing its friendship with the United States, and a longstanding beacon of welcome to those arriving in New York from distant shores—serves to remind readers of Martí's transnational travels. In addition, Ponte's reference to Argentine writer and statesman Domingo Faustino Sarmiento's correspondence with Argentine-French writer Paul Groussac again highlights the ways in which identities shift and move through time and space. Groussac was born in France, but lived most of his life in Argentina; Martí was born in Cuba, but lived many years elsewhere.

In "Martí: los libros de una secta criminal," Ponte further advances the argument he makes in "El abrigo de aire" and "Martí: historia de una bofetada," pointing once again to the need to move beyond reductive readings of Martí to allow the nineteenth-century figure to take on new life in the present. Writing in this essay of the books on Martí published in Cuba, Ponte describes them as the books of a "sect" in a nod to his provocative title, stating that "Son libros de una secta criminal, hechos para justificar crímenes de Estado. Se imprimieron para justificar la complicidad de José Martí con Fidel Castro" [They are books of a criminal sect, created to justify crimes of the State. They were published to justify the complicity of José Martí with Fidel Castro].[43] Martí, Ponte contends, is repeatedly—but also reductively—tied to Fidel Castro by the sect-like writers who analyze him in Cuba, in a bid to bring the two together as the body and soul of a singular Revolution writ large.

At the same time that Ponte continues to make the case for a productive rip in the fabric of the national myth in "Martí: los libros de una secta criminal," he also continues to associate Martí with the spaces that together comprise the wider *arcubiélago*. He begins to set up this argument in "Martí: los libros de una secta criminal" by recounting a visit he made during his early years in Madrid to Cuban writer Gastón Baquero's apartment. For Baquero, Ponte writes, Cuban books marked a clear association with the nation. It was not titles penned by well-established Cuban authors that were key in this regard, however, but rather, "unos títulos prácticamente desconocidos, de autores opacos, [. . .]. aquella era la biblioteca de las mareas y de los derelictos, el exilio" [some practically unknown titles, by opaque authors, [. . .]. that was the library of the tides and the derelicts, exile]. For Ponte, the books of Baquero's library mark the separation that results from exile. The same books, however, might also signal the connections between an archipelagic constellation of spaces. Considered in this regard, it is of note that Ponte writes that "lejos de aquí, océano por medio, en otras librerías, esos libros y yo nos habíamos visto las caras" [far from here, an ocean in between, in other bookstores, those books and I had seen each other's faces].[44] With books cast adrift in Havana washing ashore in Madrid, the books that Ponte references are emblematic of the archipelagic connections between seas and cities, waterways and shorelines. At once separate and sutured together, the spaces that Ponte describes form part of a larger, archipelagic whole.

As is true of the books in Baquero's library, Martí too is for Ponte an archipelagic, larger-than-life figure that proves resistant to the strictures to which those belonging to what Ponte describes as a devoted "sect" in Cuba seek to reduce him. If sectarian writers seek to tie Martí to the space of the island nation and its longtime leader(s), Ponte demonstrates that Martí slips through their grasp, much as might an "abrigo de aire" [coat of air], to more freely roam the space of the transnational Cuban archipelago.

Remappings That Rankle

In "El abrigo de aire," "Martí: historia de una bofetada," and "Martí: los libros de una secta criminal" Ponte points to the need to both dismantle a mythical figure and to remap the nation to which he is firmly yoked, beginning to trace the potential contours of a wider space that encompasses the aerial, the saline, and the scattered islands of the *arcubiélago*. Through the stories included in *Cuentos de todas partes del Imperio* [*Tales of the Cuban Empire*], as well as through his work on the *Diario de Cuba*, Ponte further limns some of the ways in which the space of Cuba might be productively rankled and remapped.

In an interview, Ponte tellingly states that he considers the space of Cuba to be that of an empire:

> Pienso Cuba como un imperio. Lo pensé en broma para mi libro *Cuentos de todas partes del Imperio*, y lo pienso seriamente para un libro dilatadísimo (como todas las cartografías imperiales) que gira alrededor de *The Tempest* y el Caribe, y que se llamará *La Tempestá*.
>
> [I think of Cuba as an empire. I thought of it as a joke for my book *Tales from the Cuban Empire*, and I am thinking about it seriously for an expansive book (like all imperial cartographies) that is about *The Tempest* and the Caribbean, which will be called *La Tempestá*.][45]

For Glissant, the empire represents the opposite of Relation: "The empire is the absolute manifestation of totality. [. . .] The empire [. . .] usually attempts to forestall conflicts throughout its territory. But imperial peace is the true death of Relation."[46] In his tongue-in-cheek characterization of Cuba as imperial, Ponte implies that the construct of the nation is in some ways inescapable, even as he also references the ongoing need for rhizomatic rankling rather than imperial peace. In telling the tales of the scattered spaces of the *arcubiélago*, Ponte once more emphasizes the need to reimagine the space of Cuba as inherently relational and errant, as well as transnational and interconnected.

In *Cuentos de todas partes del Imperio*, there is no mention of Martí, nor, indeed, does the word "Cuba" appear in print.[47] Rather, the "stories" in the collection tell of the multiple pathways that Cubans travel across the globe without ever invoking the name of the "empire" itself. "Las lágrimas en el congrí" ["Tears in the Congrí"], for instance, tells of students banding together in a cold and distant locale, recalling (without explicitly stating) the experiences of Cubans sent to study in the former USSR. "A petición de Ochún" ["At the Request of Ochún"] narrates the experiences of a butcher in the Chinese Quarter who twice cuts elephant meat without ever tasting it, chronicling the little-known exploits of a city, replete with *santos*, reminiscent of Havana. And "Por hombres" ["Because of Men"] chronicles the tale of a woman who returns to an airport of the country where she was born—an airport remarkably similar to the Havana airport named after none other than José Martí—after traveling (at times against her will) across the world.

Although Cuba is not mentioned by name in the *Cuentos*, there are several references to the island. The island is specifically invoked, for instance, in what is perhaps the best-known story of the collection, "Un arte de hacer ruinas" ["A Knack for Making Ruins"]. "Un arte" tells of the *tugurs* who attempt to over-crowd—and thus overload—a city's precarious buildings (so similar to those for which Havana is known), causing them to fall below. The *tugurs* seek to achieve this seemingly paradoxical goal, the narrator of the story explains, through the construction of what Cubans call "barbacoas" [barbecues]: lofts added to living quarters to accommodate more people in a limited space, with the high temperatures that give the elevated spaces their colloquial name. As professor Damaris Puñales-Alpízar reminds us:

> Aunque el número de inmigrantes de otras provincias y ciudades ha seguido creciendo [en Habana], la oferta de vivienda se ha mantenido bastante inmóvil. [. . .] los nuevos habitantes de la ciudad [. . .] han comenzado a fragmentar edificios, antiguas residencias. La ciudad ha comenzado a crecer hacia adentro, [. . .] expandiéndose por dentro [. . .]

> [Although the number of immigrants from other provinces and cities has continued to rise [in Havana], the amount of available housing has remained relatively unchanged. [. . .] the new residents of the city [. . .] have begun to fragment buildings, historic residences. The city has begun to grow toward within, [. . .] expanding within [. . .]][48]

The need to surpass the limited space of the singular island is implicit in the *tugurs'* toppling of overpopulated edifices. At one point, the narrator asks his advisor, the enigmatically named Professor D, why the *tugurs* work to ensure buildings' collapse. In his response, the professor invokes the island, stating: "Son [los *tugurs*] de sombra ligera, tienen sangre de nómadas [. . .]. Y es duro ser así en una isla pequeña" [They're footloose [the *tugurs*], rolling stones, they have nomadic blood [. . .]. And it's hard to be like that on a small island].[49]

Recalling Virgilio Piñera's description of the "peso" [weight] of the island, here the professor suggests that life on the island is difficult for those born to wander.

The protagonist discovers the results of the *tugurs'* efforts to satisfy their "no-madic blood"[50] and move beyond the limited space of the singular island when he first pockets, then puts to use, one of the odd coins he discovers in his advisor's apartment: a coin that bears the words "'A mí me ronca arriba'" ['For me it rankles above'][51] on one side of its rough surface.[52] After following a mysterious stranger to a hidden tunnel, the narrator walks along the underground passage-way until he is stopped by a woman who intonates the words on the coin. Giving her the mysterious *moneda*, the narrator replies with the words printed on the other side: "'A mí me ronca abajo'" ['For me it rankles below'].[53] He is then allowed to proceed to an underground city that mirrors the one found above:

De no salir inmediatamente, tendría que reconocer que allí existía una ciudad muy parecida a la de arriba. Tan parecida que habría sido planeada por quienes propiciaban los derrumbes. Y frente a un edificio al que faltaba una de sus paredes, comprendí que esa pared, en pie aún en el mundo de arriba, no demoraría en llegarle.

[. . .] Tuguria, la cuidad hundida, donde todo se conserva como en la memoria.

[If I didn't get out immediately, I would have to accept that a city very similar to the one that existed above ground existed below it. So similar that it must have been planned by those who caused the buildings to collapse. In front of a building lacking one of its walls, I understood that the missing wall, still standing in the world above, would not take long to get here.

[. . .] Tuguria, the sunken city, where everything is preserved as in memory.[54]

Recalling the fantastic stories of Borges, or the thought-experiment work of science fiction, Ponte offers a parodic rendition of "imperial" Cuba as a small island rebuilding itself from below.

Redrawing the map in "Un arte de hacer ruinas," as that which was once above is now below, Ponte also calls to mind the restoration of Old Havana and the way in which the meticulously renovated buildings and streets of this part of the city now serve as a living museum for tourists, alongside dilapidated (yet still inhabited) ruins. Reminiscent of the restoration of Viejo San Juan in Puerto

Rico, or the Ciudad Colonial in the Dominican Republic, the restoration of Old Havana recalls, more generally, continental discourse on islands. This discourse, Elizabeth DeLoughrey notes, "commonly relegates island spaces as 'museums' for tourism, anthropological inquiry, or sociological praxis."[55] If the carefully restored buildings of Old Havana (or the city's much-photographed ruins) form part of the prevalent discourse on islands as museum exhibits, the *tugurs'* drive to topple buildings, and to go underground, proposes a radical refiguring of island(s) and nation alike.

Ponte's efforts to craft an alternate, archipelagic space are also apparent in the preface to the *Cuentos*. Here, in a piece titled "Rogación de cabeza por Scherezada" ["Plea for the Head of Scheherazade"], Ponte references the narrator of *The Thousand and One Nights* at the same time that he offers what could be considered a sly nod to his essay "El abrigo de aire":

> Encendidos los cigarros, servido el café, confiadas ya las más bien tristes nuevas de cada rincón de donde vienen, no demora en comprobarse que el Imperio consiste únicamente en ese aroma amargo que sale de las tazas, en el humo picante del tabaco, en palabras, en música. Aire todo, en fin.

> [Cigarettes lit, coffee served, the rather sad news of each corner from which the travelers come now divulged, it quickly becomes apparent that the Empire consists only of that bitter aroma rising from their cups, the pungent smoke of the tobacco, the words, the music. Nothing but air, after all.][56]

For Carlos J. Alonso, Ponte to some degree remains within the confines of established mappings of the island (or what lies beneath) in recounting the tales of a far-flung "empire." For if the Preface manifests Ponte's desire to map an alternate space in his *Cuentos*, this desire is undermined by the focus on the island, and on Cuba writ large, in the collection as a whole.[57] Yet if Cuba is an empire, as Ponte suggests, it is ultimately an empire that—like Martí's coat—is nothing but air, or, as Ponte writes, no more than "ese aroma amargo que sale de las tazas, [. . .] el humo picante del tabaco, [. . .] palabras, [. . .] música. Aire todo, en fin" [that bitter aroma rising from their cups, the pungent smoke of the tobacco, the words, the music. Nothing but air, after all].[58] Omnipresent and immaterial, like Martí's *abrigo*, the empire must also be rankled to remain relevant; and it must be remapped to take into account its ruins.

Considered from this vantage point, Professor D's words to the narrator are a suggestive indication of how space, for Ponte, might be productively reimagined. When one has no other option, Professor D states, it is necessary to "Buscar la conexión de la isla con el continente, la clave del horizonte" [Search for the connection of the island with the continent, the key of the horizon].[59] That which rankles above may still rankle below; but, by mapping the connections between island and continent, the land above the waterline and the salty sea beneath, it is possible to remap and reform space to allow access to an alternate, archipelagic space of identity.

In addition to remapping the space of Cuba in *Cuentos de todas partes del Imperio*, Ponte also rankles traditional renderings of the nation through his work on the *Diario de Cuba* (www.diariodecuba.com), an alternative online news service that he helped to found and where he now works as Vice Director. As *Diario* editor Pablo Díaz Espí explains in a 2014 interview, "Our goal was to create what a democratic society would consider a news media, in order to help reconstruct Cuban society. Those were and continue to be our objectives. We see the variety and scope of information in Cuba as deficient."[60] Ponte has worked on the *Diario* since its inception in 2009.[61] The *Diario* is not readily available for perusal online in Cuba, where the government considers it to be a dissident publication. As of this writing, however, those able to access it from elsewhere can browse sections titled "Cuba," "Internacional" [International], "Derechos humanos" [Human Rights], "Cultura" [Culture], "Deportes" [Sports], and "De leer" [To Read].[62] In an open invitation to English speakers, visitors can also peruse articles in this language in the "In English" section.

One way in which Ponte offers a potential remapping of Cuban space through his work on the *Diario* is in his publication of the work of a new generation of Cuban writers, many of whom—such as poet Ramón Hondal—still live in Havana. Commenting on this aspect of his work during our conversation in Philadelphia, Ponte noted that he—perhaps in contradistinction to writers such as Baquero, whose suffering he describes in "Martí: los libros de una secta criminal"—did not miss Cuba. This, he surmised, was because he continues to work on Cuba, and, through his work on the *Diario*, is able to be in touch with emerging Cuban writers.[63]

In addition to mapping a more open, archipelagic space by publishing writers who remain in Cuba, Ponte and his collaborators on the *Diario* also foreground alternative perspectives on Cuban identity, politics, and culture on the site. A 2019 piece in the "Cultura" section published shortly before this book was submitted to press promised readers insights into "'Cuba en USA': Emilio Cueto hace un recuento de la presencia cubana en EEUU" ["'Cuba in the USA': Emilio Cueto Recounts the Cuban Presence in the United States"]; another, published in "De leer" and penned by Ponte, established the shared, transnational history of Cuba and the United States through a focus on "En Manhattan: Cuba, azúcar, tabaco y revolución" ["In Manhattan: Cuba, Sugar, Tobacco and Revolution"].

In the *Diario* Cuba is again characterized as transnational and interconnected—as archipelagic—in articles included in the section of the publication titled "Cuba." Here, in addition to articles on Cuban President Miguel Díaz-Canel, inaugurated in 2018, readers can find articles such as "'La pequeña Habana' es una playa: más de 600 cubanos varados en una localidad colombiana" ["'Little Havana' Is a Beach: More than 600 Cubans Run Aground in a Colombian Locale"].[64] Reformulating the meaning of "Little Havana," traditionally associated with Miami, this article—on Cuba and Colombia, or, perhaps, on Cuba *as* Colombia—draws attention to the new migratory trends that cause Cubans to be "beached" in Colombia. Similarly, "Un grupo de 700 cubanos marcha en caravana hacia EEUU desde Tapachula [Mexico]" ["700 Cubans March in Caravan Toward United States from Tapachula [Mexico]"] underscores the new—and increasingly varied—routes traversed by Cubans on the move throughout the spaces of the transnational Cuban archipelago. And, in the same vein, "Un carpintero cubano en México narra cómo fue una de las fugas de emigrantes en Chiapas" ["A Cuban Carpenter in Mexico Narrates One of the Emigrant Escapes in Chiapas"] details an escape by Cuban emigrants in Chiapas.

Through such mechanisms, Ponte and his collaborators on the *Diario* portray the space of Cuba as varied and variable, insinuating—as Ponte does as well in his *Cuentos de todas partes del Imperio* and his essays on Martí—that Cuba surpasses the space of any one island to encompass the archipelagic spaces of the beaches in Colombia where migrants wash ashore, and the roads of Tapachula, Mexico, where *cubanos* trod on toward the United States following the end of the U.S. "wet foot/dry foot" policy and the resulting changes in migration patterns. Through his work on the *Diario*, Ponte thus amplifies and extends the space crafted in the pages of his essays and stories, as well as in the *encuentros* [encounters] with *letrados* [literati] near and far, "above" and "below," online and in-person.

. . .

While Ponte's "El abrigo de aire" met with widespread outrage for its proposal to resignify, and even sully, José Martí—a rankling call to arms that was amplified in "Martí: historia de una bofetada" and "Martí: los libros de una secta criminal"—the same is not true of his errant, relational depiction of Cuba(s) as a constellation of interconnected spaces. Yet Ponte's description of how Cubans are *already* re-engaging with Martí as a material and metaphoric figure might be profitably employed in the case of the nation as well. In a telling anecdote in "El abrigo de aire," Ponte describes how the image of Martí on the Cuban *peso* is folded up to allow it to tell new tales, be they of *abrigos* or other topics: "Trucamos con pliegues la efigie suya en los billetes para inventarle historias" [We fold up bills with his effigy on them to invent stories for him].[65] I would suggest that the traditional map of the island(s) might similarly be folded—or disassembled and reassembled again—to take flight, as it did for Martí, and to reveal the previously hidden yet already-present convergences of land and sea, island(s) and continent(s), that characterize the multiple "historias" [histories/ stories] of the *arcubiélago*.

Rethinking Cuba as island(s) in such a way would allow for a productive re-conceptualization of the ties that link national and transnational communities and spaces. In the specific case of Cuban writers from the 1990s and 2000s, considering Cuba as part of a wider transnational archipelago would also allow us to visualize a space that includes not only those writers who, like Ramón Hondal and Ricardo Alberto Pérez, remain in Cuba, along with those who, like Reina María Rodríguez, travel to and from Havana but also those who, like Ponte himself, have relocated on a full-time basis elsewhere. More generally, as occurs with Martí's map that, in taking flight, unintentionally signals the contours of a wider, archipelagic space that bridges air and sea, land and paper, for Ponte the island of Cuba has become but one in a larger, transnational constellation of spaces: a constellation of spaces that, in constituting a whole that is larger than the sum of its parts, is archipelagic.

6

Timeless Rhetoric, Special Circumstances

In December 2014, U.S. President Barack Obama announced that diplomatic relations would resume between the United States and Cuba after 50 years of embargo. In a speech announcing the historic policy change, Obama reminded his listeners that "the city of Miami is only 200 miles or so from Havana. Countless thousands of Cubans have come to Miami—on planes and makeshift rafts; some with little but the shirt on their back and hope in their hearts."[1] Following Obama's directives, the United States implemented policy changes designed to ease travel to Cuba, facilitated banking and commercial ties, and reopened its embassy in Havana. With these changes, the number of U.S. visitors to Cuba increased, and Cubans on the whole welcomed the resulting improvement in their economic prospects.

The ties between the United States and Cuba referenced in Obama's 2014 speech, as well as the intense debates regarding Cuban identity that the policy change brought to the fore, are highlighted in the work of writer Zoé Valdés. Born in 1959, the year of the Cuban Revolution, and living in exile in Paris since 1995, Valdés is one of the best-known authors of her generation. With humorous accounts of Special Period scarcities that cause detergent bottles to be coveted as water pitchers, for instance, her *La nada cotidiana* [*Yocandra in the Paradise of Nada*] (1995) received acclaim from reviewers upon its publication for its "testimonio de la Cuba actual" [testimony of Cuba today] and its ability to "denuncia[r] mejor que cualquier ensayo" [denounce better than any essay][2] the exigencies of life during the Special Period. The following year, her novel *Te di la vida entera* [*I Gave You All I Had*] (1996) was a finalist for the prestigious Premio Planeta. Valdés has also been criticized, however, for attempting to profit from Cuba's despair, due in no small measure to the over-the-top imagery she employs.[3]

Taking a step back in time to analyze some of Valdés's best-known titles from the 1990s, it becomes clear that the outsized nature of many of the images the author uses in her fiction, along with the polemic surrounding her strident critiques of Fidel Castro, at times threatens to obscure her evident desire to transcend the space and time of the present in her work. Thinking *with* the archipelago and departing from the idea of history as time allows for a greater understanding of this aspect of her work. Following scholar Jonathan Pugh:

> History as time is linear and sequential; it separates out, arranges and judges people and places according to such binary categories as "the modern" (Western) and "the residual" (Caribbean); "developed" and "developing" countries; "central" and "periphery"; "mainland" and "island." History as time conflates and downplays the importance of space; it reduces the importance of spatiality, different spatial trajectories and differences that are the central concerns of many associated with the spatial turn. It reduces island life to the sorts of dichotomies that Stratford et al. suggest thinking with the archipelago can challenge.[4]

Invoking a sense of timelessness through her use of sex and symbols, song and sea, Valdés gestures toward an archipelagic space out of time for what might be described, following Michael Warner, as a transnational counterpublic of readers: a group, forged through the reception of a common corpus of texts, that maintains a distance from authority. Writing and singing islands in *La nada cotidiana* and *Te di la vida entera*, as well as *El todo cotidiano* [*The Daily Everything*] (2010), Valdés seeks to surpass the space and time of the present to contribute to new outcroppings of the *arcubiélago*.[5]

Zoé Valdés and *La nada cotidiana*

Valdés is a prolific writer who has published more than 25 titles over her three-decade career. In addition to *La nada cotidiana*, *Te di la vida entera*, and *El todo cotidiano*, her novels include *Sangre azul* [*Blue Blood*] (1987), *Café Nostalgia* (1997), *Traficantes de belleza* [*Beauty Traffickers*] (1998), and *La eternidad del instante* [*The Eternity of the Instant*] (2004). Valdés has also published several volumes of poetry, including *Respuesta para vivir* [*Answer for Living*] (1986), *Vagón para fumadores* [*Smoking Car*] (1996), and *Cuerdas para el lince* [*Cords for the Lynx*] (1999).[6] Valdés is the author of *Vidas paralelas* [*Parallel Lives*], the screenplay for the film of this name (*Parallel Lives*, Pastor Vega, 1993); and she

Figure 12. A Havana used book market. Valdés's work is not widely available in Cuba. Photo by author.

maintains an active presence online through her blogs "Zoé en el metro" [Zoé in the Metro] and "Zoévaldés.net." Valdés's work has been published in England, Finland, France, Germany, Greece, Hungary, Italy, Poland, Portugal, Spain, Sweden, Russia, Turkey, and the United States.[7] Her work is not widely available in Cuba, however, and online access to her blogs on *la isla* is similarly limited. (See Figure 12.)

Valdés is known for playing a central role in inaugurating the dramatic increase in the foreign consumption of Cuban literature, music, and film in the 1990s. As professor Esther Whitfield maintains, "Special Period fiction" published during this decade often includes a "complex gesture that pits representations of authenticity (what Cuba is now) against stimuli of nostalgia (for what Cuba once was or might have been), thereby exposing ideological fissures in both the Cuban Revolution itself and outsiders' interests in it."[8]

Published in 1995, at the height of the Special Period, *La nada cotidiana* is arguably Valdés's best-known work, emblematizing the acerbic style for which she is known. In this novel, Valdés invokes a rhetoric of timelessness through her use of sex and symbol, gesturing toward a space out of time in which a counter-public of readers might gather to find an escape from the scarcities of the Special Period. The similarities between her rhetoric and that of the Castro regime, however, signal the thorny difficulties of any such attempt to craft a space that defies the norm.

Valdés begins and ends *La nada cotidiana* with an evocation of islands, telling of a woman who has returned from the liminal space of Purgatory (where she meets a cherub, an angel, and the all-knowing Nada) to the island whence she came: "*Esa isla que, queriendo construir el paraíso, ha creado el infierno*" [*the island that in wanting to build paradise has created hell*].[9] The woman—who resembles "*cualquier mujer, salvo que abre los ojos a la manera de las mujeres que habitan las islas*" [*any other woman, except that she opens her eyes in the manner of the island women*][10]—is hungry, existing between life, death, and laughter:

> *Tiene hambre y nada qué comer.* [. . .] *En su isla, cada parte del cuerpo debía aprender a resistir. El sacrificio era la escena cotidiana, como la nada. Morir y vivir: el mismo verbo, como por ejemplo reír. Sólo que se reía para no morir a causa del exceso de vida obligatoria.*

> [*She is hungry and has nothing to eat.* [. . .] *On her island, every part of the body learned to resist. Sacrifice was the order of the day, as was nada, nothingness. To die and to live: the same verb as to laugh, except that you laughed in order not to die from an excess of compulsory living*].[11]

Implying that life and death are equivalent states of being, the narrator here jokingly references Cuba's national anthem, which valiantly proclaims that "morir por la patria es vivir" [to die for the nation is to live].[12] Yet if *morir* [to die] is *vivir* [to live], both are also *reír* [to laugh] in 1990s Cuba, with laughter—in Purgatory as in the pages of *La nada cotidiana*—offering a conduit for escape, a way to transcend an impossible conflation of opposites and escape the clutches of death.

What might be termed the novel's *choteo* [or joking], following Cuban writer Jorge Mañach, thus serves as a means of social critique and a harbinger of potential freedom in the novel. Mañach writes that "Un choteo, es decir, confusión, subversión, desorden . . . comporta una negación de jerarquía . . . Todo orden implica alguna autoridad. Ordenar es sinónimo de mandar. En el desorden, el individuo se puede pronunciar más a sus anchas" [A *choteo*, which is to say, confusion, subversion, disorder . . . involves a negation of hierarchy . . . All order implies some authority. To order is to command. In disorder, the individual is able to pronounce oneself more easily].[13] Upending established hierarchies, death is life and both are laughter in the novel's opening pages. In much the same way, the notion of the space of the Cuban nation is dramatically refigured to expand beyond the narrow confines of the singular *isla*, or island, to encompass the wider seas and spaces of the transnational Cuban archipelago. This is apparent as the novel continues and the narrator, Patria, tells the story of her birth:

> Cuenta mi madre que era el primero de mayo de 1959, ella tenía nueve meses de embarazo, ya sabía que yo era niña. Cuenta que caminó y caminó desde La Habana Vieja hasta la Plaza de la Revolución para escuchar al Comandante. Y en pleno discurso comencé a cabecearle la pelvis, a romperle los huesos.

> [According to my mother, it was the first of May, 1959. She was nine months pregnant and already knew I was a girl. She walked and walked, she says, all the way from Old Havana to the Plaza de la Revolución to hear the Comandante. And in the middle of his speech I started to raise such a ruckus in her pelvic region that she thought her bones would break.][14]

As her name indicates, Patria's birth closely parallels that of the Revolutionary nation, her arrival serving as a corporeal repetition of the nation's (new) beginnings. Patria, it would seem, is destined to be synonymous with the vaunted Revolución.

After a long labor, however, Patria is born not on May 1, May Day, but on May 2, which, as the doctor reminds her father, is "el Día de los Episodios Nacionales, los Fusilamientos en Madrid" [the Day of the Madrid Uprising, the Executions in Madrid].[15] The slippage in the date of her birth—from a day dedicated to the celebration of the worker, to one marking the conquest of a nation by a tyrant—gestures toward the problematic genesis of a nation that has missed its opening beat. At the same time, the slippage signals the nation's transnational ties. As such, Patria's birth both mimics and mocks that of the singular Revolutionary nation. Offering what Homi Bhabha refers to in his discussion of mimicry as "the representation of a difference that is itself a process of disavowal,"[16] the birth of the Patria, in the pages of *La nada cotidiana*, signals that the singular *isla* is an outmoded rhetorical artifact rather than a material reality.[17]

Patria again underscores difference and reformulates space in the repeated references to *nada*, or nothingness, that she includes in her narrative. In her title, Patria references the lack of basic foodstuffs—of *pan cotidiano*—during a time of extreme scarcities. In her narrative as a whole, she refigures what Fidel Castro implies are undesirable and non-revolutionary acts in his 1961 "Palabras a los intelectuales" ["Words to the Intellectuals"]. While Castro denigrates *nada* as anti-Revolutionary in this speech, for Patria *nada* is something of possible value, and, indeed, comes to represent everything to her: "Busco cualquier pretexto en cada mínimo objeto que me rodea para no seguir pensando más. Para no comprometerme con algo que no sé si podré hacer, si tendré ovarios: describir la nada que es mi todo"[18] [I'm casting my eyes about at every object around me, however small, to keep from thinking. To keep from getting into something I may not be able to pull off: describing the *nada* that is my everything].[19] Underscoring that her "todo" [everything] is both transnational and archipelagic, the narrator incorporates not only the words of her friend la Gusana (living in exile in Madrid) in her text, but also those of her friend el Lince (living in Miami after being accused of counter-Revolutionary activities in Cuba).[20]

As Patria states after receiving a call from el Lince, the "nada" that is simultaneously her "todo" allows for a space that exceeds that of the island to encompass the constellation of spaces of the wider *arcubiélago*:

> Estamos muy cerca, muy cerca. Mira, Lince, estás aquí: en la yema de mis dedos, te me sales por las uñas y me entras por cada ínfima porción de la piel. ¿Qué enemigo, coño, dentro y fuera de esta puta isla, podrá quitárteme de encima, de mí misma, amigo mío, hermano, amante, hijo, *mon semblable* como en el poema de Jaime Gil de Biedma?

> [We are near, very near. You are here, my Lynx, beneath my fingernails, entering me through every pore. No one inside or outside this miserable country will ever be able to tear you away from me, my friend, my brother, my lover, my child, *mon semblable*, to quote Jaime Gil de Biedma.][21]

Claiming el Lince (and, by extension, the Cuban population living abroad) as the very flesh and blood of the Patria, the narrator neatly posits an alternate space of identity. Bridging the longstanding divide between the island(s) and its diasporas, the narrator instead gestures toward an archipelagic, embodied space that allows her to incorporate el Lince in her very being, without regard to "dentro" [within] or "fuera" [outside].

The alternate space of identity that Patria seeks to establish is characterized by its sexual and textual inclusiveness, as well as by its encompassing of an archipelagic grouping of spaces ranging from Miami (where el Lince resides) to Madrid (where la Gusana moves to live with her Spanish lover). Patria includes a range of U.S. and European intertexts in her narrative, often linking the consumption of these texts with the consummation of her desires. As she recounts re-creating the film *Nine ½ Weeks* (Adrian Lyne, 1986) in her very own boudoir, watching *Taxi Driver* (Martin Scorsese, 1976) with friends, and making out with her lover while *The Doors* (Oliver Stone, 1991) flickers in the background, Patria once again destabilizes Revolutionary rhetoric, in effect chronicling a circuit of texts that stands in contradistinction to what the Castro regime envisioned as its all-inclusive *todo*: "a national and a revolutionary *book*: produced in Cuba, its contents written in Cuba or translated in Cuba and with a specific Cuban 'look.'"[22]

Testifying to the range of contemporary Cubans' textual indulgences, *La nada cotidiana* fractures the idea of the nation as a singular imagined community, pointing to the need to recognize instead what Michael Warner denominates as "publics."[23] Through her references to difficult-to-procure U.S. and European films and novels, Valdés portrays (and invites readers to join) a specific type of public, defined against a dominant authority, that Warner terms a "counterpublic": "The discourse that constitutes it [a counterpublic] is not merely a different or alternative idiom but one that in other contexts would be regarded with hostility or with a sense of indecorousness."[24] In employing this "indecorousness"[25] in her discourse, Patria effectively appeals to (and demonstrates the existence of) a transnational, archipelagic counterpublic. On the one hand, she reaches out to readers who might have similar literary and cinematic tastes; on the other hand, she chronicles the existence of a like-minded counterpublic in Havana.

Foregrounding—and indeed performing—her gender and sexuality as part of her appeal to a counterpublic, Patria utilizes a "política del cuerpo . . . que propone sexualidades y erotismos, morbos y escatologías como prácticas liberadoras del sujeto" [a politics of the body . . . that proposes sexualities and eroticisms, sicknesses and scatologies, as liberating practices of the subject].[26] Reading against the grain, Patria challenges as well the scripted discourse of heteronormative Revolutionary desire. As a teenager, for instance, Patria falls in love with a highly acclaimed Revolutionary writer whom she nicknames el Traidor [the Traitor]. In recounting how their relationship begins, she pokes fun at the romanticized discourse of desire that el Traidor invokes when he initially refuses to have sex with her because she is a virgin: "señorita por la vagina, pero no por c'anal'es" [my vagina was indeed virgin but [. . .] the other c(anal) was considerably less pure].[27] Unsentimentally acting in response to the older man's concerns, Patria engages in a liaison with a drunk hippie named Machoqui:

> Le di cuatro bofetones, lancé dos jarras de agua fría en su imbécil cara y comencé a besarlo para no perder la costumbre del romanticismo. En el pullman descosido y sudoroso, escuchando un bolero en la propia voz de José Antonio Méndez, él se abrió la portañuela, y se sacó el pito bien tieso. Yo ya tenía el blúmer por los tobillos. Evoqué la guillotina, y de un tirón me senté en la cabeza del rabo. Él chilló de dolor, yo no había lubricado lo suficiente. Costó trabajo, pero lo decapité. Sólo hubo un mínimo ardor y una aguada sangrecita. Mi himen había cumplido su cometido: matar a un tolete.

> [I slapped him four times, threw two pitchers of cold water on his idiotic face, and began to kiss him in order to maintain a modicum of romance. On a battered bench reeking of sweat, and to the tune of a bolero sung by José Antonio Méndez himself, he opened his fly and fished out a well-stiffened prick. I already had my panties down around my ankles. All I could think of was a guillotine. Without further ado, I sat myself down squarely on the head of his member. He was the one who let out a cry of pain; I wasn't moist enough. It took some doing, but finally I managed the beheading. It didn't hurt much, and all there was to show for it was a watery bloodstain, but my hymen had accomplished its mission: to murder a penis.][28]

Evoking the well-worn tropes of romance (the bolero playing in the background, the kisses she plants on Machoqui's face), the narrator's description of her loss of virginity is decidedly unsentimental. Rather, Patria scripts sex as a means to an end in her encounter with Machoqui: taking charge, it is she who "decapitates" him, and, in a further reversal of stereotypical gender roles, it is he who screams in pain. As a result of what she pragmatically terms her "trabajo," she achieves her goal, returning to el Traidor and jubilantly announcing that "Ya me partieron" [I've been deflowered].[29]

Patria's appeal to a counterpublic—and her condemnation of the outdated models of Cuba's past—is again evident in her tongue-in-cheek description of an encounter with her current lover, the film director she refers to as el Nihilista [the Nihilist]. Since she cannot decide what to wear, Patria awaits el Nihilista completely naked, listening not to José Antonio Méndez but to Peter Frampton, who sings "Show Me the Way."[30] When her lover arrives, he brings a special surprise: two pizzas, or "dos trozos de panes [. . .] mal redondeados, desiguales en tamaño, apestosos a queso, digo a preservativo rancio, coloreados con cualquier tinte rojo menos con salsa de tomate" [two pieces of bread [. . .] each more or less round, each a different size, both reeking of rancid cheese—I mean cheese substitute—and smeared with some reddish liquid that bears no relationship whatever to tomato sauce].[31] After savoring this rare treat, Patria and el Nihilista re-create "nuestra *nueve semanas y media*" [our Nine and a Half Weeks],[32] relying on the protagonists of *Nine ½ Weeks* to "show them the way" as they experiment with Tiger balm, anal sex, and "infinite" orgasms.[33]

In such "indecorous" pairings of sex and text, Patria chronicles—and appeals to—a Cuban counterpublic. As she does so, furthermore, she offers a means of transcending the limitations of space and time through her depiction of what Araceli San Martín Moreno and José Muñoz de Baena Simón term "un goce instantáneo, imposible de controlar" [an instantaneous pleasure, impossible to control].[34] If, as we have seen, the body of Patria offers a space able to encompass all Cubans—be they in Miami, as is el Lince; or in Madrid, as is la Gusana— the pleasure the body experiences is capable of upending time, offering a momentary reprieve from the difficult conditions that the narrator chronicles. It is noteworthy in this regard that Patria's explicit descriptions of sex often contain elements of the erotic, associated by Georges Bataille with nostalgia for lost continuity.[35] Referencing José Lezama Lima's *Paradiso* (*Paradise*, 1966), for example, in the chapter in which she relates her *Nine ½ Weeks*-inspired encounter with her lover, Patria invokes pornography and erotica in the same breath:

> Parece que los capítulos ocho de la literatura cubana están condenados a ser pornográficos.
>
> Así se expresará el censor cuando lea estas páginas. El censor que me toca por la libreta, porque cada escritor tiene un policía designado. Dictará estas palabras a su secretaria, que le tecleará el informe sobre mi novela refiriéndose, para honor mío, al capítulo ocho de *Paradiso*, de José Lezama Lima [. . .] los censores, [. . .] ni siquiera conocen la diferencia entre lo erótico y lo pornográfico. Y por eso tampoco se dieron cuenta de que no sólo el capítulo ocho, sino toda *Paradiso* es erótica de cabo a rabo, una de las novelas más sensuales de la literatura contemporánea.
>
> [It would appear that all Chapter Eights of Cuban literature are condemned to being pornographic.

Such will be the censor's report when he reads these pages. My personal censor—for every Cuban writer has his or her designated censor—will dictate those words to his secretary, who will type up the report on my novel, referring—to my credit—to Chapter Eight of José Lezama Lima's *Paradiso* [. . .] the censors, [. . .] are incapable of telling the difference between the erotic and the pornographic. And that is why they are unable to understand that not only Chapter Eight but the entirety of *Paradiso* is erotic.][36]

In her description of Hollywood-inspired sex later in the chapter, Patria clearly riffs on pornography, invoking a film (*Nine ½ Weeks*) known for its sexual explicitness. Yet in announcing that her less-than-brilliant Cuban censor will unthinkingly equate her narrative with a well-known predecessor (i.e., *Paradiso*), Patria warns readers not to fall prey to the tendencies that plague those who patrol the borders of the Revolutionary "todo," priming them to the existence of elements of the "sensual" and erotic.

In turn, Patria's subsequent description of her first sexual encounter with el Nihilista, whom she tellingly depicts as an "amante eterno" [eternal lover],[37] evidences the aforementioned desire for continuity associated with erotics:

El beso duró el resto de la película, pero no exclusivamente en la boca. Él fue descendiendo con experimentada lentitud por mi cuello, me lengüeteó desde la barbilla hasta los pezones, donde permaneció minutos de goce interminable. Al rato fue aún más despacio, de mis senos a las costillas y de ellas al ombligo, y la punta de su lengua hizo estragos en mi vientre. [. . .] Después, con sus dedos largos, apartó mis pendejos y relució, rojo y erguido, mi clítoris. Allí estampó el beso que lo consagró para la eternidad, el Nobel del cunilingüismo. Su nombre debiera aparecer en el *Guinness* como el mamalón más profesional que haya conocido la historia de la civilización.

[His kiss lasted as long as the film continued, but it didn't confine itself to my mouth. It descended, as if on an exploratory mission, slowly down to my neck, then, with little flicks of the tongue, moved from my chin to my nipples, where it lingered for several interminable minutes of pleasure. Then he slipped, even more slowly, from my breasts down my sides, and from there to my navel, where the tip of his tongue wreaked havoc. [. . .] After that, his long fingers parted my bush, to reveal, red and erect, my clitoris. He planted thereon a kiss that consecrated him, for all eternity, as a Nobel laureate of cunnilingus. His name should be etched in the *Guinness Book of Records*.][38]

Patria once again appeals to a Western reader's sensibilities through her mention of the *Guinness Book of World Records*. Patria's description of the "mamalón" she receives, however, also serves as a gesture toward a space out of time. Minutes, it would seem, somehow expand to encompass Patria's never-ending pleasure; these "minutos de goce interminable" [interminable minutes of pleasure] slow even further ("aun más despacio" [even more slowly]) as her lover explores her body, culminating in an "eternity" of consecration for the narrator.

In Patria's appeal to a counterpublic, symbols as well as erotics serve to cull into existence a space out of time for a transnational, archipelagic counterpublic. On the one hand, names such as Patria, la Gusana, and el Traidor appeal to readers abroad who may not be familiar with the nuances of Cuban history; on the other hand, such oversized, symbolic names form part of the narrator's appeal to an alternate space and time. Referencing the protagonists' names in an interview with Valdés, Enrico Mario Santí suggests that the text can be categorized as an allegory: "Una de las cosas más interesantes de tus personajes es que [. . .] son personajes alegóricos. Es decir, no tienen nombres como Pepe, María o Teresa, sino etiquetas, como el Traidor, el Nihilista, la Gusana, el Lince, etcétera" [One of the most interesting things about your characters is that [. . .] they are allegorical. That is to say, they don't have names like Pepe, María, or Teresa, but labels, like the Traitor, the Nihilist, the Gusana, the Lynx, etc.].[39] In allegories, however, there is generally a distinction between referenced and referent. Scholar Rafael Rojas states:

> El relato alegórico o parabólico permite narrar una fábula a través de la trama de otra. [. . .] La naturaleza oblicua de una narración así facilita la articulación, bajo el Estado revolucionario, de una *voz* crítica, emboscada en la alegoría y la parábola y, por tanto, difícilmente legible y censurable.
>
> [The allegorical or parabolic tale allows the narration of one fable through the plot of another. [. . .] The oblique nature of a narrative thus facilitates the articulation, under the revolutionary State, of a critical voice, hidden in allegory and parable and, for this reason, only with difficulty legible and censurable.][40]

In *La nada cotidiana*, in contrast, referenced and referent largely coincide: Patria *is* the patria, even if this patria is capable of encompassing counterpublics; la Gusana *is* an exile; and el Traidor *is* a traitor: "Tú vives en la traición. Eres el traidor de ti mismo" [You live in betrayal. You're betraying yourself].[41]

While Valdés invokes the allegorical, it is thus perhaps more accurate that she lampoons the popular genre of the political allegory, which is often favored by authors who fear censorship, including, in the case of Cuba, Reinaldo Arenas, Alejo Carpentier, and Lisandro Otero;[42] and that she opts instead for what might be characterized as the more easily digestible symbol. In her use of the symbol, Valdés chooses a trope that, as theorist Paul de Man maintains, attempts to cover the tracks of time:

> In the world of the symbol it would be possible for the image to coincide with the substance, since the substance and its representation do not differ in their being but only in their extension: they are part and whole of the same set of categories. Their relationship is one of simultaneity, which, in truth, is spatial in kind, and in which the intervention of time is merely a matter of contingency, whereas, in the world of allegory, time is the originary constitutive category.[43]

As is evident most clearly in the case of the narrator, image and substance repeatedly coincide in *La nada cotidiana*, as de Man argues will occur in the realm of the symbolic: specifically, the substance of the counterpublic "nation" that Valdés seeks to conjure into existence proves equivalent in "being" if not in "extension" to its representation. Patria, that is, can locate her exiled friend el Lince in her fingertips; while he may spill a bit out of her nails, he can enter again through her skin. Such spatial simultaneity of image (i.e., the narrator Patria) and substance (i.e., the more perfect and inclusive patria of which she dreams) underscores Patria's attempts to collapse time—the "originary constitutive category" of the allegory she mocks—through sex and erotics.

Even as the narrator of *La nada cotidiana* seeks to destabilize Revolutionary rhetoric through *choteo* and to gesture toward an alternate, archipelagic space of identity through the use of sex and symbol, however, the repetitive nature of daily life in Cuba suggests that wholesale escape is doubtful. The text's appeal to a counterpublic is problematized by "representations" that prove part and parcel of a larger whole. For, as Patria's narrative makes clear, the demands of the Special Period in effect erase the distinctions between one day and the next, making *lunes* [Monday] the same as *martes* [Tuesday] in the 1990s and creating an "eternal 'now.'"[44] Patria's daily routine, for instance, varies little: she goes to work, engaging in a simulacrum of productivity for a magazine that she knows will never be published; contemplates what she will eat for her next meal and where she will find the ingredients; and alternates evenings with el Traidor (whom she marries, divorces, and takes as a lover) and el Nihilista. Speaking of an electrical outage that effectively ends her workday, Patria underscores the incessant, unproductive repetition of even the most basic tasks, with information that has been entered into a database having to be re-entered *ad infinitum* due to power outages.[45] All writing, too, begins to repeat itself. El Traidor, for instance, finds himself confined to two sentences, which he repeats time and again in his manuscript: "'Todos me persiguen. No puedo escribir porque todos me persiguen'" [Everyone is after me. I can't write because everyone is after me].[46]

Describing the conditions under which Cuban intellectuals must write, el Traidor's repetitive prose also indicates a leveling out of workers in an era in which, as philosopher Walter Benjamin suggests, art has lost its aura due to the pernicious effects of mass reproduction.[47] The office assistant and the esteemed author, after all, do not differ greatly in their tasks. While implying a profound rhetorical deficit in Cuba that mirrors the shortage of goods and comestibles on the island, such repetitions also problematize the very idea of a counterpublic, which is fundamentally dependent on difference. For when all writing is subject to repetition, even the exceptional proves routine. Patria, for instance, decides as a teen to change her name to Yocandra, el Traidor's ephemeral muse. Rebelling against the nationalistic fervor that led her parents to associate her identity with that of their country, Patria assumes the name of the woman she hopes to become.

The name Patria chooses, however, demonstrates the difficulties of escaping the oversignified realm in which she exists, as el Traidor's reaction reveals: "llevo años de años buscando un nombre extraño, sugerente, que sea un gancho para los editores, le pongo a mi libro *Los versos de Yocandra*, y vienes tú, maldita pulga 'cuatro pelos', a robarme mi título" [For years I racked my brain, trying to find a title that publishers would find intriguing. *Poems of Yocandra's*. And then a ridiculous little twerp like you comes along and steals it!].[48] As the (common) Patria, the narrator was asked to serve as a synecdoche of the nation, representing the Revolutionary zeal that had inspired her father when he decided on her name. As a (proper) Yocandra, the narrator attempts to assume an individual identity—the "yo" the name incorporates—yet finds herself once more relegated to the realm of the repetitive, a reified and marketable concept.[49]

In her final lines to the reader in *La nada cotidiana*, the narrator affirms the importance of gathering together all Cubans through the body and the word:

> [. . .] hay amigos muy grandes que murieron, otros que se fueron y otros que se quedaron. Todos aquí, dentro de mí. Dentro de las palabras que no sé más si soy yo quien las escribe. O si son ellas las que me escriben a mí:

Ella viene de una isla que quiso construir el paraíso . . .

[[. . .] I have had friends who have died, others who have fled, still others who have remained. They are all inside me. Inside the words. I no longer know if I have written them. Or if they have written me:

She comes from an island that had wanted to build paradise. . . .][50]

The repetition of the novel's opening words and the ellipsis at its end signal the narrative's circularity, evoking once again a space out of time in which the norms of chronology do not apply—a space, perhaps, fit for a counterpublic that might return time and again to the pages of a text whose circulation helps to create (but does not contain) a group of readers willing to laugh along at stock symbols of the nation, and to lose track of time as the protagonist tells of her sexual exploits. In this instance, as in the blog "Del Palenque . . . y para . . . ," the ellipsis might also be considered to suggest the archipelagic interconnections between a series of spaces (emblematized in the dots that comprise the ellipsis) that are simultaneously singular and plural. Yet if the narrator intends for this space to exist in contrast to the dominant, normative discourse of Castro's Cuba, it is unclear to Patria/Yocandra herself who writes (to) whom: the body of the Patria continues to encompass the body politic, but the words the narrator writes are perhaps the "Palabras" [words] that write her.[51]

Sounding the Archipelago in *Te di la vida entera*

In the multimedia production *Te di la vida entera* [*I Gave You All I Had*], Valdés once again seeks to overcome the strictures of time, employing in this instance the lyrics to guarachas, rumbas, mambos, tangos, and boleros that fill the pages of the novel,[52] as well as the tracks of its self-proclaimed "soundtrack," *Te di la vida entera: Grupo Café Nostalgia.*[53] To my knowledge, the novel and its soundtrack are sold separately; a search for the novel on Amazon in English and Spanish returns the CD as the second item listed, suggesting that they are easily purchased together. As of this writing (May 2022), the soundtrack is also available as a user-posted playlist on Spotify.

As Valdés states in the liner notes to this CD, which she orchestrated to accompany the novel, the songs are meant to communicate the passage of time: "I finished the first manuscript [of *Te di la vida entera*] while still in Cuba. After I was in exile, it occurred to me that each chapter should comprise a decade, from the thirties to the nineties, and that certain songs could highlight each stage in the life story of Cuca Martínez [. . .] Cuca Martínez's story follows exactly the words of each bolero, each *guaracha*, each *son,* each cha-cha-cha, and later, of each Revolutionary hymn."[54] To wit, each chapter of *Te di la vida entera* starts with an epigraph from a song; lyrics are also often incorporated into chapter titles, and are scattered throughout the text of the narrative itself.

The lyrical thus serves to situate *Te di la vida entera* in both time and space, and to influence its main events. Yet the longing communicated in the boleros, in particular, frequently also holds out the promise of a universal language understood by all, pointing to the possibility of an alternate, archipelagic space outside the constraints of time.[55] As scholar Iris M. Zavala notes in this regard:

> La multiplicación de los niveles comunicativos [en el bolero], como en la poesía lírica de todos los tiempos, crea un espacio de percepción abierto, por encima del espacio de percepción real del autor/a. Se instala una suerte de segundo espacio perceptivo al margen de las restricciones espacio-temporales y de las presuposiciones que los receptores tengan de una situación concreta.
>
> [The multiplication of the communicative levels [in the bolero], as in the lyrical poetry of all times, creates a space of open perception, above the space of real perception of the author. A sort of second perceptive space is installed at the margins of the space-time restrictions and the presuppositions that the receivers may have of a concrete situation.][56]

With origins in the fin de siècle, around the time of Cuba's independence from Spain, the bolero would appear to be well suited to new imaginings of (trans) national identity, appearing to offer a space open to publics and counterpublics alike.[57]

Valdés's multimedia project thus speaks (and sings) to both the possibilities and the limitations of transnational, multimedia productions intended to foment archipelagic ties. As it is recorded on page or (sound)track, the written and vocalized word serves to release the reader-listener from the moorings of time and space and to offer a potential new space—what Zavala terms a "sort of second perceptive space"[58]—in which a transnational, archipelagic counterpublic might gather. At the same time, any given character's ability to communicate through song is often shown to be dependent on his or her preexisting knowledge of language and lyrics, suggesting the ongoing need for localized knowledge even in an increasingly transnational era. As such, Valdés's multimedia production suggests both the possibilities and the limitations of employing the written and vocalized word to forge alternate, archipelagic spaces for far-flung readers and listeners.

Intimating the need for the alternate space that Valdés seeks to create through the lyrical, *Te di la vida entera* chronicles the life of Cuca Martínez, a woman who is born in the small town of Santa Clara in the 1930s, and who moves to pre-Revolutionary Havana as a young woman to work as a maid.[59] It is here that the protagonist—whose name, of course, is close to Cuba (but no cigar)—discovers the pleasures of the capital city's dancehalls and cabarets; and it is here that she meets Uan Pérez, the "one" whom she immediately determines is the love of her life. Cuca's passionate affair with Uan, however, is soon interrupted by the 1959 Cuban Revolution. As a self-starter who has become involved with the mafia, Uan emigrates to the United States and leaves behind Cuca (now some months pregnant) and his most important possession, a dollar bill. The remainder of the novel chronicles the years of hardship that follow for the protagonist, who struggles to survive and raise her daughter during the Special Period.[60]

Situating her narrative in time and space, Valdés leverages a stark critique of Fidel Castro's regime that echoes the one offered in *La nada cotidiana*. The contrast between the portrayal of the splendors of pre-Revolutionary Havana and the struggles of the Special Period in the novel offers one indication of Valdés's oppositional stance. After arriving in Havana, Cuca revels in the pleasures of life in the years before 1959, enjoying what history professor Louis A. Pérez describes as the "Music [that] served as both source and setting of the North American meditation on sex and sensuality."[61] Foregrounding the pleasures of Havana clubs and dancehalls, and evoking the pre-Revolutionary period through the boleros and music she includes,[62] Valdés references a time in which music promised tourists (as well as recent arrivals to the city) access to an island dream. After the triumph of the Revolution, though, Cuca is forced to march to the beat of a different drum. During the 1990s, in particular, she must raid local dumps for basic household items, forgo needed medication due to a lack of basic supplies, and cope with severe and ongoing food shortages.

By offering a diachronic portrayal of a utopia turned dystopia in *Te di la vida entera*, Valdés critiques the policies and practices of Fidel Castro's government. In addition to challenging the policies of the Castro regime in this way, Valdés also unfetters desire in *Te di la vida entera* in a critique of the heteronormative status quo, as she did as well in *La nada cotidiana*. The protagonist, for instance, is shocked to discover her sickly brother engaged in a homosexual tryst before she departs for Havana, and a same-sex relationship between her roommates surprises Cuca when she moves to the capital city. Shivering in her bed as she lies sick with the flu just after her arrival, she hears the blissful sounds of the women with whom she is to share her living quarters: "Tetas contra tetas. Raja contra raja. Los dedos llenos de sortijas baratas pajeaban los clítoris a una velocidad de años luz" [Tit to tit and clit to clit, they mashed so hard they gave off sparks. In a flash of cheap rings, fingers were strumming clits at the speed of light].[63] Chronicling and appealing to a transnational, archipelagic counterpublic, Valdés here challenges what she considers to be the repressive policies of Fidel Castro and his regime's attempts to limit the space of the nation to the space of the (heteronormative) island.[64]

If *Te di la vida entera* is temporally situated, however, it is also unleashed from the moorings of time and space, communicating a sentiment that exceeds the boundaries of both. As Whitfield argues, the novel focuses not only on specific moments in time—moving from pre-Revolution splendors to Special Period scarcities—but also on the excess of feeling experienced by the protagonist. This is indicative in the dual focus in the novel on *el dólar*—the U.S. dollar that Uan leaves with Cuca when he departs for Miami, and that motivates his return to Havana—and *el dolor* (which might be translated as pain, as well as sorrow). The translation of the novel's title into French (*La douleur du dollar*) foregrounds the aforementioned relationship between pain and money, and the novel plays with the semantics of the terms as well. When Uan returns to Cuba to ask Cuca for his *dólar*, for instance, needing its serial number to access funds deposited in a Swiss bank account some thirty-odd years ago, Cuca is overwhelmed with emotion, understanding *dolor* instead of *dólar* and responding accordingly.[65]

The association between pain and money in *Te di la vida entera* might be considered part of the author's capitalist proclivities, recalling criticisms leveraged at the author in the 1990s for seeking to benefit financially from a nation's suffering. Yet the *dólar-dolor* wordplay also points to the fact that Valdés seeks to craft a space that surpasses that of the singular island in *Te di la vida entera*. As occurs with the repetition of sex and symbol in *La nada cotidiana*, furthermore, in *Te di la vida entera* the boleros that permeate and motivate the novel remit the reader to a space outside the normal constraints of time: a space that is both transnational and archipelagic.

The lyrics that begin (and motivate) the first chapter of *Te di la vida entera* encapsulate "la multiplicación de los niveles comunicativos" [the multiplication of communicative levels] referenced by Zavala,[66] and also signal the author's desire to employ the lyrical to cull a transnational, archipelagic space into existence. The chapter is entitled "Be careful, it's my heart" (in English) and the chapter opens with an epigraph (in Spanish) from this song by Irving Berlin, interpreted by Bola de Nieve ("Snowball"): "Ten cuidado / que es mi corazón / no mi reloj lo que tienes / en la mano."[67] The reader who has purchased the soundtrack can pair written lyrics and vocalized sound by listening (and perhaps even singing) along to the soundtrack clip, which is in English: "Be careful / it's my heart / it's my heart / It's not my watch you're holding / It's my heart." The motivated reader can also contextualize the lyrics by reading through the liner notes to the soundtrack. As the notes explain of "Be careful, it's my heart," for instance, the song was originally written by Irving Berlin but "bears the inimitable stamp of arrangements by Cuban pianist and composer Ignacio Villa Fernández," otherwise known as Bola de Nieve. This version, the liner notes explain, "alternates Bola's voice with Omar Hernandez's. The listener can enjoy Hernandez's arrangements, which blend Bola de Nieve's piano solos with the music of Grupo Café Nostalgia."[68]

At the same time that Valdés uses the lyrical to move the novel forward through time, she thus also signals the possibility of creating a space out of time for her readers. For here, even as the novel chronicles Cuca's life in Cuba over the course of various decades, the lyrical serves as well as a means of accessing a space open to all readers (or listeners) across the transnational Cuban archipelago willing to sing along. Bola de Nieve and Omar Hernández, after all, come together thanks to the possibilities of digital remixing; if I sing along, I can join them (although, in my case, I will almost certainly be somewhat out of tune).

Considered from this vantage point, the distinction between what Zavala describes as the "space of real perception" and the "space of open perception" is clear even from chapter 1's epigraph. "Ten cuidado / que es mi corazón" echoes (indeed, translates) the chapter title, "Be careful, it's my heart,"[69] establishing a clear distinction between the affective (the heart) and the temporal (the watch). The repetition of the lyrics' first lines signals the lack of individuality communicated by the boleros, which allows listeners to assume their words as their own, appropriating them as a vehicle for their emotions. Reinforcing what Zavala terms the "multiplication of communicative levels" and the collective nature of the experience promised by the bolero, the novel codes information regarding author and artist as secondary, relegating it to a parenthetical, visually subordinate space: "(De Irving Berlin. Interpretada por Bola de Nieve)" [By Irving Berlin, as sung by Bola de Nieve].[70] The song may be written by Berlin, that is, and interpreted by Bola de Nieve, but Omar Hernández can sing it too, as might you or I.

As the first chapter draws to a close, "Be careful, it's my heart" is integrated into the novel's plot. In a key moment, Cuca hears the song on the radio while en route to the club where she will meet Uan for the first time:

> Cuquita sintió inmediatamente un filón (de *feeling*) inexplicable con esa canción, y eso que ella no entendía ni pitoche de inglés, pero algo espiritual, o de espiritismo, le decía que ésa era su canción, o al menos la que definía su estado de ánimo en aquel mismo instante: *Remember, it's my heart, the heart with the wishes old . . . Be careful, it's my heart . . .*

> [And even though she didn't know squat when it came to English, Cuquita immediately felt a tingling, as if some sainted or fetish-tainted thing was telling her that this was her song. At any rate, it was a tune singularly attuned to her mood at that time. "*Remember, it's my heart, my heart filled with old desires. . . . Be careful, it's my heart . . .*"][71]

Translated from Spanish to English, as occurs on the CD as well, the song assumes a different form, yet its malleability does not preclude Cuca's strong affective identification with the music she hears.

Cuca then requests clarification regarding the song's meaning ("-Ay, ¿qué quiere decir esa canción?" [What's he saying?][72]): a question also included on the soundtrack, at the end of the track of "Be careful." In response, her friend Mechunga first downplays the importance of the lyrics, then offers a translation that provides yet another iteration of them:

> —Nada, tú, una bobería del corazón . . .—y Mechunga comenzó a cantarla en español, con voz chillona y pésima traducción: *Recuerda, es mi corazón, mi corazón lleno de viejos deseos . . . Ten cuidado, es mi corazón, la, la, la . . .* No me sé la letra.

> ["Nothing, some foolishness about the heart." And La Mechunga started singing a poor Spanish rendition in her screechy voice: "*Recuerda, es mi corazón, mi corazón lleno de viejos deseos . . . Ten cuidado, es mi corazón, la, la, la . . .* I forgot the words."][73]

Saberse la letra [knowing the words], however, would not seem to be of primary importance; listeners can appropriate the song's lyrics and assume them as their own, changing words and language at will.

Lest the reader-listener think it possible to transcend time and space willy nilly, however, the lyrics at the beginning of chapter 5, "Un cubano en Nueva York" ["A Cuban in New York"], begin to hint at the difficulties of creating a time-space that is open to all, even as they again encapsulate the tension between the "space of real perception" and the "space of open perception." In this chapter, Uan has left Havana for the United States, and, at first glance, the lyrics to this *guaracha* from 1940 (recorded on the CD by soloist Luis Bofill and the Café Nostalgia musicians) seem to offer a brief synopsis of the timeless experience of exile in the United States.

Ponte duro, cubano,
que tú estás en Nueva York.
A este país llegué yo,
cuando mi Cuba dejé,
y pronto me enamoré
de una joven que pasó.
Ella me dijo: I don't know
speak to you, cubano.

[Hey, fellow Cubano,
time to get tough now,
this is New York now.
I, too, left my Havana,
was new to this city,
lost my heart
to the first passerby
"I don't know speak to you,
Cubano," she said.][74]

The lyrics, however, also foreshadow Uan's first encounter with the woman who becomes his wife (whom he meets and marries in the United States), at the same time as they insinuate themselves into his recounting of their meeting:

Reparé en su presencia [. . .] Sucumbí a ese *ni p'a ti, ni p'a mí, ni p'a todos los que están aquí* que se arma cuando un nalgatorio y un par de tetas saben cómo bambolearse [. . .] Como aún chapurreaba el inglés, decidí lanzarme en español:

—Oye, tú eres cubana, no me digas que no—le solté en la misma entrada del Empire.

—*I don't know speak to you*, cubano.

Ripostó con odio transitorio en la mirada. Fue cuestión de identificar-nos, y nos echamos a reír.

[I picked her out [. . .] I fell for her "too sexy for you, too sexy for me, too sexy as far as the eye can see" way of flouncing down the street. She had me going with her rolling tits and ass [. . .] As I still spoke broken English, I went for it in Spanish:

[. . .]—"Hey there, you're Cuban, right? Don't tell me you're not." We were right in front of the Empire State Building.

"I don't know speak to you, *Cubano*," she said, and there was a momentary hardness in her eyes. But the recognition had been mutual, and we both started laughing.][75]

It is worth noting that the CD liner notes describe the *guaracha* as "a song style that often depicts amusing situations in Cuban life"[76]—and, recontextualized, the lyrics here allow Uan and his future wife to share a joke. Laughing together, the two find that they speak a language that is both universal and specific to the Cuban exile; it may not be important for Mechunga to *saberse la letra*, or "know the words," but it proves critical that Uan "knows" how to speak.

Given the possibilities and limitations of the lyrical, as seen in the afore-mentioned examples from *Te di la vida entera*, it is worth asking whether sing-alongs and multimedia productions can allow a transnational, archipelagic readership to join together—even briefly—in a space out of time. Valdés in some ways seems to hope that the answer is yes. *Te di la vida entera*, after all, uses songs both to organize and mark time, and to open up a possible new space for a community of readers and listeners willing to sing (or at least hum) along, translating and appropriating lyrics for their own purposes at the same time that they come together in song. Even as Valdés's production hints at the rich, polyvalent range of possibilities inherent in the use of the written and recorded word to form transnational communities, however, her novel also points to the limitations of the lyrical, as protagonists and readers alike must often depend on preexisting knowledge and linguistic competency to com-municate fully with each other.

From this perspective, the novel's penultimate chapter, "Perdóname, concien-cia" ["Forgive Me, Conscience"], sounds a cautionary note on the difficulties (and perhaps even the dangers) of using the lyrical to transcend time and place. Here, as the novel draws to a close, Uan and Cuca have just been released by government officials who have subjected them to torture. Uan has been exiled from the country, and Cuca has been left on the streets of the town where she was born. As recounted in a parenthetical commentary, Cuca now sings the words to what the narrator describes as an "antigua grabación" [very old recording][77] by Moraima Secada that she hears on the radio.

Perdóname, conciencia,
razón sé que tenías,
pero en aquel momento
todo era sentimiento,
la razón no valía.

[Forgive me conscience,
I know you were right
but at the time
only feeling mattered,
reason did not count.][78]

A plethora of characters serve as narrators of *Te di la vida entera*: Cuca and Uan narrate chapters; a story-telling cadaver (later determined to be Cuca and Uan's daughter María Regla) announces her presence; a scribe makes a brief appearance at the end of the novel as Zoé Valdés; and a disembodied, parenthetical voice identifies itself as Pepita Grillete, the narrator's conscience. Here, in comments included in parentheses (and thus attributable to Pepita Grillete), song lyrics provide a bridge from organized narrative to the repetitive fragments that mark Cuca's descent into madness. For as with a vinyl record that begins to skip, the final words of the song repeat again and again:

La razón no valía. La razón no valía. La razón no valía. La razón no valía. La razón no valía. La razón no valía. La razón no valía. La razón no valía. La razón no valía. La razón no valía. La razón ... ¡Crach! Piiiiiiiiiiiiiiiiiiiiii iiiiiiiiiiiiiiiiiiiiiiiiiiiiiiiiiiiiiiiiiiiiiiiiii. Isquemia. Arteriosclerosis. Muerte cerebral. Un vegetal. Un buen recurso para la salvación.

[Reason did not count. Reason did not count. Reason did not count. Reason did not count. Reason did not count. Reason did not count. Reason did not count. Reason did not count. Reason did not count. Reason did not count. Reason ... Crash! Piiiiiiiiiiiiiiiiiiiiiiiiiiiiiiiiiiiiiiiiiiiiiiiiiiiiiiiiiiiiiiiiiiiiiiiiiiiiiiiii. Ischemia. Arteriosclerosis. Brain death. Vegetable. One way to salvation.][79]

While boleros offer themselves up for repetition and recontextualization, in this case meaning is lost, rather than gained, through Cuca's stuttered, skipping re-iteration. For the protagonist, sentiment again prevails over reason, as the lyrics suggest; the repetition of the words "La razón no valía" [Reason did not count] signals once more a break in time, when—with each sentence repeating the one that comes before—the order of the verses ultimately lacks importance.

Closing the Book in El todo cotidiano

Considered together, La nada cotidiana and Te di la vida entera might be taken as one indication that much work remains to bridge the global rift over Cuba, and to restore sense and sanity to a discussion in which, as singer Moraima Secada warns us, "reason" does not always "count."[80] Analyzing these works within an archipelagic framework contributes to this project, as thinking *with* the archipelago sheds new light on the ways in which space and identity are negotiated. Following Pugh in this regard: "Thinking with the archipelago denaturalizes space so that space is more than the mere backcloth for political or ethical debate. Instead, reflective of a spatial turn in thinking, it emphasizes more fluid tropes of assemblages (Tsai, 2003), mobilities, and multiplicities associated with island-island movements."[81] The need to think *with* the archipelago, and to have a more nuanced conversation throughout the *arcubiélago*, is underscored in the years following the 2016 election of U.S. President Donald Trump. Dashing the hopes of many Cubans (but fulfilling the desires of countless others), Trump moved quickly to repeal Obama-era policies and reinstate limitations on U.S.-Cuban commerce and relations.

In El todo cotidiano [The Daily Everything] (2010), published shortly after Obama's 2008 election, Valdés more specifically engages the question of politics even as she continues to signal the need for a transnational, archipelagic space. Valdés states in an interview that "Although El todo cotidiano is not a continuation of La nada cotidiana, we can talk about it as Part Two, because the people, for the most part, are the same."[82] As the novel begins, Yocandra has departed Cuba on a makeshift raft, or *balsa*. After the minimum time in Miami necessary to get her papers, Yocandra departs for Paris, where she moves into an apartment building inhabited by an international cast of characters, including many Cubans. Yocandra soon welcomes her mother, "La Ida," to her Parisian abode; marries a fellow Cuban who promises to help her secure the necessary papers to allow el Nihilista to leave Cuba; and, following her new husband's betrayal, reunites with el Nihilista (now identified as César Figueroa Richard) in Madrid. As she travels between New York and Miami, and between Paris, Normandy, and Madrid, Yocandra continues to eke out a living as a writer, employing her blogs, in particular, to launch harsh critiques of Fidel Castro and the government he inaugurated.

In a departure from *La nada cotidiana* and *Te di la vida entera*, Valdés chronicles a life lived in the plenitude of exile in *El todo cotidiano*, where "todo" is at least nominally accessible. In a shift from the allegorical rhetoric employed to conjure up a space out of time in *La nada cotidiana*, furthermore, Valdés here appeals explicitly to a post-Castro future rather than a timeless present. In the penultimate chapter of the novel, Yocandra reflects on what Fidel Castro's death and Barack Obama's election might mean:

> Entonces intenté nuevamente predecir cómo acogeríamos la noticia [. . .]: <<Fidel Castro acaba de morir>> [. . .]. ¿Cuánto nos quedaría? ¿Hasta cuándo la retahíla, la misma candanga? Abrí los ojos. Por lo pronto, Barack Obama había sido investido presidente. ¿Qué cambiaría en nuestras vidas? Poco, el daño que nos hizo el primero está hecho, y es irreversible. El segundo tiene frente a él un breve camino para recomponer Estados Unidos, y el mundo [. . .].

> [Then I began again to predict how we would take the news [. . .]: 'Fidel Castro just died' [. . .] How much longer do we have? How much longer with the same hassle? I opened my eyes. In the meantime, Barack Obama had been sworn in as president. What would change in our lives? Little, the damage from Castro is done, and is irreversible. Obama has ahead of him a brief stretch in which to remake the United States, and the world [. . .].][83]

And indeed, when Fidel Castro did die in November 2016, some six years after the publication of *El todo cotidiano*, Valdés ebulliently told an interviewer from Radio Televisión Martí that she had not stopped celebrating since hearing the news: "no he parado de festejar; continúo celebrando y celebraré mientras viva" [I haven't stopped celebrating; I continue celebrating and will celebrate as long as I live].[84]

Even as she marks time in *El todo cotidiano*, Yocandra invokes the sea to offer a poignant reminder of the ongoing need for an alternate, archipelagic space. After reuniting with el Nihilista in Madrid and relocating with him to Paris, Yocandra travels with el Nihilista to Normandy, where the two swim together.

Describing the differences between the waters of the North Sea and those of the Caribbean, Yocandra highlights the history of bloodshed of the shores off which she swims:

> Mientras acudía a su encuentro, a nadar tranquilamente en aquellas aguas densamente azules, tan distintas de las cristalinas, verdes esmeralda, aguas del Caribe, pensé cuántas historias guardaban aquellas playas, las del desembarco de soldados norteamericanos, definitivo para la liberación y la victoria de la segunda guerra mundial.

> [As I went toward him, to swim peacefully in those densely blue waters, so different from the crystal, emerald green waters of the Caribbean, I thought of how many histories those beaches kept, those of the disembarking of U.S. soldiers, definitive for the liberation and victory of World War II.][85]

As a self-identified *balsera* from Cuba, Yocandra knows firsthand the power and perils of the water, with her swim in Normandy reminding her of "las voces de la gente que se fueron muriendo en la balsa" [the voices of the people who died in the *balsa*] as she approached the United States.[86] Tying together these spaces in a bid to portray them as interconnected and archipelagic, Valdés calls to mind not only the deaths of World War II soldiers storming the beaches of Normandy, but also those of so many who perished seeking passage to the United States (or, in the more distant past, when forcibly removed from Africa and sold into slavery in Cuba).

In *El todo cotidiano*, Valdés thus chronicles her protagonist's sojourns throughout the *arcubiélago* and remits readers to an alternate, archipelagic space. In so doing, the author signals the ongoing importance of the counterpublic that she both chronicles and helps to inaugurate, and points to the continuing need for an alternate space of identity. Bringing home this point at the end of *El todo cotidiano*, Valdés insinuates that Yocandra is herself unable to put words on the page and that *La nada cotidiana* is, in fact, the transcription of a surreptitious recording of her voice:

> —<<Ella huyó de Aquella Isla . . .—susurró vacilante—. Una isla que quiso construir el paraíso y creó el infierno.>>
> —Continúa, Yocandra, vas bien.—El hombre garrapateó los nombres de nuevos medicamentos en una receta.
> La mujer cerró los párpados y se puso a contar [. . .] El hombre en-

treabrió una gaveta cuidadosamente, manipuló un pequeño aparato en el interior, con sumo cuidado, sin que Yocandra percibiera que hasta la más mínima inflexión de su voz, y de su respiración, serían grabadas.

[—<<She fled from That Island . . . she whispered hesitantly. An island that wanted to construct paradise and created hell.>>

—Continue, Yocandra, you're doing well.—The man scrawled the names of new medications on a prescription.

The woman closed her eyes and began to speak [. . .] The man opened a cabinet carefully, manipulated a small device inside, very carefully, without Yocandra realizing that even the smallest inflection of her voice and her breathing would be recorded.][87]

In *La nada cotidiana*, it is el Traidor who is unable to write more than a single sentence; in *El todo cotidiano*, it is Yocandra who submits "trescientas y pico páginas en blanco" [some three hundred blank sheets of paper]. Seemingly unaware that she sits with a stack of empty pages in front of her as she speaks, Yocandra narrates her tale of *nada* surrounded by *todo*: the ellipsis that follows the word Isla ("Ella huyó de Aquella Isla . . .") echoes the ending of *La nada cotidiana*, establishing a tie between the 1995 title and its 2010 sequel.

Closing the book by establishing the importance of both the *Isla* in the Cuban imaginary that the author invokes and the need for a recognition of its multiplicity, Valdés ensures that the space she creates remains open and fluid, bringing together both the titles of her *oeuvre* and the landmasses and waterways of the *arcubiélago*.

Conclusion

Between 1995 and 2014, Cuban authors across the *arcubiélago* employed a range of approaches to writing islands into existence, bridging the geographic separations of land and water with text. Casting aside a rooted tack, authors forged instead a rhizomatic series of interconnected spaces in which a like-minded group of readers might gather. In so doing, they sought to employ the poetics of Relation to supersede the longstanding divisions between *islas* and waterways, and to cull into existence a transnational, archipelagic space both materially, or *in situ*, and metaphorically, in their work.

As is true of the archipelago as sketched on a map or outlined in an atlas, the islands, islets, and keys of the *arcubiélago* vary in size and extension. The larger (textual) islands I have detailed here are the best known and have been written into existence by some of the biggest names in Cuban literature of the 1990s and 2000s: Reina María Rodríguez, Antonio José Ponte, and Zoé Valdés. The smaller islands I analyze are still gaining prominence, and have been textualized more recently by less-well-known authors such as Ramón Hondal, Ricardo Alberto Pérez, and the Grupo del Palenque. While the larger islands might have more ink, so to speak, they are by no means more important than their smaller companions, or the waterways in between. Rather, as is true of the archipelago as a decolonizing trope that destabilizes longstanding dichotomies between "large" continents and "small" islands, the *islas* written into existence throughout the *arcubiélago* contribute, together, to the formation of a constellation-like whole that is larger than the sum of its parts.

The dates I have chosen as bookends for this study are somewhat mobile, as are the contours of the archipelago, but are designed to capture a particular, if fleeting, moment in time. Analyzing a series of precarious perches, a collection of artistic collaborations, and an ephemeral series of blog posts created between

2007 and 2014 illuminates how writers conjure new spaces into being, both on the ground and on the page.

I made my first trip to Cuba to research this book in 2013, a decade after my first trip to Havana in 2003. Throughout this time, the printed book had occupied a privileged place in the Cuban imaginary. Clandestinely shared among friends, swapped with new acquaintances in town for a visit, or purchased at the Feria del Libro [Book Fair], the printed book had consistently served as a conduit that connected literati into a public or a counterpublic.

By 2020, when I visited Havana to conduct my final interviews with authors and artists, this had changed dramatically. With the resumption of the long-standing U.S. embargo under President Donald Trump, the economic crisis of close ally Venezuela, and cash-flow difficulties, there was a paper shortage reminiscent of the Special Period of the 1990s, and a shift in rhetoric toward the perceived benefits of the digital. The Pabellón de Cuba—traditionally one of the largest sites of the Feria, outside the Morro—was almost empty in 2020, with a relatively miniscule number of books available for sale. Internet access was increasing, although still spotty: with pre-paid cards, I could join throngs of others accessing wifi in designated public spaces. Even though speeds were still comparatively slow, Cuban authors and readers were thus encouraged to go online.

Although I did not know it at the time, the way in which publics and counterpublics alike gathered throughout the *arcubiélago* was also on the verge of a seismic shift in early 2020 as a result of the global COVID-19 pandemic. The novel coronavirus was already circulating when I made my final research trip to Havana for this book, but its full reach was not yet known: when I mentioned the virus to one of my contacts, she reassured me that there was no need to worry, as Cuban scientists had a vaccine ready. This overly optimistic projection would be belied by the events of the years ahead, with millions of lives lost worldwide. Throughout the *arcubiélago*, shutdowns, social distancing, and travel restrictions hastened the shift to digital platforms for communication and gatherings.

The tectonic changes of 2020 followed on the heels of the smaller but nonetheless significant changes of the preceding years. In December 2014, following months of secret negotiations, President Barack Obama had announced that the United States would reopen diplomatic relations with Cuba and would begin to lift the decades-old restrictions of the embargo. The tides changed once again, however, in early November 2016, when newly elected President

Trump promised to rescind many Obama-era policies. Fidel Castro died later that month, bringing to a close fifty years of Cuban history defined by his leadership.

Even before Trump took office, Cuban migration patterns had changed in anticipation of the end of the longstanding "wet-foot/dry-foot" policy that had been a contested cornerstone of U.S. immigration policy since 1995. Inaugurated in that year by President Bill Clinton, the policy mandated that Cuban migrants caught in transit on the water were returned to Cuba. Those who reached U.S. shores, or crossed by land, could remain legally in the country. The potential end of this decades-old accommodation under Obama had the unintended consequence of encouraging Cubans to attempt to gain access to the United States before the policy changed. In 2015 and 2016, Cubans increasingly sought entry to the United States by traveling through Central America and Mexico to cross at the U.S.-Mexico border.[1] Following the change in policy under Obama on January 13, 2017, and the inauguration of Trump on January 20, deportations of Cuban migrants increased by a factor of seven between fiscal year 2017 and fiscal year 2018.[2] Cubans were now in the same boat as other migrants from across Latin America and the Caribbean.

Climate change also brought increasingly ferocious hurricane seasons to Cuban shores in the 2010s, with promises of more to come. In 2017, Hurricane Irma proved particularly damaging throughout the Caribbean. The hurricane slammed Cuba's northern coast and caused widespread devastation, as well as flooding and property damage. Newspaper photographs showed Havana residents wading through waist-deep water along city streets, recalling the futuristic scenes of *Habana Underguater* [*Havana Underwater*] in Erick J. Mota's specular novel of this title.[3]

In 2018, the same year that Raúl Castro stepped down from his post as President of Cuba, the ripples across the *arcubiélago* spread with the Movimiento de San Isidro [San Isidro Movement]. Led by performance artist Luis Manuel Otero and rapper Maykel Osorbo, the San Isidro Movement was founded to protest the limitations imposed by Decree 349, which threatened to severely restrict all cultural activities not explicitly sanctioned by the Ministry of Culture. As the movement gained traction, writers and artists took to social media and the streets to protest the limitations on their expression and the increasing restrictions on what constituted cultural production "dentro de" [within] the Revolution. On Thursday, November 26, 2020, state forces raided the Movement's headquarters, located in the largely Afro-Cuban neighborhood of San Isidro that gives the movement its name. The following day, Friday, November 27, in a surprisingly public rebuke of the government's actions, hundreds of protesters gathered outside the ministry to demand that their voices be heard.[4]

Texts published throughout the *arcubiélago* reflected these societal shifts that occurred between 2014, when the Palenque poets stopped posting regularly to their blog, and 2020, when I made my final visit to Havana to wrap up the research for this book. Science fiction writer Jorge Enrique Lage's *Archivo* [*Archive*] (2015), in particular, both anticipates and reflects many of the changes referenced above with regard to shifting migration and reading habits, as well as the digitalization of media and communication.[5] As promised in its title, *Archivo* offers readers an archival collection of fragmentary materials, evidently compiled by an agent working for the state. In an interview with writer and cultural critic Carlos Aguilera, Lage states that he considers *Archivo* to be a "desconexión" [unplugging]: "*Archivo* fue una desconexión. Tiene la estructura de una lista" [*Archivo* was an unplugging. It has the structure of a list].[6] The ephemera contained in *Archivo* are numbered from 1 to 153; 153 containing no more than the number used to identify it. Pulling the plug on the traditional novel, Lage thus employs the form of the archive to offer readers access to the scattered materials that might, in other instances, lead to the production of a nominally more finished narrative with a beginning, middle, and end.

Construing *Archivo* as a "desconexión" [unplugging], Lage references in his title not only the brick-and-mortar archives that collect and store valuable ephemera, but also the more routine *archivos* [files] stored on disk drives and, in the case of Cuba, increasingly used to swap and share files in the 2000s. And yet while digital archives are often construed as a freeing means of disconnecting from State control to access a wider world of media and material, in *Archivo* official bureaucracy spills over into social media feeds. As scholar Yairamaren Román Maldonado writes in this regard, the novel points to the omnipresence of state surveillance:

El sector más susceptible a la vigilancia es representado por la generación más joven, que aparece en la novela constantemente conectada a la red. La relación entre las redes sociales y las redes de la Seguridad se hace patente en la descripción un tanto paranoica de uno de los personajes: 'Nacida en Myspace y criada en Twitter y Facebook, Lily Allen era una estrella que brillaba con luz propia en medio de las ruinas de Centro Habana. Toda su vida había estado bajo la lupa de la Seguridad del Estado.'

[The sector most susceptible to surveillance is represented by the youngest generation, which appears in the novel constantly connected to the Internet. The relationship between social networks and Security networks is manifest in the somewhat paranoid description of one of the characters: 'Born in Myspace and raised on Twitter and Facebook, Lily Allen was a star who shone with her own light in the ruins of Central Havana. Her whole life had been under the scrutiny of State Security.']⁷

The protagonists are to some degree conscious of the ways in which they are subject to the gaze of the State, and yet they continue to engage with the very technology that monitors them. The aforementioned Lily Allen, social media influencer and small-time "star," for example, works as a *jinetera* [escort] in Havana. Aware of the danger to which she subjects herself as she speaks, be it online or in bed, she inks a message to herself on her arms:

Una vez intuyó el peligro. Se hizo en cada brazo un tatuaje que decía: CÁLLATE.

"Así, cuando esté hablando demasiado, al mover los brazos podré ver los tatuajes y seguir el consejo."

[Once she intuited the danger. She put a tattoo on each arm that said: SHUT UP.

"That way, when I'm talking too much, when I move my arms I'll be able to see the tattoos and follow their advice."]⁸

Here, as Antonio José Ponte argues is true of Cuba more generally in *Villa Marista en plata: Arte, política, nuevas tecnologías* [*Villa Marista in Silver: Art, Politics, New Technologies*], the State continues to *vigilar*, now utilizing the tentacles of the technology often heralded as a means of liberation.

Reinforcing this point, and linking social media platforms such as Myspace, Twitter, and Facebook to the State and self-surveillance, *Archivo* offers a fragmentary chronicle of agents working for the State. The narrator first introduces readers to the "Agente" [Agent], who clarifies that he is "Agente de la Seguridad del Estado. Nada de claves ni de nombrecitos falsos" [State Security Agent. Nothing about codes nor fake names].⁹ The narrator then introduces readers to a series of less traditional state agents, including Baby Zombi, Yoan/Yoani, the VirginBot, and the Médium. Although the inclusion of zombies and bots places *Archivo* squarely within the realm of sci-fi, the author's recourse to characters of such shadowy stripes also reinforces his characterization of agents as multiform and multimedia. Zombies and bots, that is, exist not only in the worlds conjured up by sci-fi authors, but also online, where individuals can assume new identities at will, and bots can impersonate humans. Indeed, Lily Allen (the Havana *jinetera*) is not, truly, Lily Allen (the British singer): "Dice llamarse Lily Allen, y de verdad se cree que es Lily Allen, aunque probablemente nunca en su vida haya oído hablar de la verdadera Lily Allen" [She says her name is Lily Allen, and she truly believes she is Lily Allen, although she has probably never in her life heard of the true Lily Allen].[10] Born and raised online, as a ward of social media, Lily Allen assumes as her own an identity manufactured from the social media feeds she consumes. Yet while the "true" Lily Allen (the singer) seems to feel free to speak out about her experiences (including, for instance, her struggle with depression), her Havana counterpart recognizes that she must remain quiet or face the consequences.

Employing what might be considered an archipelagic form for the archives in *Archivo*—a series of interconnected bodies of text, each floating in the same expanse of pages within a singular volume—Lage calls to mind the longstanding connections between archives and colonial power. For, following Enmanuel Martínez, the archives manifest "the legacies of the global history of European colonization—starting with(in) the Caribbean archipelago—[that] continue to shape our archival imaginaries, records, and repositories today in the era of postcoloniality."[11] Asking readers to recall the ties between the archive and what Aníbal Quijano terms the "coloniality of power," in *Archivo* Lage thereby sounds a warning to resist the siren call of new media. As "Lily Allen" demonstrates, multinational conglomerates such as Myspace, Facebook, and Twitter hold out the offer of freedom of expression but confine their users' identities and manipulate their data in innumerable ways. Forging ties with the State, moreover, shiny new media platforms work hand in glove with the very artifacts of the past from which they promise to liberate users. The Agent in *Archivo* can show his face and openly announce his identity because his partners now lurk in cyberspace, where we all willingly give up our privacy for the pleasure of the likes we may receive. At the same time that the dusty papers of the past are swapped for the digital USBs of the present, *Archivo* thus signals the ongoing need for decolonizing projects within and beyond the *arcubiélago*.

In February 2021, the paramount need for decolonizing endeavors throughout the *arcubiélago* was again laid bare when the San Isidro Movement released "Patria y vida" [Homeland and Life], a video production created by Havana-based rappers Osorbo and El Funky and Miami-based musicians Yotuel (of the hip-hop band Orishas), Gente de Zona (a reggaeton duo), and Descemer Bueno (a singer-songwriter). The video, which also includes shots of the San Isidro protests, soon went viral: it received 1 million views on YouTube in the first three days after it was posted, and was widely shared in Cuba on USBs.[12] "Patria y vida," the title chosen by the group of Afro-Cuban musicians, is itself a direct challenge to the Cuban government. Riffing on the longstanding Cuban slogan "patria o muerte" [homeland or death], the musicians pointedly suggest in the inclusion of "and" that it should not be necessary to choose between the two. The opening sequence of the video further confirms its critical intent: a black-and-white image of José Martí burns away to reveal the image of George Washington featured on the U.S. dollar bill underneath. The Cuban government initially responded to this clear critique by condemning the movement in speeches and on social media posts; it then jailed Movement members.[13]

It remains to be seen how "patria" and "vida" will continue to be negotiated alongside space and identity, and how the rhizomatic *arcubiélago* will continue to morph and form, in the 2020s and beyond. In April 2021, as I finished writing this conclusion from my home in New Jersey, the San Isidro Movement protests continued, and Raúl Castro announced that he would step down from his position as the Secretary General of Cuba's Communist Party, marking the end of a sixty-year era in which a Castro had held this post. (Castro had stepped down as President in 2018.) In the post-Castro era, islands will undoubtedly continue to be written, in some cases through new media; and existing shorelines and seascapes will continue to change with the currents. Whatever form the *arcubiélago* takes, the call for "patria y vida" from the San Isidro Movement serves as a reminder of the inescapable imbrication of the material and the metaphoric, in islands and archipelagos alike. Considered alongside Lage's portrayal of the *Archivo*, the rap song points to the pressing need for decolonizing methodologies throughout the transnational Cuban archipelago, and for ongoing attention to the ways in which space and identity continue to be negotiated as new islands are written into existence.

Appendix of Interviews

With Cubans increasingly residing in a variety of locales throughout the transnational Cuban archipelago, the texts that I consider in this book might be described, following Françoise Lionnet and Emmanuel Bruno Jean-François, as examples of the "small narratives and significant details that give us the texture of human interactions in the contact zones of migratory flows."[1] These small narratives offer a counterpoint to big data[2] and provide new perspectives on the stories of migration and movement that numbers alone cannot tell.[3]

The small narratives that I analyze in this book point to the connections (rather than the divisions) that exist between islands and individuals, and to what Lionnet and Jean-François describe as the power of "archipelagic voices" to unsettle received truths.[4] To allow these voices to speak for themselves in the pages of this book, I conclude *Writing Islands* with an appendix of some of the formal interviews that I conducted as I researched and wrote this book. Interviews are included in the order in which they were conducted and have been edited for space and clarity.

My thanks to the writers whose words I include here for joining in this conversation, and to Rafael Osorio for his assistance with the translations.

INTERVIEW WITH RAMÓN HONDAL

I conducted this interview with poet Ramón Hondal on February 14, 2017, in Havana. Hondal's work is analyzed in chapter 3.

Ramón, ¿cuáles han sido las influencias más importantes en tu obra?
RH: Es difícil responder a eso y ser sincero. Demasiadas, creo. Y vienen de

muchos sitios diferentes. Desde la música hasta la literatura misma. Sería una lista . . . No sabría por dónde empezar. Lo más obvio, en literatura, puede ser Samuel Beckett, Margarite Duras. Pero, como te digo, son muchas realmente. En cuanto a la música puede ser Miles Davis, las interpretaciones que hizo Jacqueline Du Pré (interpretar es un fenómeno menospreciado). He sido muy abierto a ver y explorar, y eso trabaja, creo, muy detrás, en lo inconsciente de lo que puedo decir como influencia. Eso sí, me siento más cómodo consumiendo que produciendo. Entonces, la producción luego del consumo me intriga, saber, digo, de qué parte se toma, ¿no? Así que es seguro que te mienta si te digo exactas influencias.

Quería saber, ¿qué espacios o lugares han sido las influencias más importantes en tu obra?

RH: Me cuesta mucho entrar en otro espacio. Soy de mi casa, me gusta estar en mi "hueco." Puedo estar ahí mucho tiempo sin que eso sea un problema. Digamos que es una protección, estar en mi cuarto, por mucho tiempo. Soy de espacios reducidos. Pero también me gusta salir, y por un tiempo me gustó mucho caminar de noche solo por la ciudad, lo disfrutaba. Creo que eso duró un tiempo, de ahí salió *Scratch*, después no lo he vuelto a hacer. Soy, creo, de la ciudad. Me gusta también el campo. Me gusta ir al campo, me gusta entrar en contacto con lo natural. Pero sé que no pertenezco a ese espacio. Sé que ya estoy excluido de lo natural, no podría estar una semana viviendo en una casa de campaña en el campo. He vivido siempre en la misma casa y quizás por eso sea así, de un mismo sitio. Y eso reduce también mi escritura, ¿no? El espacio de mi casa, estar ahí, leer, releer, ver cine, escuchar música. Por supuesto, me gusta compartir con los pocos amigos queridos, pero, bueno, también puedo estar solo.

Sé que has asistido a eventos en la Azotea, en la Torre de Letras. ¿Esos espacios tienen importancia en tu obra, en tu formación? ¿O no son lo más importante en cuanto a tu escritura y el proceso de escribir?

RH: Bueno, hace más de quince años que conocí a Reina María Rodríguez y al proyecto de La Torre. Y yo no sé si yo he participado, porque, bueno, Reina me dice "fantasma." Y eso tiene que ver con muchas cosas. Tiene que ver con nuestras conversaciones: nosotros hablamos más por teléfono de lo que nos vemos. Yo también le digo "fantasma" a ella, somos fantasmas los dos. Pero me cuesta participar. Y por esto mismo que te decía, que me gusta más estar fuera. Ahora, haber conocido a aquel grupo de escritores que iban a La Torre cambió mi manera de ver lo que es la literatura. Allí estaban los Dia(s)poras, Reina, Antonio José Ponte, Juan Carlos Flores, etc., gente muy inteligente y creo que única en el pobre panorama intelectual de Cuba, con un interés serio e inteligente acerca de la literatura. Ha sido el encuentro más significativo de mi vida intelectual hasta ahora. Les debo muchísimo y agradeceré por siempre.

Hemos hablado un poco de eso ya, pero ¿crees que formas parte de una comunidad más amplia de escritores? Pero no sólo de escritores, sino también artistas, o gente que trabaje incluso con los libros, en las editoriales, o lo que sea, intelectuales, digamos. Y si es que sí, ¿puedes describir la comunidad, y decir cuál ha sido el efecto en tu obra?

RH: Estoy bastante alejado de grupos, y cosas así. Tengo amigos, y con ellos comparto ideas, cosas. Tengo dos amigos que son artistas, con los que tengo ideas de hacer cosas así, entre todos. Con uno de ellos, Lester Álvarez, tengo un proyecto de hacer un corto, con un guion que escribí. Cosa que está abierta todavía, porque hace falta financiamiento, y es difícil encontrarlo, ¿no?, pero, bueno, tenemos ya la idea de lo que vamos a hacer, una idea que está abierta, porque no está definida todavía. Una vez que arranque, que ya tengamos el dinero, que podamos hacerlo, y que arranque, estamos abiertos a explorar qué pasa, ¿no? Creo que sí, que se puede aprobar. Pero siempre tomo un poco de distancia. Porque no creo que forme parte de nada . . . Son amigos míos, con quienes comparto gustos de cine, de música, de literatura, sobre todo el arte, y con quienes . . . nada, conversamos, y a veces sale algo, pero no me siento parte de ninguna "comunidad." Ni me gustan las reuniones de escritores, de artistas, no voy a nada que tenga que ver con exposiciones, porque, o sea, no me gusta el ambiente. Prefiero el individuo al grupo.

Hablemos un poco de Diálogos. *¿Cómo empezó ese proyecto? ¿Y cuál era el mensaje, o los mensajes, que querías comunicar en este libro?*

RH: Difícil. Como siempre, fue una forma de procesar algo que me pasaba en mi vida, algo personal, algo que me había sucedido, una separación. Empecé a escribir eso así, como ejercicio de salida, para sanar un poco, y se fueron reuniendo textos, así, y, bueno, se fue construyendo eso poco a poco. Nunca pensé que iba a terminar en un cuaderno. No me interesan los "mensajes," eso está del otro lado, la lectura que se haga, pero es obvio que detrás de esos "diálogos" hay un intento por develar el vacío de lo que llaman comunicación.

Después de escribir Diálogos, *escribiste otro libro, que se llama* Scratch. *¿Podrías hablar un poco de este proyecto? ¿De cómo surgió?*

RH: Casi fue lo mismo que el primero. La misma sensación, pero con diferentes matices. *Scratch* tiene que ver con música, con lo circular, tiene que ver con algo más social, ¿no? De alguien que interactúa más con lo que hay afuera. Fue algo parecido, tiene más contacto, quizás, en cuanto a la estructura. Y lo que hay en el libro en sí es más cercano a la música. Y pensaba en el sonido que se ha convertido en algo insalvable, de lo que hace falta, en un disco, en el scratch. Y pensé en este ruido, ¿no?, que hay detrás del sonido, que debería ser limpio pero nunca lo es. Entonces, hablar de cómo este scratch está en las relaciones, ¿no?, y en la misma escritura. Fue algo muy diferente a *Diálogos*. Y de ahí partió la idea de hacer tres libros para hacer una trilogía. Fueron *Diálogos*, *Scratch* y el último que es *Prótesis*, que ya es más físico, con mayor sensación corporal. Parten de la misma idea, pero son diferentes en cuanto a lo que se ve en ellos, en la estructura y en lo que tratan. Pero parten de la misma idea.

Entonces, Prótesis *tiene que ver más con lo físico, ¿verdad? ¿Cómo se nota eso en el libro mismo?*

RH: En los otros libros hay una especie de personaje, que ronda el libro. En *Prótesis* no hay nada. Lo único que hay son gestos. Y gestos físicos, es decir, corporales. Una mano, un ojo. Ya la escritura se convierte en algo físico, muy anatómico. Es estar más desolado ante cualquier intento de comunicación, porque ya no hay comunicación con nadie. Queda solamente un ser que, bueno, es la nada. Una especie de historia que es solo un cuerpo que se derrumba, digamos, y narra su decadencia, es decir, usa el lenguaje ante la ausencia, ¿no? Por eso Prótesis.

. . .

Ramon, what have been the most important influences on your work?

RH: That's a difficult question to answer honestly. Too many, I think. And they come from many different places. From music to literature itself. It would be a list . . . I wouldn't know where to begin. The most obvious, in literature, could be Samuel Beckett, Margarite Duras. But, as I say, there are many. In terms of music, it could be Miles Davis, the renditions of Jacqueline Du Pré (renditions are an underappreciated phenomenon). I've been very open to seeing and exploring, and that works, I think, in the background, on an unconscious level of what I could give as an influence. I should say that I feel more comfortable consuming than producing. Then, the production after consumption intrigues me, knowing from what part something is taken, right? So it's true that I would be lying to you if I told you exact influences.

I wanted to know, what spaces or places have been the most important influences on your work?

RH: It is hard for me to enter another space. I'm a homebody, and I like to be in my "hole." I can be there for a long time without it being a problem. Let's say that it's a form of protection, being in my room, for a long time. I belong to small spaces. But I also like to go out, and for a time I liked walking at night, alone through the city, I enjoyed it. I think this lasted for a time, *Scratch* came from this, afterward I haven't done it again. I belong, I think, to the city. I also like the countryside. I like to go to the countryside, I like to be in contact with nature. But I know that I don't belong there. I know that I'm excluded from nature, I couldn't spend a week living in a house in the countryside. I've always lived in the same house and perhaps for this reason I'm like this, of one place. And this also reduces my writing, no? The space of my house, being there, reading, re-reading, watching films, listening to music. Of course I like to share with a few dear friends, but, well, I can also be by myself.

I know that you have attended events in the Azotea and the Torre de Letras. Are those spaces important in your work, in your training? Or is it that they are not the most important in terms of your writing and the process of writing?

RH: Well, it was more than fifteen years ago that I met Reina María Rodríguez, and got to know the Torre project. And I don't know if I've participated, because, well, Reina calls me the "ghost." And that has to do with many things. It has to do with our conversations: we speak more by phone than we see each other. I call her "ghost" as well, we are both ghosts. But it is an effort for me to participate. And that's because of what I told you before, that I prefer to be outside. Now, having met that group of writers that went to the Torre changed my way of seeing literature. There were the Dia(s)poras, Reina, Antonio José Ponte, Juan Carlos Flores, etc., very intelligent people, I think unique in the impoverished intellectual panorama of Cuba, with a serious and intelligent interest in literature. It has been the most significant encounter in my intellectual life to date. I owe them so much and I will be forever grateful.

We have already talked a bit about this, but do you think you are part of a wider community of writers? Not only writers, but also, let's say, artists, or people who work with books in publishing houses, intellectuals? If so, can you describe this community and say what its effect has been on your work?

RH: I am relatively distant from groups and things like this. I have my friends, and I share ideas and other things with them. I have two friends who are artists, with whom I exchange ideas about doing things like this, together. I have a short film project with one of them, Lester Álvarez, with a script that I wrote. Something that is still open, because we have to find financing, and it's difficult, no? But, well, we already have an idea of what we are going to do, an idea that is open, because it is not defined yet. Once it starts, once we have the money, and we can do it, and it's going, we're open to exploring what happens, no? I think that yes, it can be approved. But I always keep my distance. Because I don't think that I form part of anything . . . They're friends, with whom I share my taste in cinema, music, literature, above all art. And with whom . . . well, we talk, and sometimes something comes of it, but I don't feel part of any "community." I don't like gatherings of writers, artists. I don't go to anything that has to do with exhibitions, because, I mean, I don't like the atmosphere. I prefer the individual to the group.

Let's talk a little bit about Dialogues. *How did this project begin? And what was the message, or the messages, that you wanted to communicate in this book?*
RH: Difficult. As always, it was a form of processing something that was happening in my life, something personal, something that had happened to me, a separation. I started to write that like this, as a way to get over it, to heal a bit, and the texts were piling up, like this, and, well, the book came together little by little. I never thought that it would end up as a book. I'm not interested in "messages," what is done on the other side, in the reading that is done; but it's obvious that behind the "dialogues" there is an attempt to unveil the void of what is called communication.

After writing Dialogues, *you wrote another book called* Scratch. *Could you talk a little about this project? How did it come about?*
RH: It was almost the same as the first. The same sensation, but with different nuances. *Scratch* has to do with music, with circularity, it has to do with something more social, right? With someone who interacts more with what is out there. It was something similar, but it has more contact, perhaps, in terms of structure. And what is in the book is closer to music. And I thought of the sound that has become an insurmountable part of that which is needed, in a record, in the scratch. And I thought of this noise that is behind the sound, which should be clean but never is. So, talking about how this scratch is in relationships, right? And in writing itself. It was something very different than *Dialogues*. And from there came the idea of writing three books that could form a trilogy. *Dialogues, Scratch,* and the last one, which is *Prosthesis,* which

is more physical, with a greater corporeal sensation. They stem from the same idea, but they are different in what is seen, in their structure, and in what they deal with. But they start from the same idea.

So Prosthesis *has more to do with the physical, right? How is this apparent in the book?*

RH: In the other books, there is a kind of character that roams the book. In *Prosthesis* there is nothing. There are only gestures. And physical gestures, that is to say, corporeal gestures. A hand, an eye. The writing becomes something physical, anatomical. It's about being more desolate in front of any attempt at communication, because there isn't any more communication with anyone. All that remains is someone who, well, is the void. A kind of story that is just a body that collapses, let's say, and it narrates its decadence, using language in the face of absence. And thus: *Prosthesis.*

INTERVIEW WITH CARIDAD ATENCIO, RITO RAMÓN AROCHE, AND JULIO MORACEN

I conducted this interview with "Palenque" poets Caridad Atencio, Rito Ramón Aroche, and Julio Moracen on February 16, 2017, in Havana. The "Grupo del Palenque" [Palenque Group] is analyzed in chapter 4.

Quería empezar pensando en su identidad como poetas del Palenque, así se dice, por lo menos. Entonces quería saber, si me podrían decir, ¿cómo es esta identificación?

JM: Ayer, el poeta venezolano Juan Calzadilla, cuando Basilia [Papastama-tiu] le habló de nosotros, él nos preguntaba, "¿Por qué palenque?" Y Basilia dice no, porque es un lugar donde se reúnen los negros esclavos que huyen. Y ella le dijo que nosotros éramos todos negros. Y eso le llamó la atención. Y él comenzó a buscar en su cabeza, si ese palenque tenía, y nosotros negros, tenía que ver con, si nosotros éramos herederos de una tradición poética negra, que es un gran problema dentro del pensamiento literario, ¿no? Porque son los movimientos específicos literarios, y principalmente el movimiento fundamental que fue el movimiento del negrismo literario, en Estados Unidos, el Harlem Renaissance, esos movimientos cómo quedaron colocados en su tiempo, y si hubo personas [que] intentaron seguir esos movimientos, quizás por el hecho de ser un movimiento donde la cuestión negra tuvo gran importancia, y lo que deriva de eso con la cuestión de que los países todavía siguen siendo países comprime negros, quizás por eso no haya tenido seguidores, sea, que continúe haciendo ese tipo de poesía, las de vanguardia, parecida a la poesía de Nicolás Guillén, o Luis Palés Matos. Eso significa que nosotros no somos continuadores, supuestamente, de estos movimientos. Nosotros somos, sí, escritores negros. Pero, lo que nos une, quizás, es que nosotros, en la época como vivimos nosotros, dentro de la Revolución Cubana, lo que se conoce como la Revolución Cubana, la cuestión de la información con relación al mundo que nosotros queríamos vivir, que el mundo de la literatura, eso es algo que fue muy difícil, en relación a una estructura de información que tenía el país. [. . .] Al final, somos un grupo, si lo pensamos, utilizando la filosofía del palenque, o sea, normalmente los que viven dentro de esta institución, eran los de la casa grande, y los que trabajaban en eso, como si nosotros saliéramos de esta estructura institucional, que pasa por grupo no sé qué, y nosotros fuéramos realmente los que habían escapado de la plantación. Y nosotros estuviésemos en ese espacio. [. . .]

RRA: Bueno, hace unos años, y ahora tendríamos que precisar la fecha, nos encontramos en un evento de crítica nacional, en Pinar del Río, y había una poeta que vive en Cuba, desde hace muchísimos años, los años 60, que se llama, ella es poeta y ensayista, ella se llama Basilia Papastamatiu, que es cubana-griega-argentina. Bueno, los argentinos dicen que ella no es una poeta argentina, los cubanos dicen que ella no es una poeta cubana, que ella es una poeta argentina, y así. En fin, estando en ese evento, ella me pregunta, pocos minutos antes de dar su charla, o leer su conferencia, si podía, que iba a hablar de nosotros, y yo le pregunté que quiénes éramos nosotros, y dice "Uds."

Es decir, este grupo, para ella, este Uds., se componía de la siguiente forma: Caridad Atencio, Rito Ramón Aroche, Ismael González Castañer, Antonio Armenteros, Dolores Labarcena y Julio Moracen, y Julio Mitjans. Y que no todos estábamos ahí, en ese evento. Pero, entonces, yo le pregunté que ¿cuál era la preocupación? Porque a ver si les puedo denominar a Uds. el Palenque. Entonces, yo le pregunté ¿a qué venía eso de decirnos Palenque? Bueno, porque todos son negros, escriben bien, andan juntos y son amigos, ¿no? Entonces, yo dije, [. . .] Ud. es la crítica, ¿no? Ud. puede decir ahí lo que su investigación arroje, ¿no? Pero se le hace partícipe a los dos amigos no estando viviendo en Cuba en este momento, Julio Moracen y Dolores Labarcena, que está en Barcelona, actualmente acaba de publicar dos novelas, y tiene un libro de poesía [. . .]. Y entonces cuando les enviamos correos a ellos, contándoles lo que nos había pasado en este evento de crítica, nos dice, ah, pero eso está muy bien. Porque así entonces ahora podemos crear un blog que se llame Del Palenque . . . y para . . . Tres puntos suspensivos, ¿no?, para los amigos. Esto creó mucho ruido, porque era como que en Cuba, se había creado un grupo [. . .] Y entonces, bueno, ya surgía la preocupación, de muchos otros colegas, de que si teníamos un manifiesto, si teníamos una revista, así. Bueno, no teníamos nada, sencillamente teníamos ese blog donde colocábamos nuestras cosas, ya todo el mundo sabe que la red es muy democrática, quizás demasiado, y, bueno, incluso ya vamos a recibir correo de mucha gente que lo revisaba, diciendo de que era muy interesante, esta gente es de dentro, preocupada de por qué tiene que hacerse llamar el Palenque. Y esta es la versión más o menos vivida por mí, porque fue a mí que se me preguntó [. . .] si nos podían poner el Palenque. Entonces el grupo es variopinto, cada cual tiene su propio camino.

CA: Disculpa, disculpa que te interrumpa, pero quizás debemos hablar de cómo estas personas influyentes que nos pusieron "El Palenque" al grupo, trataron de unificar las personas que estábamos aquí, y diferenciarlas de lo que fue el grupo Diásporas que se había ido, y como una manera de, no sé, de llenar un lugar que estaba vacío . . .

RRA: Estaba pensando si lo decía o no. El problema es que ya casi estaban los influjos del Grupo Diásporas, por lo cual, nosotros no veíamos ¿por qué tenían que ponernos el Palenque? Y yo sí entendí rápidamente que era que nos querían diferenciar de Diásporas. Porque Diásporas era como una cosa, ¿no? y se habían radicalizado políticamente, ya la radicalización venía literariamente, pero después ya, y casi todos se habían ido del país, pero todavía; de hecho todavía, sigue influyendo, pero bueno, querían separarnos. Y en Diásporas, no había una diferenciación entre blancos y negros, ni nada de eso. Pero nosotros tampoco decíamos, nosotros sencillamente andábamos juntos, nos uníamos, compartíamos criterio, pero también discutimos muchas cosas, no quiere decir que estemos de acuerdo en todo, ¿no? Entonces, por ahí anda la cosa.

¿Piensan en Cuba como una isla, o en Cuba como un archipiélago u . . . otra cosa?
CA: Me parece que, los creadores también se definen por lo que niegan, o a lo que se niegan. Porque aquí, hay una línea en la poesía más contemporánea, que es la idea esa del agua por todas partes, de la isla, de la maldición. Ya nosotros hemos reaccionado un poco contra eso, porque todo el mundo está en eso. [. . .] Entonces, uno trata, bueno, de ponerlo todo en función de tratar de lograr la originalidad en lo que escribe. Y esto es bastante difícil, y te lleva toda una vida. [. . .]

I wanted to start by asking about your identity as Palenque poets, at least, that's how it's said. So I wanted to know, if you could tell me, how did you come up with this identity?

JM: Yesterday, when Basilia [Papastamatiu] told the Venezuelan poet Juan Calzadilla about us, he asked us, "Why the palenque?" And Basilia said no, because it is a place where the Black slaves who fled met. And she told him that we were all Black. And that caught his attention. And he began to mull over, if the Palenque identity and us being Black, had to do with, if we were the inheritors of a Black poetic tradition, which is a big issue in literary thought, right? Because they are specific literary movements, and especially the fundamental movement that was the literary negrismo movement, in the United States, the Harlem Renaissance, how those movements were situated in their time, and if there were people [who] tried to follow those movements, perhaps due to being a movement where the Black question was of great importance, and what derives from that with the issue of how countries continue to repress Blacks, maybe that's why they haven't had followers, I mean, people who continue to do that kind of poetry, vanguardia poetry similar to the poetry of Nicolás Guillén, or Luis Palés Matos. That means that supposedly we are not the continuation of these movements. Yes, we are Black writers. But, what unites us, perhaps, in the time that we live in, within the Cuban Revolution, what is known as the Cuban Revolution, is the issue of information in relation to the world that we wanted to live in, the world of literature, that is something that was very difficult, in relation to a structure of information that the country had. [. . .] In the end, we are a group, if we think about it, using the philosophy of the palenque, that is, normally those who lived and worked inside this institution, the ones who belonged to the big house. It's almost as if we left this institutional structure, through I don't know what group, and we were truly the ones who had escaped from the plantation. And we were in that space. [. . .]

RRA: Well, a few years ago, and now we would have to specify the date, we were at a national criticism event, in Pinar del Río, and there was a poet who has lived in Cuba for many years, since the 60s, her name is, she is a poet and essayist who is Cuban-Greek-Argentine, her name is Basilia Papastamatiu. Well, the Argentines say that she is not an Argentine poet, the Cubans say that she is not a Cuban poet, she is an Argentine poet, and so on. Anyway, at that event, a few minutes before giving her talk, or reading her paper, she asks me if she could, that she was going to talk about us, and I asked her who we were, and she says "you guys." This group, for her, this "you guys," was as follows: Caridad Atencio, Rito Ramón Aroche, Ismael González Castañer, Antonio Armenteros, Dolores Labarcena, Julio Moracen, and Julio Mitjans. And we were not all there, at that event. But then, I asked her, what is the issue? "Because I wanted to see if I can call you guys the Palenque." So I asked, what is this about, calling us Palenque? "Well, because you are all Black, you write well, you hang out together and you are friends, right?" So I said, [. . .] you're the critic, right? You can say there what your research produces, right? But this involved our two friends who were not living in Cuba at that time, Julio Moracen and Dolores Labarcena, she is in Barcelona, she recently published two novels, and she has a book of poetry [. . .]. And then when we emailed them, telling them what had happened during the national criticism event, she said, ah, but that's very good. Because now we can create a blog called Del Palenque . . . y para . . . An ellipsis, no? For our friends. That generated a lot of noise, because it was like, in Cuba, a group had been created [. . .] And then there was the concern, from many other colleagues, about whether we had a manifesto, if we had a magazine. Well, we didn't have anything, we just had that blog where we put our things. Everyone knows that the Internet is very democratic, maybe too much so, and, well, we were already receiving emails from many people who reviewed it, saying that it was very interesting. These people were from inside, worried about why it has to be called Palenque. And this is the version of the story I have lived through, basically, because she asked me [. . .] if she could call us El Palenque. The group is diverse, everyone has their own path.

CA: Excuse me, excuse me for interrupting you, but perhaps we should talk about how the influential people who put the name "El Palenque" on our group, tried to unify the people who were there, and differentiate them from the Diásporas group that had left, and as a way of, I don't know, filling a space that was empty . . .

RRA: I was thinking whether or not to mention it. The problem is that the influences of the Diásporas Group were almost already there, so we didn't see why they had to call us El Palenque? And I quickly understood that they wanted to differentiate us from the Diásporas Group. Because Diásporas was one thing, right? and they had become radicalized politically, and the radicalization came through literature, but afterward, almost everyone had left the country, but still; in fact, it is still influential, and, well, they wanted to separate us. And in Diásporas, there was no differentiation between Whites and Blacks, or anything like that. But we also never said, we just hung out together, we met, we shared suggestions, but we also debated many things, that doesn't mean we agree on everything, no? So, that's where we ended up.

Do you think of Cuba as an island, or an archipelago or . . . something else?
CA: I think that creators also define themselves by what they deny, or by what they refuse. Because here, there is a line in more contemporary poetry, that is the idea of water everywhere, the island, the curse. We have reacted a little against that, because everyone is in that. [. . .] So, one tries to put everything toward trying to achieve originality in what one writes. And this is quite difficult, and it takes a lifetime. [. . .]

INTERVIEW WITH RICARDO ALBERTO PÉREZ

I conducted this interview with poet Ricardo Alberto Pérez (known as "Richard") on February 9, 2018, in Jaruco. Pérez's work is analyzed in chapter 3.

Richard, ¿puedes hablarme un poco de cuáles han sido las influencias más importantes en tu obra?
RAP: Bueno, las influencias más importantes en mi obra han sido varias. [. . .] Pero bueno, creo que sería imperdonable no hablar de mi primera gran influencia como poeta, específicamente, que fue la del poeta sevillano Luis Cernuda. Creo que Cernuda fue, yo lo reconozco como mi primer gran influencia poética. Fue un poeta que leí descarnadamente, con gran pasión, y que creo que me enseñó dos o tres cosas, y su obra me dejó impregnado de otras cosas, de las cuales inclusive, después yo he leído mucho y he tenido otros ídolos literarios, me dio a una lectura que ha venido de distintas lenguas, distintas culturas, y en todo ese marasmo de cultura, Cernuda ha sobrevivido de alguna manera. Yo creo que ese es mi primera influencia puntual. [. . .] Después vinieron otras influencias. [. . .]

Yo me influencio ahora de otra manera, por ejemplo: no influencias de autor específico, sino influencias de modos de ser. Y en este caso, la poesía brasileña me ha influido enormemente. Y llegó un momento, en que ya las influencias, que han sido, quizás la última década, no son tantas literarias, son influencias de imágenes. [. . .] David Lynch, lo reconozco como una influencia tan grande como Samuel Beckett, o como Luis Cernuda. David Lynch, Cronenberg; porque ahora cuando veo la realidad, y la proceso, yo digo que la mente del poeta es como una máquina de moler carne, la proceso para regresar esta carne molida a la página; casi siempre esa carne molida pasa por estos recuerdos tremendos que tengo de las imágenes del cine de David Lynch, de Cronenberg, [. . .] o por la cosa tan rara de Michael Haneke [. . .]

¿Cuándo empezó, o surgió, ese interés que tenías en la poesía? ¿En qué momento surgió este interés?

RAP: Siendo niño. Iba de visita los fines de semana a una casa de campo, una finca, y una de estas veces estaba, me gustaba mucho dormir en el suelo, y uno de esos días, pues, tuve el deseo de escribir algo, que no era lo que normalmente uno escribía en la escuela, o un mensaje normal. Era algo que era una metáfora. Y creo que fue la primera vez, como a los doce años. [. . .] yo pertenezco de algún modo a una generación, que se formó en una cosa institucional, que había en Cuba, que se llamaba Taller Literario. Jamás fui a un taller literario. Yo me hice escritor underground, era roquero, en realidad andaba de roquero, por las playas, campaña, y así fue que entendí la poesía. Nunca fui a una oficina, a una casa de institución del estado [. . .]. Eso para mí no existió nunca. [. . .]

Pero así fui, descubriendo la cosa, así, sin que nadie me dijera no, hasta que, en los, a mediados de los ochenta, conocí a muchos que fueron miembros de Diásporas. A Rolando [Sánchez Mejías]. Y Rolando tenía, era un gran lector, tenía un excelente duro disc. Y fue quien me iba pasando todos esos libros, poco a poco, que te mencioné, a Bataille, a Becquer. [. . .]

¿Y cuándo estuviste en Brasil?

RAP: Estuve de 1998 hasta el 2002. [. . .] Y digamos, creo que fue, cuando hablas del espacio, juro que era un espacio lleno de cosas que yo no conocía. Creo que cuando retorné de Brasil, retorné sobre todo con mucho menos prejuicio. Una visión del mundo mucho más libre, mucho más abierto. La cuestión de la lengua, de los sonidos, [. . .] El portugués ejerció sobre mí una especie de misterio sonoro, para decirlo de algún modo. Que yo me doy cuenta de que cuando escribo en español, está por detrás esa, esa influencia secreta. Del portugués. Y de todas las cosas que implica la música brasileña, Carnaval, la pasión por el fútbol. Es una cultura, una cultura, y un modo de ser de las personas. Como una idea de la esperanza, [. . .] hasta de las personas que son, como he pensado mucho, hice amistad con mendigos, me hablaban con optimismo de la vida, siendo mendigos. Hasta en el peor de los casos, ¿no? Y creo que eso . . . Eso me hizo pensar que existía una literatura, que algún modo existiera un reflejo de esa filosofía de vida, de ese modo de vivir. Y por ahí también he leído los brasileños desde esta perspectiva. Por eso te digo: Brasil. Y la calle, la calle, la calle. Han sido los lugares, los espacios fundamentales. Como diría en Brasil, en la rua, la rua, la rua.

Durante una época, asistías a, como por ejemplo, las reuniones de la Azotea; o las reuniones de Reina. ¿Y cuándo cambió todo eso, desde tu perspectiva? ¿En qué año, en qué época? ¿Y por qué?

RAP: A ver. Yo creo que cambió, entre otras cosas, por el flujo migratorio tan fuerte. En principio, ese flujo ha hecho que no estén los actores. Los actores, los protagonistas. En segundo lugar, cambió cuando quisieron disfrazar, es decir buscar una solución para este país. En el que todo cambió. Porque para hacer algo, hay que tener dinero. Si no tienes dinero, no lo puedes hacer. Si quieres tener un buen café, tienes que tener dinero; si quieres hacer una salida nocturna, tienes que tener dinero. Entonces, todo aquello que existía, que eran espacios literariamente populares, desaparecieron. Y se creó una especie de, digamos, de vacío espiritual, yo creo. [. . .] Y entonces, la verdadera bohemia, no tiene más cómo ser, ¿no? Y porque había una, decadencia de todos los varones, muy grande, en tercer lugar, que puede ser en primer lugar. (Risa.) Y el estado ha propiciado una especie de falta de todo, de todo lo que sea seriedad. Promueve cosas, que no son realmente las que son. Y crea una gran confusión, donde, de pronto, en los espacios, que tú puedes ir a una feria de libro, o a una institución, están personas que realmente no tienen ningún talento. Pero esa cosa participativa, que genera las propias instituciones, de un estado que realmente no tiene cómo respirar. Esa especie de anarquía, que es malo para las personas que realmente tienen proyecto, talento, una obra.

Ya hablamos un poco de los cambios que has visto en las comunidades de los escritores, ¿no? No sé si querías decir algo más de eso.

RAP: Yo creo que el vínculo del poder político cubano, con los escritores, o los creadores de cualquier ámbito, no ha cambiado un milímetro. Todo es una fantasía. Y una especie de cosa muy externa. El hecho de que haya cien restaurantes, y veinticinco cafeterías, no significa que la posición del poder, ante lo que se puede y no se puede decir haya cambiado. Ni un milímetro. Todo es muy disfrazado. [. . .] hay cosas que . . . no sé . . . no puedo decir, en los periódicos oficiales, lo que yo pienso. Y cuando lo digo en lo no oficial, de igual cae, de alguna manera u otra, en una lista negra. Entonces todo es muy hipócrita. Es que ha salido una imagen de democracia, y de permisividad, que es muy dudosa. Es lo que yo pienso. [. . .]

¿En qué proyectos estás trabajando ahora?
RAP: Voy a seguir escribiendo sobre arte. Inclusive, mis mayores amistades son, críticos de arte, artistas. Pero mi proyecto es tratar de, es decir, de entender cada día, cada día. Yo creo que un día es, y dentro de ese día, caben diez o cien palabras. Las que quepan. Y todo hay días cuando no cabe una sola palabra. Si uno vive en ese sentido, pues, ese para mí es escritor, artista, creador auténtico. [. . .] Me interesa la vida, como una cosa, un influjo, donde hay cultura, donde hay desastre, donde hay erotismo, sobre todo.

. . .

Richard, can you tell me a little about the most important influences on your work?
RAP: Well, I've had various important influences on my work. [. . .] But, I think it would be unforgivable not to mention my first great influence as a poet, specifically, the Sevillian poet Luis Cernuda. I think Cernuda was, I recognize him as my first great poetic influence. He was a poet I read starkly, with great passion, and I think he taught me a thing or two. His work left me imbued with other things, so that even after I've read a lot and had other literary idols, reading works from different languages, from different cultures, and in all that cultural morass, Cernuda has survived in some way. I think that he is my first timely influence. [. . .] Then came other influences. [. . .]

I'm influenced now in another way, for example: not influences of a specific author, but influences of ways of being. And in this case, Brazilian poetry has influenced me tremendously. And there came a moment, perhaps in the last decade, in which the influences are no longer as literary, but are visual influences. [. . .] I recognize David Lynch as an influence as important as Samuel Beckett, or Luis Cernuda. David Lynch, Cronenberg: because now when I look at reality, and I process it, I say that the mind of a poet is like a meat-grinding machine, I process it to return this ground meat to the page, this ground meat almost always passes through these tremendous memories that I have of the cinema of David Lynch, of Cronenberg, [. . .] or that strange thing by Michael Haneke [. . .]

When did the interest you had in poetry begin, or arise? In what moment did this interest arise?
RAP: When I was a boy. I went to visit a country house, or a farm, on the weekends, and one of these times, I liked to sleep on the floor, and one of those

days, back then, I had the desire to write something, which was not what one normally wrote in school, or a normal message. It was something that was a metaphor. And I think that was the first time, around twelve years old. [...] I belong in a way to a generation that was formed in an institutional environment, that existed in Cuba at that time, which was called the Literary Workshop. I never went to a literary workshop. I became a writer underground, I was a rocker. Truthfully I acted like a rocker, on the beaches, the fields, and so that's how I came to understand poetry. I never went to an office, an institutional [literary] house that belonged to the state [...]. For me, that never existed. [...]

But that's how I was, discovering it, without anyone telling me no, until, in the mid-80s, I met many of those who were members of the Diásporas group, like Rolando [Sánchez Mejías]. And Rolando was a great reader, he had an excellent hard drive. And little by little, he gave me all the books that I mentioned, Bataille, Becquer. [...]

And when were you in Brazil?
RAP: From 1998 to 2002. [...] And let's say, I think it was, when you talk about space, I swear it was a space full of things I wasn't aware of. I think that when I returned from Brazil, I returned with much less prejudice. With a much freer, much more open view of the world. The question of language, of sounds [...] Portuguese exerted a kind of sonorous mystery over me, to put it one way. I realize that when I write in Spanish, that secret influence lies behind it. From Portuguese. Everything that Brazilian music implies, Carnival, the passion for soccer. It is a culture, a culture, and a way of life for people. It's like an idea of hope [...] even of the people who are, I've thought about it a lot, I made friends with beggars. They spoke to me with optimism about life, being beggars. Even in the worst cases, no? And I think that ... That made me think that a certain literature existed, that somehow there was a reflection of that philosophy of life, that way of living. And from there I have also read Brazilian works from this perspective. That's why I tell you: Brazil. And the street, the street, the street. These have been the places, the fundamental spaces. As one would say in Brazil, in the street, the street, the street.

During a time, you attended, for example, the meetings of La Azotea; or the meetings Reina hosted. And when did all that change, from your perspective? In what year, in what period? And why?
RAP: Let's see. I think it changed, among other things, because of the strong

migratory flow. At the beginning, this flow meant that the principal actors were not here. The actors, the protagonists. Secondly, it changed when they wanted to disguise, that is, to look for a solution for this country. Where everything changed. Because to do something, you have to have money. If you don't have money, you can't do it. If you want to have a good coffee, you have to have money; if you want to have a night out, you have to have money. Then, everything that existed, everything that was a popular literary space, disappeared. And a kind of, say, spiritual emptiness was created, I believe. [...] And then, the real bohemia, can't really exist, right? And third, which might be the most important, because there was a decadence in all the boys, a very large one. (Laughter.) And the state has fostered a kind of scarcity of everything, of everything that should be taken seriously. It promotes things that are not really what they are. And it creates a great confusion, where, suddenly, in the spaces, like, you can go to a book fair, or to an institution, and there are people who really do not have any talent. But that participation, promoted by the institutions themselves, exists in a state that really does not have room to breathe. It's a kind of anarchy, which is bad for people who really have a project, talent, a work of art.

We already talked a little about the changes you've seen in the writers' communities, right? I don't know if you had anything more to say.
RAP: I believe that the link between Cuban political power and writers, or creators in any field, has not changed a bit. It is a fantasy. And a kind of very external thing. The fact that there are a hundred restaurants, and twenty-five coffee shops, does not mean that the position of power, in the face of what can and cannot be said, has changed. Not one bit. Everything is very disguised. [...] there are things that ... I don't know ... I cannot say what I think, in the official newspapers. And when I say it unofficially, it ends up, in some way or another, on a blacklist. So everything is very hypocritical. I guess it's that an image of democracy has emerged, and of permissiveness, which is very dubious. That's what I think. [...]

What projects are you working on now?
RAP: I will continue writing about art. Also, my greatest friends are art critics, artists. But my project is to try to, that is, to understand every day, every day. I believe that a day is, and within that day, there is room for ten or a hundred words. Those that fit. And there are days when there is not a single word that fits. If one lives in that sense, then, for me, that person is a writer,

an artist, an authentic creator. [. . .] I am interested in life, as a thing, an influence, where there is culture, where there is disaster, where there is eroticism, above all.

INTERVIEW WITH ANTONIO JOSÉ PONTE

I conducted this interview with writer Antonio José Ponte over email, with Ponte responding on May 11, 2019, in response to questions sent a few weeks earlier (on March 28, 2019). Ponte's work is analyzed in chapter 5.

¿Cuáles han sido las influencias más importantes en su obra?

AJP: La guerra de Troya, desde la infancia, primero en una versión infantil de *La Ilíada*, ahora en mi propósito (que no sé si cumpliré) de aprender griego para leer el original. La poesía de varios poetas modernistas hispanoamericanos recitada de memoria por mi abuela paterna Alicia Doyhenard, buenos y malos poemas, Rubén Darío especialmente y su entonación de ciertos versos de "Sonatina," que reproduzco también de memoria en esa entonación. Verne y una de sus novelas menores pero más extrañas: *El castillo de los Cárpatos*. La poesía clásica china leída en español o en inglés. La poesía arcaica griega, también en esos dos idiomas. El Señor de la Montaña, que es como llama Quevedo a Michel de Montaigne. Marcel Proust, sobre quien escribí un libro primerizo impublicado. Alice en Wonderland y A través del espejo, con los poemas de Lewis Carroll. Fernando Pessoa, todavía más después de haber vivido en Portugal y leer portugués. Los libros sobre la memoria artificial, a partir de la lectura de Frances Yates y los de otros autores cercanos o pertenecientes al Warburg Institute. Isak Dinesen, memorialista y cuentista. José Lezama Lima y, cuando ya se me estaba haciendo sofocante, Jorge Luis Borges como triaca contra el veneno Lezama Lima, y viceversa. Octavio Paz, ya no tanto el ensayista como el poeta, donde vuelvo a encontrar, pero en versión más bárbara todavía a los poetas modernistas que leía y recitaba mi abuela paterna. Shakespeare. Arquíloco y el dilema de su escudo perdido y un fragmento donde dice que se le aflojan los nervios de su verga. Wallace Stevens. La intersección de comunismo y catolicismo y homosexualidad en Pier Paolo Pasolini, intersección y puja de esas tres fuerzas. La lucha con y por y contra José Martí. Virginia Woolf. Santa Teresa de Jesús. El Nuevo Testamento, que leo siempre a finales de año. Y los testimonios del otro prendimiento y sacrificio, el de Sócrates en Platón y en Jenofonte. Y vuelta a empezar, *La Ilíada* y mi deseo de aprender griego antiguo para leerla en el original.

¿Qué espacios o lugares han influido más en su obra?

AJP: Los espacios de la memoria de mis abuelos, donde no cabían carteles guevaristas ni castristas, no se prometía nada del futuro y, por otra parte, no se podía contar del todo, entre lo secreto y la desmemoria. Ese espacio ha encarnado para mí en ciudades, en La Habana principalmente, y en unos lugares que se repiten en sueño, unas terrazas que he pensado que podría ser la Quintana dos Mortos e dos Vivos en Santiago de Compostela y también la terraza de jade de un poema de Tsu-Tung Po. Y otro espacio recurrente en sueños de la torre de un reloj y una librería de viejos en una callecita que hay detrás.

¿Ud. cree que forma parte de una(s) comunidad(es) de escritores? Si es que sí, puede describir esta(s) comunidad(es) y decir cuál ha sido su efecto en la obra de Ud.?

AJP: Como en la plaza compostelana de la que hablaba antes, creo participar de una comunidad de muertos y de vivos, escritores muertos y escritores vivos. Con confusión de límites evidentes, porque los vivos están casi siempre muy muertos y los muertos casi siempre muy vivos. Habiendo participado en transacciones para poder publicar o no llegar a publicar, esa comunidad no solo incluye a escritores, sino que ha estado forzosamente poblada también por censores y comisarios políticos. Simples aduaneros, por supuesto. Y, hablando de aduanas, además de la frontera entre vivos y muertos, ha existido la frontera entre escritores censurados y escritores publicados. Así que la cartografía de esa comunidad a la que creo pertenecer arroja mapas bastante complicados.

¿Qué cambios ha notado Ud. en la(s) comunidad(es) de escritores e intelectuales con la(s) que se asocia, después de su llegada a Madrid?

AJP: En los últimos años de mi vida en La Habana tuve que aprender a vivir una vida literaria discreta. Fue una enseñanza dura, dada mi costumbre sostenida de hacer crítica literaria sin cortapisas. Me negué a publicar libros allá adentro, luego me negaron toda posibilidad de publicar o de hablar en público. Y, paradójicamente, aprendí de esas sanciones. De manera que cuando empecé a vivir en Madrid no tenía deseo ninguno de entrar en la vida literaria de esta Villa y Corte. No estaba dispuesto a perder el tiempo en presentaciones de libros o mesas redondas. Y he hecho mínimos esfuerzos de cortesanía. No solamente por la lección de apartamiento obligado que traía de La Habana, sino por la calidad del panorama literario español, que es tan pobre.

¿Me podría contar la historia de la publicación del ensayo "El abrigo de aire"?

AJP: Empezó siendo un encargo por el centenario de la muerte de Martí, en

1995. Un encargo de Bladimir Zamora, que lo publicaría en *El Caimán Barbudo*, pero en una edición de esa revista a publicarse en el extranjero, para otros lectores. Era la época en que algunas revistas cubanas intentaron comercializarse en otros países americanos. Colombia, por ejemplo, para la que fueron editada uno o varios números de *Unión*, por ejemplo. Sería, digamos, una edición internacional de *El Caimán Barbudo*. El encargo me llegaba cuando ya tenía yo deseos de decir públicamente dos o tres cosas sobre Martí y la administración estatal de Martí. Me puse a escribirlo, se lo pasé a Bladimir Zamora . . . Ah, olvidaba decir: me pagarían en dólares, no una cantidad muy alta, pero en dólares y no en pesos cubanos. En la moneda que más había utilizado Martí. Y, bueno, la historia del abrigo podía pasar, pero todo lo que yo decía a propósito de esa historia, no. De manera que di a publicar el abrigo y me quedé con el envoltorio para el abrigo que me había fabricado, y lo publiqué íntegramente en una revista mexicana, y luego Jesús Díaz me pidió reproducirlo en *Encuentro de la Cultura Cubana*, la revista fundada por él y que años más tarde yo dirigiría. Y para contrarrestar la no publicación dentro de Cuba, hice una lectura del ensayo en La Azotea, en el espacio que Reina María Rodríguez sostuvo durante años en su casa construida en una azotea. Fue una lectura muy animada en sus preparativos, porque llegaron muchos avisos de movimientos de segurosos, de agentes de Seguridad del Estado preocupados por lo que iba a leerse, y el actual viceministro de Cultura Fernando Rojas se apareció allí como público, en un gesto muy inusual. Pero, bueno, era de esperar todo eso dado el culto estatal martiano.

¿Piensa escribir otro ensayo sobre Martí?
AJP: [. . .] No tengo planes de volver sobre el tema. Y, a diferencia de Borges que decía no dejar pasar un día sin pensar en Stevenson (¿o era Chesterton?), puedo pasar semanas sin pensar en Martí. No es escritura sagrada para mí, pero sí que es una figura emocionante, cuya discusión me emociona, y en cuyas vicisitudes pienso a veces. Es algo crístico, tengo que confesar. O socratiano con cicuta.

¿Piensa Ud. en Cuba como una isla? ¿Cómo un archipiélago? O . . . ¿como otra cosa?
AJP: Pienso Cuba como un imperio. Lo pensé en broma para mi libro *Cuentos de todas partes del Imperio*, y lo pienso seriamente para un libro dilatadísimo (como todas las cartografías imperiales) que gira alrededor de *The Tempest* y el Caribe, y que se llamará *La Tempestá*.

What have been the most important influences on your work?

AJP: Ever since I was young, the Trojan War, starting with a children's version of *The Iliad*, and currently with my goal (I'm not sure I'll achieve it) of learning Greek to read the original. The poetry of several Spanish-American modernist poets recited from memory by my paternal grandmother Alicia Doyhenard, good and bad poems, Rubén Darío especially, and her intonation of certain verses of "Sonatina," which I also repeat from memory in that intonation. Verne and one of his lesser but stranger novels: *The Carpathian Castle*. Classical Chinese poetry read in Spanish or English. Archaic Greek poetry, also in those two languages. The Lord of the Mountain, which is what Quevedo calls Michel de Montaigne. Marcel Proust, about whom I wrote an unpublished book. Alice in Wonderland and Through the Looking Glass, with the poems of Lewis Carroll. Fernando Pessoa, even more after living in Portugal and being able to read Portuguese. Books on artificial memory, starting with those of Frances Yates and other authors who are close or belong to the Warburg Institute. Isak Dinesen, memoir writer and storyteller. José Lezama Lima and, when he makes me feel suffocated, Jorge Luis Borges as a remedy for Lezama Lima's poison, and vice versa. Octavio Paz, not the essayist so much as the poet, where I find again, but in a more barbaric version, the modernist poets that my paternal grandmother read and recited. Shakespeare. Archilochus and the dilemma of his lost shield and a fragment where he says that the nerves of his cock loosen up. Wallace Stevens. The intersection of communism and Catholicism and homosexuality in Pier Paolo Pasolini, an intersection and battle of those three forces. The struggle with and for and against José Martí. Virginia Woolf. Saint Teresa of Ávila. The New Testament, which I always read at the end of the year. And the testimonies of the other arrest and sacrifice, that of Socrates, in Plato and in Xenophon. And going full circle, *The Iliad* and my desire to learn ancient Greek to read it in the original.

What spaces or locations have most influenced your work?

AJP: The spaces of the memories of my grandparents, where there were no Che or Castro posters, where the future held no promises and, on the other hand, between secrets and forgetfulness, they couldn't tell you everything either. That space has become embodied for me in cities, mostly in Havana, and in places that repeat themselves in dreams: some terraces that I have thought could be the Quintana dos Mortos and the Quintana dos Vivos in Santiago de

Compostela, and also the jade terrace in a poem by Tsu-Tung Po. And another recurring space in my dreams is a clocktower and an antique bookstore on a small street behind it.

Do you think you are part of a community (or communities) of writers? If so, can you describe this community and say what its effect has been on your work?
AJP: Like in the plaza of Santiago de Compostela, which I just spoke of, I believe that I am part of a community of the dead and the living, dead writers and living writers. With the confusion of evident limits because the living are almost always very dead and the dead almost always very alive. Having participated in transactions to be able to publish, or not, that community not only includes writers, but has also been necessarily populated by censors and political commissioners. Simple customs officers, of course. And, speaking of customs, in addition to the border between living and dead, there has been a border between censored writers and published writers. So, the cartography of the community to which I believe I belong produces quite complicated maps.

What changes have you noticed in the community (or communities) of writers and intellectuals with which you are associated, after your arrival in Madrid?
AJP: In the last years of my life in Havana I had to learn to live a discreet literary life. It was a difficult lesson, given my sustained habit of making literary criticism without constraints. I refused to publish books there [in Cuba], then they denied me any possibility of publishing or speaking in public. And, paradoxically, I learned from those sanctions. So when I started living in Madrid, I had no desire to enter into the literary life of this "Town and Court." I wasn't willing to waste time on book presentations or roundtables. And I have made minimal efforts of courtesy. Not only because of the lesson about forced separation that I brought with me from Havana, but because of the quality of the Spanish literary scene, which is very poor.

Could you tell me the history of the publication of the essay "The Coat of Air"?
AJP: It began in 1995, as a piece commissioned for the centenary of Martí's death. An assignment from Bladimir Zamora, who would publish it in *El Caimán Barbudo*, but in an edition of that magazine published abroad, for other readers. It was a time when some Cuban magazines tried to be commercialized in other Latin American countries. Colombia, for example, for which one or various issues of [the Cuban magazine] *Union* were edited. It would be, say, an international edition of *El Caimán Barbudo*. I received the assignment when I already wanted to publicly say two or three things about

Martí and the state administration of Martí. I started writing it, I passed it along to Bladimir Zamora . . . Oh, I forgot to say: I would be paid in [U.S.] dollars, not a very high amount, but in dollars and not in Cuban pesos. In the currency that Martí had used the most. And, well, the history of the coat could pass, but everything I said about that history, not so much. So I gave the piece about the coat to be published, and I kept the wrapping for the [story of the] coat that I had made, and I published it in its entirety in a Mexican magazine. Then Jesús Díaz asked me to reproduce it in *Encuentro de la Cultura Cubana*, the magazine he founded and that I would later direct. And to counter the essay's non-publication in Cuba, I did a reading of the essay in the Azotea, in the space that Reina María Rodríguez maintained for years in her house built on a roof. The reading was very lively in its arrangements, because there were many warnings about police movement. State Security agents were worried about what was going to be read, and the current Vice Minister of Culture Fernando Rojas showed up as an audience member, in a very unusual gesture. But, well, that was all to be expected considering the state's cult of Martí.

Do you plan to write another essay on Martí?
AJP: [. . .] I have no plans to return to the subject. And, unlike Borges who said he could not let a day pass without thinking about Stevenson (or was it Chesterton?), I can spend weeks without thinking about Martí. I don't consider it sacred writing, but he is an exciting figure, whose discussion excites me, and whose vicissitudes I sometimes think about. It's something Christic, I have to admit. Or Socratian, with hemlock.

Do you think of Cuba as an island? As an archipelago? Or . . . as something else?
AJP: I think of Cuba as an empire. I thought of it as a joke for my book *Tales from the Cuban Empire*, and I am thinking about it seriously for an expansive book (like all imperial cartographies) that is about *The Tempest* and the Caribbean, which will be called *La Tempestá*.

INTERVIEW WITH REINA MARÍA RODRÍGUEZ

I conducted this interview with poet Reina María Rodríguez over email, in a series of messages sent back and forth between May 5 and May 7, 2019, in response to questions sent a few weeks earlier (on April 23, 2019). Rodríguez's work is analyzed in chapter 2.

Cuando nos vimos en la Habana, hablamos un poco de . . . te daré de comer como a los pájaros . . . , un libro que no se identifica ni como prosa ni como poesía. ¿Podría hablar un poco más de qué significa este texto para Ud., y de cómo se escribió?

RMR: Sobre *Te daré de comer como a los pájaros* viene más bien de la idea de un libro que Roland Barthes quiso hacer y no llegó a escribir donde cupiera todo: las recetas de médico, las cartas, todo! Sin una jerarquía y yo pensé en uno de varios planos a la vez que fue muy difícil de lograr porque no había en La Habana programas digitales entonces, ni yo tenía computadora! Lo mandé a una amiga escritora afuera y se perdió! Años después lo pude reconstruir gracias a un amigo que pasó las bandas de los tres planos: la escritora, la vida cotidiana, y las cartas a alguien que ya había escrito para un hombre que nunca me quiso! La idea de que Katerina Mansfield muere en el priorato de Gurdjieff junto a las vacas para saber si ella tiene alma o no es el centro de un libro que no tiene centro! He visto mi vida más que desde la realidad desde las lecturas, por eso—aunque en aquella época nos influyera tanto Gerald Genette con *Palimpsestos*, no pretendía ser intertextual, sino usar las lecturas como parte de la vida vivida: esos espacios míos que incorporé de una forma pasiva.

Pensando en cómo treinta años casi atrás, escribía en una máquina portátil negra y amarilla con cintas recicladas muchas veces teñidas y vueltas a teñir! Una banda primero y la otra luego, creyendo que si diseccionaba la realidad en partes, y contraponía una—la de creerme una escritora—, con un lenguaje más edulcorado a la otra que vivía aquella vida entre desechos y entresacaba de mis diarios o libretas de lavandería como los llamo, la realidad, con lenguaje directo o coloquial, todo ingenuamente cogería volumen y haría más espesa esa tensión entre el deseo del imaginario por convertir la supervivencia en algo más! Darle espesor a lo que no lo tenia. Por eso, *Te daré de comer . . .* trata de la alimentación que puede matar a un pájaro atragantado en mi mano; que puede matar a una escritora que no sabe bien cómo llenar los espacios y carece de un centro para sobrevivir a duras penas en un tiempo real tan miserable donde no encuentra nada ni paisaje ni seres ni alimentos: solo barbarie! Por eso también convivía en esos espacios paralelos desmontando al personaje hasta donde se puede y ficcionando a la vez la miseria a través de las lecturas y convirtiéndome en la que pretendía ser: Cualquier otra de los libros con esa esquizofrenia galopante! Gracias por recordármelo con tu pregunta! Ahora veo que todo libro trata de rebasar esos planos y crear la ilusión de que somos diferentes cuando el horizonte se ve chato sin distancia y sin relieve. Al menos lo resistí! No sé si el libro que fue la herramienta para sobrevivir lo resistirá!

Ud. se ha identificado con una serie de espacios creados para que los poetas e intelectuales cubanos—y a veces no cubanos—se encuentren: la Azotea, la Torre, el Instituto Cubano del Libro. ¿Podría hablar del efecto de estos encuentros en su poesía, y en la poesía (la obra) de otros? También se ha identificado con un proyecto para crear libros cosidos a mano, y para traducir libros claves al español. ¿Podría hablar de estos proyectos, y de la relación que tienen con su escritura?

RMR: Sobre los espacios creados el primero fue Paideia antes de los 90s! Después la Azotea y finalmente la Torre de Letras! Ha sido mi deseo de encuentro con los otros en sitios alternativos con la ilusión de que un espacio nos protegerá! En estos tres espacios las propuestas y las obras eran heterogéneas, un conjunto a partir de las diferencias y las voces. Paideia tuvo como lugar de sus conferencias el centro Alejo Carpentier y no solo reunió escritores sino artistas plásticos, dramaturgos, etc. La Azotea fue más personal y sucedió en mi casa, más íntimo, y ocurrió con los que quedábamos allí en momentos muy difíciles para la supervivencia y solo había escritores ya! Y la Torre es un híbrido que se produjo en el Palacio del Segundo Cabo de La Habana Vieja, en una torre frente a la Giraldilla en el punto más alto de La Habana colonial donde radicaba el Instituto del libro. Aquí la idea era llevar la literatura a través de las lenguas y sacar traducciones de autores cubanos en una colección bilingüe por ahora en cinco lenguas y dar charlas sobre estos procesos de traducción y lecturas de autores también. Los libros son cosidos con un cosido japonés ideado por Jorge Miralles traductor de francés y la imprenta pertenece al ICL [el Instituto Cubano del Libro] la selección, la confección es nuestra y logramos hacer también una revista que se llamó Azoteas y que tuvo sólo siete números. La idea de la revista era unir a los amigos desperdigados por el mundo, una revista manufacturada a la usanza del siglo XIX y que fuera además un útero! Creo que estos han sido deseos ingratos que nunca logré! Tentativas! Ganas de crear espacios públicos bajo la mano de los artistas no de los funcionarios de la cultura! Algo casi imposible!

En los últimos años, ha ganado dos premios sumamente importantes: el Premio Nacional de la Literatura de Cuba y el Premio Neruda. ¿Cuál ha sido el impacto de estos premios en su obra? ¿En su vida?

RMR: Sobre los premios recibidos son importantes porque dan una posibilidad de resistencia en el momento y los agradezco mucho, aunque a la larga se conviertan en techos muy altos para alcanzar! Me siento aplastada por ellos!

Mandé a tantos concursos y aún mando para resolver la precariedad de la sobrevivencia cotidiana, no por vanidad, y si la tuve alguna vez, durante la ruta la perdí! Pues siento que muchos autores latinoamericanos lo merecerían incluso antes que yo. Como el poeta argentino Arturo Carrera para mencionar a uno. Eso me provoca sentirme que me paro en puntas y no logro tocar el techo! Quiero desandar, desescribir, deshacer no solo los géneros, las hilachas de lenguajes, los ripios del lirismo con los que trabajé, por eso ahora construyo maquetas, porque solo los libros incluso con fotos como *Travelling* o *La caja de Bagdad* no logran el espesor que quisiera, los volúmenes.

Se está hablando mucho de los cambios recientes en la política estadounidense en cuanto a Cuba; y sé que está ahora varios meses del año con su hija, en Miami. ¿Cuáles han sido—y cuáles serán—los efectos de estos cambios en las comunidades de poetas e intelectuales cubanos con las que se asocia?

RMR: Volviendo a tus preguntas y para rematar la anterior, siempre he creído en los espacios como lugares de apertura por los crucigramas que el arte arma! Las conversaciones, las discusiones incluso, la retroalimentación con los otros que se convierten en espejos. Al venir a dar charlas aquí en diferentes universidades [en los Estados Unidos], quise exponer algo que no tiene casi lugar ya, y que es mi deseo y obsesión: el delirio por las lecturas, y los autores con los que conviví y la literatura como ese otro lugar, ese país. Provengo de un mundo detenido cuyo único lujo dentro de tanta precariedad fue tener el tiempo para mal vivir y dedicárselo a los libros, a las películas, a la música! Un lujo como contrapartida a la necesidad, la carencia de casi todo, lo perentorio. Este lujo no crea una mayor espiritualidad y tampoco nos hizo mejores! Por lo que ahora veo solo restos de un naufragio donde todo se ha desperdigado y trato de sobrevivir entre tanta pérdida afianzada todavía a los párrafos como si fueran mástiles! Pero el motivo esencial de esta prolongación fue estar con mi hija y ver también a los amigos! Poder conversar normalmente con ellos así sea mediante el teléfono! Oírlos, saber cómo transcurren sus vidas reales! Comprender lo real y la velocidad que tiene con todas sus contraindicaciones! Salir del ahogo, de la falta de contrastes, luces y sombras!

. . .

When we met in Havana, we talked a little about . . . te daré de comer como a los pájaros . . . , a book that is not identified as either prose or poetry. Could you talk a little more about what this text means to you, and how it was written?

RMR: *Te daré de comer como a los pájaros* came from the idea for a book that Roland Barthes wanted to do but did not get to write that would encompass everything: doctor's prescriptions, letters, everything! Without a hierarchy. And I thought about one with several planes, which was difficult to achieve because there were no digital programs in Havana then, nor did I have a computer! I sent it to a writer friend abroad and it was lost! Years later I was able to reconstruct it thanks to a friend who passed the bands of the three planes: the writer, daily life, and letters I had written for a man who never loved me! The idea that Katherine Mansfield dies in the priory of Gurdjieff next to the cows to know if she has a soul or not is the center of a book that does not have a center! I have viewed my life more from readings than from reality, that's why—although at that time we were influenced so much by Gerard Genette's *Palimpsests*—I didn't intend it to be intertextual, but to use the readings as part of the life lived: those spaces of mine that I incorporated passively.

Thinking of how, almost thirty years ago, I wrote on a black and yellow typewriter with recycled ribbon that was dyed and re-dyed many times over! One side first and then the other, believing that if I dissected reality into parts, and counterposed one—that of believing myself to be a writer—, using a more sugarcoated language, to the other one that lived life amidst the debris, and pulled from my diaries or notebooks, laundromat booklets as I call them, reality, with direct or colloquial language, everything would ingeniously densify and thicken that tension in between the desire of the imaginary to turn survival into something else! Give density to that which didn't have any. That's why, *te daré de comer . . .* is about the food that can kill a bird choking in my hand; that can kill a writer who doesn't know how to fill the spaces and lacks a center to barely survive through a miserable time where she finds nothing; not a landscape nor people nor food; just barbarism! That's why I also cohabited those parallel spaces, unraveling the character as far as possible and at the same time fictionalizing the misery through the readings and converting myself into what I aspired to be: anyone from the books with that galloping schizophrenia! Thank you for reminding me with your question! Now I see that every book tries to go beyond those planes and create the illusion that we are different when the horizon looks flat without distance and without relief. At least I resisted it! I don't know if the book that was the key to survival will be able to resist it!

You have been identified with a series of spaces created for Cuban (and sometimes non-Cuban) poets and intellectuals to meet: the Azotea, the Torre, the

Cuban Book Institute. Could you talk about the effect of these encounters on your poetry, and on the poetry (the works) of others? You have also been identified with a project to create hand-stitched books, and to translate key books into Spanish. Could you talk about these projects, and the relationship they have with your writing?

RMR: In terms of the created spaces, the first was Paideia which came before the 90s! Then the Azotea and finally the Torre de Letras! It has been my desire to meet with others in alternative places with the dream that a space will protect us! In these three spaces the proposals and works were heterogeneous, a set based on differences and voices. Paideia's conferences took place in the Alejo Carpentier Center and not only brought together writers but also visual artists, playwrights, etc. The Azotea was more personal and it took place in my house. It was more intimate, and it happened with those who remained on the island in very difficult times for survival, and there were only writers! And the Torre is a hybrid that took place in the Palacio del Segundo Cabo in Old Havana, in a tower in front of the Giraldilla at the highest point of colonial Havana where the Cuban Book Institute was located. Here the idea was to bring literature through multiple languages and to publish translations of Cuban authors in a bilingual collection, for now in five languages, and to give talks about the process of translation and author readings as well. The books are sewn with a Japanese stitching designed by French translator Jorge Miralles, and the printing press belongs to the Cuban Book Institute. The selection and the crafting is ours, and we also managed to make a magazine called Azoteas, which only lasted seven issues. The idea of the magazine was to unite the friends scattered around the world, a magazine manufactured in the style of the nineteenth century and that would also be a uterus! I think these have been thankless, unrealized desires! Attempts! The desire to create public spaces under the steady hand of artists, not cultural officials! Something that is almost impossible!

In recent years, you have won two extremely important prizes: the Cuban National Prize for Literature and the Neruda Prize. What has been the impact of these awards on your work? On your life?

RMR: In terms of the awards received, they are important because they give me a chance for resistance in the moment and I am very grateful for them, even though in the long run they become very high ceilings to reach! I feel crushed by them! I sent work to so many competitions and I still send work to help with the precariousness of daily living, not out of vanity, and if I ever had it, I lost it on the way! Well, I feel that many Latin American authors deserved it even more than me, like the Argentine poet Arturo Carrera, to name just one. That makes me feel like I'm standing on my tiptoes and I can't reach the ceiling! I want to retrace, unwrite, undo not only the genres, but the threads of languages, the riff of lyricism with which I worked. That's why I build mock-ups now, because books alone, even books with photographs like *Travelling* or *Caja de Baghdad* do not achieve the density that I would like, the volumes.

Much is being said about recent changes in U.S. policy regarding Cuba; and I know that you now spend several months of the year with your daughter, in Miami. What have been—and what will be—the effects of these changes in the communities of Cuban intellectuals and poets with whom you associate?
RMR: Going back to your questions and to finish the previous one, I have always believed in spaces as places of openness for the puzzles that art puts together! The conversations, the discussions even, the feedback with the others who become mirrors. When I came to give talks here in different universities [in the United States], I wanted to expose something that hardly exists any-more, and that is my desire and obsession: the delirium for reading, and the authors with whom I lived, and literature as that other place, that country. I come from a detained world where the only luxury in such precariousness was having the time to live poorly and dedicate oneself to books, movies, and mu-sic! A luxury as a counterweight to the need, the lack of almost everything, the imperative. This luxury does not create a greater spirituality and neither did it make us better! So now I see only the remains of a shipwreck where every-thing has been scattered, and I try to survive in the midst of so much loss still entrenched in the paragraphs as if they were masts! But the essential reason for this prolongation was to be with my daughter and also to see my friends! To converse normally with them even if it's on the phone! To hear them, to know what happens in their real lives! To understand reality and the speed of it with all of its contraindications! To leave the anguish, the lack of contrasts, lights, and shadows!

Notes

Introduction

1. "Archipelago," Oxford English Dictionary, n.p.
2. Ette, "Una literature sin residencia fija," 749.
3. I draw on the valuable extant research on Cuba as island and diaspora, further discussed in chapter 1, to inform my analysis.
4. Here Pérez-Firmat invokes the "Rubik's Cuba": "Soy un ajiaco de contradicciones, / un puré de impurezas: / a little square from Rubik's Cuba / que nadie nunca acoplará" (*Bilingual Blues*, 28). On the associations of "cubo" implicit in the title of *Cubista Magazine*, see also Morán, "Cuba.com," 153–54.
5. Maldonado-Torres, "The Decolonial Turn," 114. My decolonizing approach coincides with scholars undertaking decolonial projects in an array of fields, including Diaspora Studies, Global Studies, Migration Studies, and World Literature Studies.
6. "Archipelago," Oxford English Dictionary, n.p. The treaty is dated 30 June 1268.
7. Martínez-San Miguel, "Colonialismo y decolonialidad archipielágica," 42. All translations are mine unless otherwise noted.
8. My own work is informed by the insights of these scholars, as well as the others with whom I participated in the 2015–2016 Rutgers Center for Cultural Analysis Seminar on Archipelagos.
9. Stratford et al., "Envisioning the Archipelago," 114. See also Stratford, "Disciplinary Formations, Creative Tensions, and Certain Logics in Archipelagic Studies."
10. Roberts and Stephens, *Archipelagic American Studies*, 15.
11. Maldonado-Torres, "The Decolonial Turn," 122.
12. de la Nuez, "El destierro de Calibán," 140.
13. de la Nuez, "El destierro de Calibán," 139.
14. de la Nuez, "El destierro de Calibán," 139.
15. Stratford convincingly argues that the archipelago be understood as both a material and a metaphoric formation ("Disciplinary Formations").
16. On the artificiality of the divisions of the sea—as well as an overview of its history—see Lewis, "Dividing the Ocean Sea."
17. Stratford et al., "Envisioning the Archipelago," 114.
18. Glissant, *Poetics of Relation*, 34.
19. Suggestive of a recent archipelagic turn, López and Matute Castro invoke Glissant in writing of the need for a more "archipelagic thinking" in their introduction to a special 2013 issue of the *Revista Iberoamericana* titled *Trazos de islas*: (dis)locaciones narrativas y territorios culturales en la República

Dominicana y Cuba [*Lines of islands*: Narrative (dis)locations and cultural territories in the Dominican Republic and Cuba].

20. Glissant, *Poetics of Relation*, 12, 18.

21. See Wiedorn, who contends that Glissant's works are also archipelagic: "They too adhere to a pattern: they are a reflection of the archipelago form" (*Think Like an Archipelago*, 117).

22. Quoted in Wiedorn, *Think Like an Archipelago*, 113.

23. Puri, "Finding the Field," 70, 59.

Chapter 1. Islands and Archipelagos

1. The Feria del Libro is organized by the Instituto Cubano del Libro and the Cámara Cubana del Libro with an estimated 296,692 visitors. Uribe Schroeder et al., *Las ferias del libro*, 15, 120.

2. Events and readings take place all across Havana during the week the Feria is held in Cuba's capital city.

3. In 2013, for instance, 140 exhibitors and 200 intellectuals from more than 30 nations participated, with events and panels featuring their work. "Feria Internacional del Libro de La Habana," n.p.

4. "Feria Internacional del Libro de La Habana," n.p.

5. Rodríguez Díaz, *Compendio insular*, 46–47.

6. See Martínez-San Miguel for an analysis of the colonial-era "Archipiélago de México" [Mexican Archipelago] ("Colonial and Mexican Archipelagoes"), as well as for a discussion, more broadly, of the relationship between colonialism and archipelagic decoloniality in the Caribbean ("Colonialismo y decolonialidad").

7. Rodríguez Díaz, *Compendio insular*, 46–47.

8. Piñera, "La isla en peso," 26; Piñera, "The Weight of the Island," 27. Also, see del Risco, "Piñera y profecía," for a discussion of the controversy surrounding the publication of "La isla en peso"; see Goldman, *Out of Bounds*, for a discussion of the importance of the topic of insularity in Piñera's work.

9. Piñera, "La isla en peso," 26; Piñera, "The Weight of the Island," 27.

10. "Insular," n.p.

11. DeLoughrey, *Routes and Roots*, 9. DeLoughrey offers a comparative analysis of Caribbean and Pacific Island literature.

12. Stratford et al., "Envisioning the Archipelago," 113.

13. DeLoughrey, *Routes and Roots*, 3.

14. DeLoughrey, "'The litany of islands,'" 23.

15. Quijano, "The Coloniality of Power," 533.

16. Hau'ofa, "Our Sea of Islands," 7.

17. See Bethell, *Cuba: A Short History*, for a succinct yet detailed overview of Cuban history; see Pérez, *On Becoming Cuban*, for an overview of U.S.-Cuban relations and tourism.

18. Goldman, *Out of Bounds*.

19. DeLoughrey, *Routes and Roots*, 2.

20. Stratford et al. compare the archipelago to a constellation ("Envisioning the Archipelago," 122); Benítez-Rojo, in contrast, compares the "meta-archipelago" to "the spiral chaos of the Milky Way" (*The Repeating Island*, 4).

21. Stratford et al., "Envisioning the Archipelago," 122.

22. Glissant, *Poetics of Relation*.

23. Glissant, *Poetics of Relation*, 11.

24. Glissant, *Poetics of Relation*, 18.

25. Glissant, *Poetics of Relation*, 12.

26. Glissant, *Poetics of Relation*, 18–19.

27. Glissant, *Poetics of Relation*, 47.

28. Benítez-Rojo, *The Repeating Island*, 4.

29. See Bonilla and Hantel, "Visualizing Sovereignty," for alternative, digital cartographies of the Caribbean that build on Benítez-Rojo's work.

30. Stratford et al., "Envisioning the Archipelago," 117.

31. Pugh, "Island Movements," 17.

32. Figueroa-Vásquez, *Decolonizing Diasporas*, 29.

33. Noting the importance of the "archipelagic turn," Figueroa-Vásquez writes that she situates her project in the "decolonial turn, which [Nelson] Maldonado-Torres argues is 'about making visible the invisible and about analyzing the mechanisms that produce such invisibility or distorted visibility'" (*Decolonizing Diasporas*, 8, 18; see also 17–22).

34. "Diaspora," Oxford English Dictionary, n.p.; "Exile," Oxford English Dictionary, n.p. Emphasis added.

35. The terms diaspora and exile of course remain valuable in many areas of study. Iraida López, for instance, opts to employ the term diaspora in her analysis of the "impossible returns" of members of the "one-and-a-half" generation (i.e., those who became adults in the United States, after leaving Cuba as children or teens), stating, however, that "the near equation of diaspora and transnationalism" may not apply in all cases she studies. López, *Impossible Returns*, 2, 13.

36. My analysis of the archipelago draws as well on the incisive work of Blum ("Introduction"), Dawson ("Archaeology, Aquapelagos and Island Studies"), Hay ("A Phenomenology of Islands"), Hulme ("Subversive Archipelagos"), and Steinberg ("Of Other Seas"), as well as on the studies of de Certeau (*The Practice of Everyday Life*), Lefebvre (*The Production of Space*), and Moretti (*Distant Reading*).

37. On the need to assess the implications of the speech in an era of post-Soviet socialism, see Navarro, "In Medias Res Publica."

38. Castro, "Palabras a los intelectuales," n.p.

39. Castro, "Palabras a los intelectuales," n.p.

40. Perhaps given the close association between Castro's oft-cited "Palabras" and the "Caso Padilla," the title of the book and Castro's words are often conflated, with Castro frequently misquoted as saying "Dentro de la Revolución, todo, *fuera* de la Revolución, nada" [Within the Revolution, all, outside the Revolution, nothing; emphasis added].

41. Castro, "Palabras a los intelectuales," n.p.

42. Castro, "Palabras a los intelectuales," n.p.; emphasis added.

43. Castro, "Palabras a los intelectuales," n.p.

44. Ette, "Una literature sin residencia fija," 749.

45. Ette, "Una literature sin residencia fija," 749.

46. The exact duration of the Special Period is subject to some dispute. For details as well as an analysis of Special Period fiction, see Whitfield, *Cuban Currency*.

47. On the transnational tourism of the Special Period and the archipelagic imaginary, see Lahr-Vivaz, "Remapping the Borderlands."

48. See Prieto, "Cuba's National Literacy Campaign," for an overview of the Cuban literacy campaign, carried out between January and December 1961. Prieto writes that "During this campaign, 707,212 persons were taught to read and write. The remaining 271,995 who did not acquire basic literacy skills constituted only 3.9% of the total population" (221).

49. Behar, "After the Bridges," 6.

50. Of course, not all Cuban immigrants to the United States relocated to Miami; it is also important to note that subsequent waves of Cubans who left were often less socioeconomically privileged than those who left in the late 1950s and early 1960s. For an overview, see Duany, *Blurred Borders*.

51. The plight of the *balseros*—Cubans who left for the United States on makeshift rafts—was foregrounded in November 1999, when five-year-old Elián González was discovered in the water off Florida, the only survivor of a journey that ended in tragedy for his mother and the ten others on

the raft. González was eventually sent home to his father in Cuba after a bitter custody battle with relatives in Miami.

52. The "wet foot/dry foot" policy, implemented by President Clinton, allowed those Cubans who reached U.S. shores to stay, while mandating that those who did not had to return. The policy was ended by President Obama in 2017, leading to new migratory patterns discussed in chapter 5 and the conclusion.

53. López, *Impossible Returns*, 39–40. López notes that these "estimates are relatively consistent with those offered by Cuban researcher Antonio Aja Díaz, who found that 119,916 Cubans lived in Europe in 2007, while in South America the number was 84,715, and in Central America, 35,943 (Aja 203). Overall, more than 16 percent of the Cuban nation has relocated outside of Cuba since 1959."

54. Following Behar, "After the Bridges," "Many Cubans who had been reluctant to leave and get embroiled in the politics of the island/exile split were able to relocate to 'third countries.' Tempted by economic, cultural, educational, and artistic possibilities available to them elsewhere, they uprooted themselves and in this way participated in redrawing the boundaries of the island" (6).

55. López, *Impossible Returns*, 56.

56. Rojas, "Hypermedia, Almenara, Bokeh," n.p. Rojas implicitly refers here to the so-called Boom of the 1960s, when Latin American authors such as Julio Cortázar, Gabriel García Márquez, and Carlos Fuentes gained increased prominence in Europe and the United States following the publication of their work by presses in Europe.

57. Morán, "Cuba.com," 152–57.

58. Morán, "Cuba.com," 157.

59. Stratford et al., "Envisioning the Archipelago," 114.

Chapter 2. Birds of a Feather

1. Reina María Rodríguez, "Resaca" ["Undertow"], *Bosque negro*, 248.

2. Writing of *Otras cartas a Milena* [*Other Letters to Milena*], for instance, Dykstra notes that Rodríguez "evokes the lingering spaces and tensions of exile, for example in a series of alternately open and coded references to Miami as a twin and opposite to the city of Havana, yet she also uses the term 'diaspora' extensively" ("Merging Exile into Diaspora," 11).

3. Glissant, *Poetics of Relation*, 34.

4. Rodríguez has also received awards from the Casa de las Américas (1984 and 1988) and the Unión Nacional de Escritores y Artistas Cubanos (1980 and 1983), as well as the *Plural* award, for *Páramos* (1992); the Premio Nacional de la crítica (1992 and 1995); and the Order of Arts and Letters, from France (1999).

5. Quoted in "Reina María Rodríguez, Premio Nacional," n.p. Unless otherwise noted, translations here are my own; I have used Dykstra's excellent translations of Rodríguez's poems when possible. Ellipses not in brackets are contained in the original.

6. Rodríguez's *oeuvre* is extensive, spanning almost four decades. I focus my analysis here on . . . *te daré de comer como a los pájaros* . . . and *Bosque negro* because both are compilations of the poet's work. The prose poem . . . *te daré de comer* . . . was written in the 1990s and contains fragments of previously published work; the anthology *Bosque negro* was published in 2013 and contains poems published from 1978 to 2007, as well as previously unpublished poems. For a discussion of Rodríguez's more recent work, see Lahr-Vivaz, "After the Azotea"; Dykstra, "On Endurance"; and Lombard and Rodríguez, "'More than a Place.'"

7. Heller, *Assimilation/Generation/Resurrection*, 157. See also Cabezas Miranda, *Proyectos poéticos en Cuba (1959–2000)*, for a detailed study of the history of Cuban poetry.

8. I follow here Heller (*Assimilation/Generation/Resurrection*, 157) and Dykstra ("'A Just Image,'" 63–64).

9. As outlined in chapter 1, in his 1961 speech "Palabras a los intelectuales" ["Words to the Intellectuals"], Fidel Castro emphasized the importance of writing "within" the Revolution: "Dentro de la Revolución, todo; contra la Revolución, nada" [Within the Revolution, everything; against the Revolution, nothing], n.p.

10. In an article published in the *Diario de Cuba*, Azucena Plasencia notes the poet's importance in this regard: "Reina [. . .] es un mito nacional, una leyenda viva de la llamada república de las letras, un ser cuya influencia alcanza a casi cuatro generaciones de narradores, poetas, artistas plásticos, músicos . . ." [Reina [. . .] is a national myth, a living legend of the so-called Republic of Letters, someone who has influenced almost four generations of narrators, poets, artists, musicians . . .], Plasencia, "Reina María Rodríguez," n.p.

11. Founded in 1967, the Instituto Cubano del Libro [Cuban Book Institute] "fomenta la creación y edita, promueve y distribuye obras de literatura en los campos del arte y la ficción, de las ciencias y la técnica, la literatura para niños y jóvenes, así como de temas de interés general, tanto de autores cubanos como de otros países" [promotes the creation of, and edits, promotes, and distributes, works of literature in the fields of art and fiction, science and technology, literature for children and adolescents, as well as topics of general interest by both Cuban writers and writers from other countries] ("Instituto Cubano del Libro (ICL)," n.p.).

12. A rich bibliography exists on the gatherings held in the Azotea; for an overview, see Dykstra ("Afterword," 190–97). Throughout the 2000s, Rodríguez continued to welcome visitors to her Azotea in Havana. As of this writing, a virtual "Azotea de Reina" is open to online visitors on the website *La Habana Elegante (segunda época)*.

13. Rodríguez, personal interview. On Paideia gatherings and writers, see Hernández Salván, *Mínima Cuba*.

14. Rodríguez, "Poesía cubana," n.p.

15. Moretti, *Distant Reading*, 12. Emphasis in the original.

16. Rodríguez also speaks of her "pollitos" [chicks] in *Después de Paideia*, stating that in the present, "me cuesta mucho trabajo incubar otros pollitos" [it takes a lot of work to incubate other chicks].

17. Bachelard, *The Poetics of Space*, 102. Emphasis in the original. I depart somewhat here from Jolas's translation. In the original, Bachelard writes that " . . . cependant il déclenche en nous une *rêverie de la sécurité*" (130, emphasis in the original). Jolas translates "sécurité" as "security," but I use "safety" instead to convey the sense of "safe haven" implicit in Bachelard's description of the nest.

18. Bachelard, *The Poetics of Space*, xxii, xxxvi.

19. Rodríguez references Bachelard by name various times in . . . *te daré de comer* . . . , although she does not specifically refer to *The Poetics of Space*.

20. Bachelard, *The Poetics of Space*, 102. Emphasis in the original.

21. Rodríguez, personal interview.

22. Dykstra's translation of Flores's *El contragolpe* was published in 2016 as *The Counterpunch (and Other Horizontal Poems)*, shortly before the award-winning poet committed suicide later that year, in September 2016.

23. Dykstra posits that "For Rodríguez herself, the ultimate ideal for the rooftop [i.e., the Azotea] was to produce work that would level hierarchies of all kinds. This ideal [. . .] mirrored her aesthetic interests, her interest in language and transgression. It also conflated domestic and intellectual spaces, challenging gender divisions." Dykstra, "Afterword," 193.

24. Dykstra, "Afterword," 191.

25. I draw here on Pascale Casanova's analysis in *The World Republic of Letters*.

26. Figueroa and Rodríguez, "En la casa," n.p.

27. Rodríguez, "te daré de comer . . . ," n.p. As Arcos writes, Rodríguez is not the first Cuban poet to employ prose poetry, as writers Eliseo Diego, Fina García Marruz, Dulce María Loynaz, José Lezama Lima, and José Manuel Poveda also wrote prose poems. See Arcos, "Una nueva visión," 42.

28. The first page of . . . *te daré de comer* . . . features only one column.

29. Rodríguez, "te daré de comer . . . ," n.p.

30. Rodríguez, . . . *te daré de comer* . . . , 9. Ellipsis in the original.

31. The references to literary figures are often accompanied by references to reading, as the poet explains what she is perusing on a given day. Some individuals are mentioned solely in the left- or right-hand columns, while others are mentioned in both. In the case of the examples mentioned here, Rich and Lezama Lima are referenced in the left-hand column; Duras is referenced in the right-hand column; and Pessoa, Cage, and Bachelard are referenced in both.

32. The poems "Isla de Wight" (56–58) and "dos veces son el mínimo" (58–61) are included as well.

33. Dykstra, "'A Just Image,'" 55.

34. Rodríguez, "te daré de comer . . . ," n.p.

35. To quote Warner, a "public" is a group connected through "the circulation of texts among strangers who become, by virtue of their reflexively circulating discourse, a social entity" (*Publics and Counterpublics*, 11–12).

36. Rodríguez, . . . *te daré de comer* . . . , 56.

37. Rodríguez, . . . *te daré de comer* . . . , 27.

38. Rodríguez, . . . *te daré de comer* . . . , 56–57.

39. Foucault, "Of Other Spaces," 3–4.

40. The space of museums and libraries differs from that of a heterotopia in that it is simultaneously "outside of time" and accessible (rather than inaccessible) "to its ravages" (Foucault, "Of Other Spaces," 7). Of course, Cuban museums and libraries are also markedly accessible to the "ravages" of time. Given the limited print run of . . . *te daré de comer* . . . , Rodríguez told me that she herself did not have a copy of the book for some time; given the difficulties of controlling climate conditions in Cuba, Rodríguez's archives are housed at Princeton.

41. Prats Sariol, "En el barrio de Reina María," 40. Emphasis in the original.

42. Rodríguez, . . . *te daré de comer* . . . , 56.

43. Foucault, "Of Other Spaces," 7.

44. Rodríguez, . . . *te daré de comer* . . . , 9. Ellipsis in the original.

45. Rodríguez has published two books with the title *Bosque negro*: the 2013 anthology that I analyze here (published by Ediciones Unión), and a 2005 thematic collection (published by Extramuros). My thanks to Dykstra for this point of clarification.

46. Defined as "A published collection of poems or other pieces of writing," the origins of the anthology are to be found in the "Mid 17th century [. . .] from Greek anthologia [. . .] In Greek, the word originally denoted a collection of the 'flowers' of verse, i.e., small choice poems or epigrams, by various authors." "Anthology," n.p.

47. Stratford et al., "Envisioning the Archipelago," 122.

48. Rodríguez, *Bosque negro*, 23.

49. Rodríguez, *Bosque negro*, 23–24. Indeed, Rodríguez's rewriting of her poems continues even after their publication: in the poem "El arca" [The Ark] included in the copy of *Bosque negro* that the poet gave me, lines have been crossed out and marks of punctuation have been added (290–92).

50. "Cúmulo," n.p. "Cúmulo" is also translated as "Cumulus."

51. Rodríguez, *Bosque negro*, 290.

52. Rodríguez, *Bosque negro*, 246.

53. Poems are included here in Spanish as published in *Bosque negro*. English translations of "las islas," "Violet Island," and "la isla de Wight" are included as published in the bilingual anthology *Violet Island and Other Poems* (translators Kristin Dykstra and Nancy Gates Madsen). As Rodríguez mentions in her preface to *Bosque negro*, there are in some cases slight differences between the originally published versions of poems (as reprinted in *Violet Island*) and those published in *Bosque negro*.

54. Rodríguez, *Bosque negro*, 48; Rodríguez, *Violet Island*, 15.

55. Rodríguez, *Bosque negro*, 48; Rodríguez, *Violet Island*, 15.

56. Dykstra, "Afterword," 164.

57. Rodríguez, *Bosque negro*, 77; Rodríguez, *Violet Island*, 49.

58. Quoted in Dykstra, "Afterword," 183.

59. Rodríguez, *Bosque negro*, 80; Rodríguez, *Violet Island*, 57.

60. Rodríguez, *Bosque negro*, 99; Rodríguez, *Violet Island*, 109. Following Dykstra, "The back-narrative of the collection is about a woman flipping through the UNESCO *Courier*, looking at photographs of other places and times" (Dykstra, "Afterword," 186).

61. Rodríguez, *Bosque negro*, 99; Rodríguez, *Violet Island*, 109.

62. Rodríguez, *Bosque negro*, 99; Rodríguez, *Violet Island*, 109.

63. Rodríguez, *Bosque negro*, 100; Rodríguez, *Violet Island*, 109. In the Spanish-language version of "la isla de Wight" included in *Violet Island and Other Poems*, parentheses are placed as they are in Dykstra and Madsen's English translation (108).

64. Rodríguez, *Bosque negro*, 99; Rodríguez, *Violet Island*, 109.

65. Rodríguez, *Bosque negro*, 100; Rodríguez, *Violet Island*, 111.

66. Rodríguez, *Travelling*, 52.

67. Rodríguez employs the language of cinema to chronicle her experiences in *Travelling* and also includes artwork and photographs. As such, she anticipates the poets' collaborations with artists analyzed in chapter 3.

68. Rodríguez, *Travelling*, 7; Rodríguez, "memory of water," n.p.

69. Rodríguez, *Travelling*, 62; Rodríguez, "first time," n.p.

70. Rodríguez, *Otras mitologías*, 55. Rodríguez writes here of the history of her friendship with poet Omar Pérez.

71. Rodríguez, *Otras mitologías*, 55.

72. Rodríguez, personal interview.

Chapter 3. Artistic Collaborations from Jaruco to Habana

1. de Certeau, *The Practice of Everyday Life*, xviii.

2. Pérez is also the recipient of a Creative Writing Fellowship from the Parlamento Internacional de Escritores. To date, there is scant critical bibliography on his work; see Dykstra, "Dispatch," and Rodríguez, "Vibraciones de R," for a discussion of his poetry.

3. I analyze Pérez's *¿Para qué el cine?*, as well as Hondal's *Diálogos* and *Scratch*, because these texts represent artistic collaborations with visual artists.

4. Now available at lahabana.com.

5. Pérez was born in the Arroyo Naranjo neighborhood of Havana, but moved to Jaruco with his family when he was 15 ("Ricardo Alberto Pérez Estévez," n.p.). For a description of one of Pérez's visits to Havana in the 2000s, see Dykstra, "Dispatch," n.p.

6. Pérez, personal interview, 9 February 2018.

7. Pérez, personal interview, 9 February 2018.

8. Pérez, personal interview, 9 February 2018.

9. The book jacket describes the collection as: "Un ingenioso juego [. . .] estamos en presencia de un poema duplo, pues dentro de su recreación reflexiva aparecen palabras subrayadas, que en una lectura aparte nos entrega otra propuesta, más descarnada, del tema dado." [An ingenious game [. . .] we are in the presence of a double poem, as inside its reflexive recreation appear underlined words, which in a separate reading give us another, more straightforward proposal of the topic at hand.]

10. Suárez's work is also featured on the cover of Pérez's *Vengan a ver las palomas de Varsovia* [*Come to See the Doves of Warsaw*] (2012).

11. I have two copies of *¿Para qué el cine?*, which I purchased (to the best of my recollection) on

separate occasions in Havana bookstores. As I double-checked page numbers just before submitting this book to press, I realized that one copy has the text underlined by Suárez, while the other does not. As a result of this *errata*, undoubtedly found in other copies as well, readers of *¿Para qué el cine?* will experience the text differently depending on which copy they happen to read. As not all readers will have access to either iteration of *¿Para qué el cine?*, which has to date been published only in Cuba, I quote the poems extensively here, with thanks to Pérez for permission to do so. The words are underlined (or included in bold) as printed in the original without the *errata*.

12. Brief introductory comments by Suárez (7) and Pérez (8) precede "La digestión a mi manera" [My Way of Digestion] (9), which Pérez describes as a "prologue" (personal interview, 9 February 2018).

13. Oxford English Dictionary, n.p.

14. de Certeau, *The Practice of Everyday Life*, xviii.

15. Similarly, in Rodríguez's . . . *te daré de comer como a los pájaros* . . . , it is possible to read solely the left-hand column, solely the right-hand column, or the two together. (See chapter 2.)

16. Pérez, *¿Para qué el cine?*, 30–31.

17. Pérez, *¿Para qué el cine?*, 37.

18. My thanks to Juan Pablo Lupi for this insight.

19. My thanks to Lupi for this point as well.

20. Pérez later told me that he hoped to offer another "Recital porcino" [Porcine Reading], this time in Havana. He planned to read his poetry to "muchos cerdos" [many pigs]—at least a hundred—that he would bring to Calle G (close to the building housing UNEAC, the Unión Nacional de Escritores y Artistas Cubanos). He would also, he described, bring cuts of pork to distribute; and would ask a filmmaker to document the performance and the reactions of passersby. Pérez, personal conversation, February 2019.

21. Pérez, "Los cerdos: retorno a la virtud," n.p. Pérez was kind enough to share this unpublished piece with me.

22. *Miedo a las ranas* was subsequently published by Casa Vacía (2018).

23. Pérez, personal interview, 9 February 2018.

24. As is true of Pérez, there is relatively scant published criticism on Hondal. See Rodríguez, "En busca de una voz," for a discussion of *Diálogos*.

25. www.diariodecuba.com and www.rialta-ed.com.

26. Hondal has also edited two other editions of titles by Gombrowicz, both of which are forthcoming from the Torre de Letras imprint: *Cosmos* and *Bakakai*.

27. In addition to Hondal, Mora and Pérez identify the following poets as members of the "Generación Años Cero": Jamila Medina Ríos, Sergio García Zamora, Larry J. González, Legna Rodríguez Iglesias, Pablo de Cuba Soria, Alessandra Santiesteban, Javier L. Mora, Oscar Cruz, Leandro Báez Blanco, Hugo Fabel, Lizabel Mónica, and José Ramón Sánchez. Simal and Dorta note that "Generación Cero" authors working in narrative also include Carlos M. Álvarez, Lien Carranza, Gleyvis Coro, Ahmel Echevarría, Carlos Esquivel, Michel Encinosa Fú, Jhortensia Espineta, Abel Fernández-Larrea, Raúl Flores, Jorge E. Lage, Polina Martínez Shviétsova, Lizabel Mónica, Anisley Negrín, Osdany Morales, Erick J. Mota, and Lia Villares (3).

28. Mora and Pérez, "La desmemoria," 14; see also Simal and Dorta, "Literatura cubana contemporánea," 2–4.

29. Mora and Pérez, "La desmemoria," 13.

30. Mora and Pérez, "La desmemoria," 17.

31. Hondal, personal conversation. Hondal recalls that he first attended events at the Torre "con el festival con los poetas de Buffalo" [with the festival with the poets from Buffalo (New York)]; the Torre was then located in the Palacio del Segundo Cabo (personal communication, 11 April 2019).

32. Hondal, personal interview, 14 February 2017.

33. Hondal, personal interview, 14 February 2017.

34. Aguilera, "Ramón Hondal habla," n.p.

35. Hondal, *Diálogos*, 17.

36. Hondal, *Diálogos*, 19.

37. de Certeau, *The Practice of Everyday Life*, 93.

38. de Certeau, *The Practice of Everyday Life*, xviii.

39. de Certeau, *The Practice of Everyday Life*, 97.

40. Hondal, *Diálogos*, 17.

41. Dykstra, "'A Just Image,'" 64. See also Mora and Pérez, "La desmemoria," 17.

42. Hondal, *Diálogos*, 11.

43. de Certeau, *The Practice of Everyday Life*, xviii.

44. Hondal, personal interview, 14 February 2017.

45. Hondal, personal interview, 14 February 2017.

46. Hondal, *Scratch*, 7, 43, 85.

47. Hondal, personal conversation.

48. As Gitelman demonstrates, the phonograph also contributes to the formation of what Anderson terms "imagined communities" (as well as what Warner describes as "publics"): "By the late nineteenth century, nonprint, inscriptive media had become rich and vigorous 'allies' to print in the construction of imagined communities, joined so obviously in the twentieth century by noninscriptive forms" (*Scripts, Grooves, and Writing Machines*, 12). See also Brady, *A Spiral Way*, which offers an overview of the early history of the cylinder phonograph and traces its ties to ethnography.

49. Hondal, *Scratch*, 75.

50. Haneke, *Caché*.

51. Hondal, *Scratch*, 14.

52. Hondal, *Scratch*, 14. The constant vigilance by unknown forces that is at the heart of *Caché*—and that is referenced repeatedly in "La Casa Haneke"—also threatens the creation of the alternate space of identity that Hondal insinuates.

53. Hondal, *Scratch*, 25.

54. Hondal, personal conversation.

55. Price, "Books to Be Looked At," 309. For more on "La Maleza" and Álvarez's work, as well as other Cuban "Books to Be Looked At," see Price's article of this title; on recent art and culture in Cuba more broadly, see *Planet/Cuba*.

56. When Álvarez decided to include *Scratch* in his "La Maleza" project, the book had not yet been published. At present, *Scratch* is still not widely available in Cuba: when I brought Hondal a copy of the Bokeh edition the year after its publication, he had not yet seen it.

57. Álvarez's project is in some ways an homage, if unintentional, to Rodríguez's Azotea, which was also constructed from scraps of building materials that she and her then-husband scavenged from city streets.

58. As of this writing, Álvarez is seeking funding for the second phase of "La Maleza," in which he plans to print a limited number of copies of the text of the books for which he has created covers, to be given away as art at the gallery openings for his work. He published one such book, Cuban writer Roman Gutiérrez Aragoneses's *Trenes van y trenes vienen* [*Trains Come and Go*] during a 2018 residency in Bilbao, Spain, and hopes to publish more in the future in Cuba. In distributing the books as art, rather than as printed material, Álvarez neatly sidesteps the requirement that all books in Cuba be published by a press recognized by the state. Private printing presses are not allowed, but the creation of books as works of art, it would seem, might allow Álvarez's works to fall into a different category that is deemed more permissible. Rodríguez's La Torre imprint might be considered to occupy an intermediate space, as it operates somewhat independently but is still affiliated with a state-run organization.

59. Álvarez did not mention restored 1950s-era U.S. cars such as the one that we took on our trip to Jaruco. These are much more expensive to rent and are used almost exclusively by tourists.

60. de Certeau, *The Practice of Everyday Life*, xviii.

Chapter 4. Blogging on (and Beyond) the Palenque

1. Here I use the conventional term in English-language scholarship to refer to Cubans of African heritage. At the same time, as I further discuss in this chapter's conclusion, I acknowledge that any one term is woefully inadequate to describe the complexities and nuances of Afro-Cuban identities (or any racial identities, for that matter). More generally, I write of race here as simultaneously a fiction and a lived reality, following renowned Cuban anthropologist and essayist Fernando Ortiz when he states that race "es un fantasma, precisamente por ser creado por la fantasía; pero el terror y el don con que se expresan los racismos no son imaginativos sino verdaderos" [is a ghost, precisely by being created by fantasy; but the terror and the ability with which racisms are expressed are not imaginary but real] (quoted in Romay, *Cepos de la memoria*, 13).

2. Following Warner's use of the term, a particular "public" might be considered to gather at this Havana party.

3. For more on the "paquete semanal," see Concepción, "Escaneando el paquete seminal (I)" y "Escaneando el paquete seminal (II)." Cearns analyzes what she describes as "socially-grounded networks of exchange stretching across the Florida Straits and beyond" in the 2000s in "'The Mula Ring'"; Bustamante analyzes the mail services from the United States to Cuba in "Cold War Paquetería."

4. See Morán, "Cuba.com," for further discussion of Cuban journals published online. These journals, Morán contends, contribute to the formulation of an alternate space of identity: the Cuba.com referenced in his title.

5. Gillis notes the connection between the Internet, islands, and archipelagos, stating: "Now we imagine cyberspace archipelagically and speak of 'surfing' the Internet, describing our Web browsers as 'navigators' (Edmond and Smith 2003, 4)" ("Island Sojourns," 276). My thanks to Enmanuel Martínez for this reference.

6. Cárdenas offers an incisive overview of the taboo topic of race in Cuba in his documentary *Contra las cuerdas*. See also Ferrer, de la Fuente, and Romay, whose insights on race and identity in Cuba have greatly informed my analysis here.

7. Gates, *Black in Latin America*, 207. In this, Fidel Castro—then serving as Prime Minister—sought to realize nineteenth-century Cuban writer José Martí's vision of a "Nuestra América" (Our America, 1891) in which differences of race are subordinated to similarities of "alma," or soul (Martí, n.p.).

8. Gates, *Black in Latin America*, 208.

9. Quoted in de la Fuente, *A Nation for All*, 279.

10. de la Fuente, *A Nation for All*, 285.

11. See Whitfield, *Cuban Currency*, for an overview of Cuba's dual economy during the Special Period.

12. Zurbano, "Soy un negro más," 97. It bears noting that membership in the Grupo del Palenque is somewhat fluid; Zurbano, for instance, does not mention Aroche, who was a member of the group from its inception, or Labarcena, who joined the group somewhat later but played a key role in the blog. The story of how the group got its name has been retold various times; for Aroche's account, see the Appendix of Interviews.

13. Labarcena noted in an interview that the poets were also referred to as the *palenqueros, los del Palenque*, or the *Grupo del Palenque* in the 1990s (personal conversation, May 2018). Papastamatiu might thus have used what was already a common moniker for the group when she "baptized" them.

14. Abreu, "La vanidad es indecente," n.p.

15. Aroche, quoted in Abreu, "La vanidad es indecente," n.p; original emphasis.

16. For more on the relationship between the "Grupo del Palenque" and the "Grupo Diásporas," see the Interview with Atencio, Aroche, and Moracen included in the Appendix.

17. Zurbano, "Soy un negro más," 97.

18. Benítez-Rojo, *The Repeating Island*, 252; original emphasis.

19. In the nineteenth century, according to Marqués de Armas, a group of white Cubans published a journal titled *El Palenque literario* (personal conversation, May 2018).

20. Labarcena, personal conversation, May 2018, emphasis added.

21. See delpalenqueypara.blogspot.com. The ephemeral nature of all Internet pages is underscored in Broussard, "Preserving News Apps," as well as in LaFrance, "Raiders of the Lost Web."

22. Posts to the blog were made by Palenque poets Dolores Labarcena (from Barcelona) and Julio Moracen (from Brazil), in coordination with poets in Cuba.

23. Schreibman, Siemens, and Unsworth, "The Digital Humanities," n.p. On Cuban blogs, see Duong ("Bloggers Unplugged"), Venegas (*Digital Dilemmas*), and Vicari ("Blogging Politics in Cuba"); see also the documentary short *BlogBang Cuba* by Claudio Peláez Sordo, which describes and analyzes the increase in Cuban blogs in the 2000s. On digital humanities—a field whose contours are still being defined and debated—see Gallon ("Making a Case for the Black Digital Humanities"); Klein and Gold ("Digital Humanities").

24. Brock, "From the Blackhand Side," 530.

25. Vicari, "Blogging Politics in Cuba," 1003.

26. Venegas, *Digital Dilemmas*, 13. Tourists were often able to access the Internet in upscale hotels or Internet salons, but this option was rarely available to Cubans.

27. Duong writes that the term was coined in 2009, when "Cuban academic Rafael Hernández coined a derogatory [and soon popular] term for the alternative blogosphere" ("Bloggers Unplugged," 382).

28. For a discussion of Sánchez's "Generación Y," as well as Claudia Cadelo's "Octavo Cerco" and Luis Felipe Rojas Rosabal's "Cruzar las alambradas," see Ponte, *Villa Marista en plata*. For an analysis of the difference between well-known bloggers like Sánchez and "anonymous" bloggers such as "Lucy" in Mexico, see Amaya, "The Cultures of Anonymity and Violence" (3821).

29. delpalenqueypara.blogspot.com/2007/04, 3 April 2007.

30. Aroche, personal interview, 16 February 2017.

31. As a point of comparison, see Brock, Kvasny, and Hales's analysis of African-American women's use of blogs to overcome the perceived "digital divide" in the United States. Brock et al., "Cultural Appropriations of Technical Capital."

32. Labarcena, "Re: fechas/pregunta."

33. Aroche, personal interview, 16 February 2017.

34. delpalenqueypara.blogspot.com/2010/03, 27 March 2010; ellipsis in original.

35. delpalenqueypara.blogspot.com/2008/06, 14 June 2008; ellipsis in original.

36. delpalenqueypara.blogspot.com/2010/10, 28 October 2010.

37. Alviárez self-identifies as Venezuelan in her user profile (accessed 25 October 2018, https://www.blogger.com/profile/04807281274034516604).

38. Labarcena, personal conversation, May 2018.

39. Benítez Rojo, *The Repeating Island*, 253–54.

40. Stratford et al., "Envisioning the Archipelago," 122.

41. Recio is identified as Profesora del Instituto Internacional de Periodismo José Martí in *BlogBang Cuba*, which Paláez Sordo completed as part of his master's program at the University of Havana.

42. Moracen, personal interview, 16 February 2017.

43. Romay, in contrast, rejects the idea of a "universal" identity: "Rendir banderas al universalismo autoatribuido a la cultura occidental, es la mejor manera de convertir la aldea en prisión" [To surrender to the universalism self-attributed to Western culture is the best way to convert the village into a prison] (*Cepos de la memoria*, 138).

44. Ferrer, *Insurgent Cuba*, 16; Martínez, *The Open Wound*, 1–2.

45. On the ways in which Cuban artists and writers dialogue with race, see Odette Casamayor Cisneros, "Huellas del esclavizamiento en la carne de la mujer negra caribeña: aproximaciones literarias y audiovisuales."

46. delpalenqueypara.blogspot.com/2007/04, 19 April 2007. Rodríguez is a Cuban-born visual artist who now lives in Madrid.

47. delpalenqueypara.blogspot.com/2007/04, 19 April 2007.

48. "Elio Rodríguez," n.p.

49. "Elio Rodríguez," n.p.

50. delpalenqueypara.blogspot.com/2007/08, 21 August 2007.

51. The line might also be read as an allusion to lynching. For an incisive study of the performance of lynching plays in the United States in the late nineteenth and early twentieth centuries, see Mitchell, *Living with Lynching*.

52. delpalenqueypara.blogspot.com/2009/10, 28 October 2009.

53. delpalenqueypara.blogspot.com/2009/10, 28 October 2009.

54. Ramírez, "Negra cubana tenía que ser," negracubanateníaqueser.com.

55. Portales Machado, "En 2310 y 8225," yasminsilvia.blogspot.com.

56. afrocubaweb.com.

57. Romay, *Cepos de la memoria*, 11.

58. As Campoalegre details, a growing number of groups in Cuba sought to address the issues of racism and discrimination, including Red Barrial Afrodescendiente, Afrocubana, Justicia y equidad racial, Red de Mujeres Negras, Club del espendrún, and Muñeca Negra. See also Faguaga Iglesias, "Vivir la pluralidad," 118.

59. *BlogBang Cuba*. The documentary does not include mention of the "Caso Zurbano."

60. Duong, "Bloggers Unplugged," 388.

61. Atencio, personal interview, 16 February 2017.

62. See also Abreu, "'For Blacks in Cuba'" (100–101), who offers as one example of Zurbano's previous work an essay featured (in excerpted form) on the "Del Palenque . . . y para . . ." blog in April 2007: "El triángulo invisible del siglo XX cubano: raza, literatura y nación" ["The Invisible Triangle of Twentieth-Century Cuba: Race, Literature, and Nation"].

63. Kristina Cordero completed the translation of Zurbano's op-ed for *The New York Times*. A revised translation was published on *AfroCubaWeb* on 20 June 2013 under the title "The Country to Come: and My Black Cuba." See the Spring 2014 issue of the *Afro-Hispanic Review* dedicated to the "Caso Zurbano" for reprints of both translations, as well as many of the key articles and essays on the controversy.

64. According to my contacts in Havana, Zurbano was first fired from the "Casa"; when he refused to leave the organization, he was then demoted from his lofty post to a position of less prominence.

65. Alex Webb/Magnum Photos.

66. Zurbano, "For Blacks in Cuba," n.p.

67. Morales, "La Revolución Cubana," 31. See also Feraudy, who references the op-ed's title in the opening lines of his piece, "*The New York Times* y los negros en Cuba" ["*The New York Times* and Blacks in Cuba"], published in *La Jiribilla* (30 March 2013).

68. Fowler, "Derivas con (por, y desde) Zurbano," 129.

69. Zurbano, "For Blacks in Cuba," n.p.

70. Gates, *Black in Latin America*, 231–2.

71. I analyze one instance of the cultural discourse surrounding race and *blanqueamiento*, or whitening, in Cuba in "'¿Qué cosa eres?': Reading Refractive Melodrama in Humberto Solás's *Cecilia*."

72. Luis, "Editor's Note," 8.

73. Cassin, "Introduction."

74. Cassin, "Introduction," xix.

75. Glissant, *Poetics of Relation*, 116.

76. Glissant, *Poetics of Relation*, 190.

77. In December 2020, after my conversation with Labarcena, and after I had submitted this manuscript to the press for review, Labarcena made one final post to the blog, titled "Para seguir leyendo" ["To Continue Reading"]. delpalenqueyparablogspot.com/2020/12, 2 December 2020.

Chapter 5. Rankling José Martí

1. Ponte, "Martí: historia de una bofetada," n.p.

2. The conference, "Cuba in War and Peace," was held at Temple University in Philadelphia on 20–21 April 2018.

3. I analyze here the versions of the essays published online. "El abrigo de aire" was republished in the online journal *La Habana Elegante* in 2003; "Martí: historia de una bofetada" appeared in the *Diario de Cuba* in 2015; and "Martí: los libros de una secta" was republished in the *Diario de Cuba* in 2019.

4. Gómez, "Simulaciones de la memoria," n.p.

5. *Encuentro de la Cultura Cubana* was founded in Madrid in 1996 with the goal of publishing the work of Cuban writers living both in Cuba and in exile. For an overview of the journal's history, see Cruz, "La revista."

6. Martí is the subject of innumerable studies and biographies, many of which are decidedly political in their take on his life and work. Space does not allow me to delve fully into this bibliography here; for overviews, see, among others, Ette (*José Martí, apóstol, poeta revolucionario*), Fernández Retamar (*Martí*), Hidalgo Paz (*José Martí, 1853–1895*), A. López ("José Martí"), and Montero (*José Martí*). For alternate perspectives, see Belnap and Fernández (eds.), whose collection presents essays on Martí from the perspective of hemispheric studies (*José Martí's "Our America"*); Lomas, who writes on Martí from the perspective of Latino/a Studies (*Translating Empire*); Austin, who writes on gender and nationalism in *Lucía Jérez* ("Monstrous Progeny"); and Hagimoto, who analyzes the connections between Martí and Philippine writer José Rizal (*Between Empires*).

7. Poet Caridad Atencio—whose work with the blog "Del Palenque . . . y para . . ." is analyzed in chapter 4—works at the Centro de Estudios Martianos in Havana, and has published numerous studies of Martí in addition to her poetry.

8. Ponte, "El abrigo de aire," n.p.

9. Ponte, "El abrigo de aire," n.p. Ponte refers here to a conversation between Cuban poet Eliseo Diego and two young writers: Diego asks the writers who they read, and when they respond "Martí," states that "Yo les pregunto cuáles autores leen, no cuál aire respiran" [I ask which authors you read, not which air you breathe.]

10. Ponte, "El abrigo de aire," n.p.

11. Ponte, "El abrigo de aire," n.p.

12. Ponte, "El abrigo de aire," n.p.

13. Castro quoted in Rojas, *Isla sin fin*, 210. Despite this claim, of course, Revolutionary discourse has undergone substantive changes through time; see also Ferrer.

14. For details, see the Appendix for the interview I conducted with Ponte.

15. Ponte, "Epílogo," n.p.

16. Ponte, "Epílogo," n.p.

17. Díaz, "Pero los dientes," 111.

18. Díaz, "Pero los dientes," 117.

19. Ponte, "El abrigo de aire," n.p.

20. Rodríguez Díaz, *Compendio insular*, 46–47.

21. Ponte, personal interview, 11 May 2019.

22. Glissant, *Poetics of Relation*, 20.

23. Glissant, *Poetics of Relation*, 12, 16.

24. Ponte, "El abrigo de aire," n.p.

25. Ponte, "El abrigo de aire," n.p.

26. Ponte, "El abrigo de aire," n.p.

27. Ponte, "El abrigo de aire," n.p.

28. Ponte, "El abrigo de aire," n.p.

29. Ponte, "El abrigo de aire," n.p.

30. Ponte, "El abrigo de aire," n.p.

31. Birkenmaier, "Antonio José Ponte," 184. See also Álvarez Borland ("Exilios secretos y sujetos invisibles"), Aldama Ordóñez ("Entre ruinas"), and Rivera-Taupier ("Recuperación de la ciudad").

32. Ponte, *La fiesta vigilada*, 232.

33. Ponte, *La fiesta vigilada*, 234.

34. Ponte, *La fiesta vigilada*, 214.

35. Morán, "Cuba.com," 152.

36. Ponte, *Villa Marista en plata*, n.p.

37. Both essays were later republished in the *Diario de Cuba*. "Martí: historia de una bofetada" was also republished in *Cuadernos Hispanoamericanos* (CHACHA) (in 2008).

38. "Martí: historia de una bofetada" was informed by Ette's *José Martí. Apóstol, poeta revolucionario: una historia de su recepción* (Ponte, "Epílogo," n.p.).

39. Ponte, "Martí: historia," n.p.

40. Ponte, "Martí: historia," n.p.

41. Ponte, "Martí: historia," n.p.

42. Ponte, "Martí: historia," n.p.

43. Ponte, "Martí: los libros," n.p.

44. Ponte, "Martí: los libros," n.p.

45. Ponte, personal interview, 11 May 2019.

46. Glissant, *Poetics of Relation*, 28.

47. There is a reference to Boyeros (a municipality of Havana) in the Epilogue (Ponte, *Cuentos*, 77; Ponte, *Tales*, 89). Miami, New York, and Africa are all referenced in the *Cuentos* by name.

48. Puñales-Alpízar, "La Habana (im) possible," n.p.

49. Ponte, *Cuentos*, 34; Ponte, *Tales*, 35.

50. Ponte, *Tales*, 35.

51. Ponte, *Cuentos*, 27; Ponte, *Tales*, 26.

52. The first "coin" he finds is a button bearing an anchor.

53. Ponte, *Cuentos*, 40; Ponte, *Tales*, 42.

54. Ponte, *Cuentos*, 40–1; Ponte, *Tales*, 43.

55. DeLoughrey, "'The litany of islands,'" 24.

56. Ponte, *Cuentos*, 7; Ponte, *Tales*, 2.

57. Alonso, "La escritura fetichizadora de Antonio José Ponte," 104.

58. Ponte, *Cuentos*, 7; Ponte, *Tales*, 2.

59. Ponte, *Cuentos*, 34; Ponte, *Tales*, 35.

60. Yusimi Rodríguez, "Interview," n.p.

61. Ponte, personal conversation.

62. 21 October 2021.

63. Ponte, personal conversation.

64. Juan Arturo Gómez Tobón, "'La Pequeña Habana' es una playa."

65. Ponte, "El abrigo de aire," n.p.

Chapter 6. Timeless Rhetoric, Special Circumstances

1. "Statement by the President on Cuba Policy Changes," n.p.

2. Quotes from *El País* and *Le Monde*, respectively. Both are included on the book jacket of the Emecé edition (1995).

3. See Whitfield, "La narrativa," for a discussion of the criticism Valdés has received, as well as an overview of the concern the (foreign) publication of *La nada cotidiana* provoked in Cuba (251–52). De

Maeseneer, for one, argues that Valdés's explanatory asides to her readers "refuerzan en el lector (occidental) cierta imagen de Cuba, fomentada tanto por las agencias de viaje como por la música y las películas nostálgicas, que se difunden por ahora en Europa y que son poco representativas de lo que pasa actualmente [en 2002] en Cuba" [reinforce in the (Western) reader a certain image of Cuba, promoted by both travel agencies and nostalgic music and films, that is being spread around Europe now and that is little representative of what is happening these days in Cuba (in 2002)]. de Maeseneer, "Denzil Romero, Enriquillo Sánchez y Zoé Valdés a ritmo de bolero," 50.

4. Pugh, "Island Movement," 14.

5. *La nada cotidiana* and *Te di la vida entera* are two of Valdés's best-known titles from the 1990s; *El todo cotidiano* takes up where *La nada cotidiana* leaves off to tell of the protagonist's life in exile. González Abellás notes as well the similarities between *La nada cotidiana* and the other works in what Valdés identifies as a "sexagonía": *Sangre azul, La nada cotidiana, La hija del embajador, La ira: Cólera de ángeles, Te di la vida entera*, and *Café Nostalgia* (*Visiones* 18). For a discussion of the connections between these novels, see also González Abellás, "Aquella isla."

6. "Zoé Valdés"; "Zoé Valdés. Biografía." For a complete list of Valdés's published work, see also "Bibliografía de Zoé Valdés."

7. Mateo del Pino and Gutiérrez, "Zoé Valdés," 59.

8. Whitfield, *Cuban Currency*, 22. Valdés is considered "a pioneer of a sub-genre of contemporary Cuban fiction that took as its material the 'special period in times of peace.'" Whitfield, *Cuban Currency*, 35.

9. Valdés, *La nada cotidiana*, 20; Valdés, *Yocandra*, 6. Original emphasis. English translations of *La nada cotidiana* in this chapter are by Sabina Cienfuegos; English translations of *Te di la vida entera* are by Nadia Benabid.

10. Valdés, *La nada cotidiana*, 13; Valdés, *Yocandra*, 1. Original emphasis.

11. Valdés, *La nada cotidiana*, 14; Valdés, *Yocandra*, 2. Original emphasis. In this passage and in the novel as a whole, *La nada cotidiana* emphasizes the importance of corporeality. See González Abellás, "Aquella isla"; Ortiz Ceberio, "La narrativa de Zoé Valdés"; and Timmer, "Cuerpo."

12. Timmer, "Dreams," 195.

13. Mañach, "La crisis," 67.

14. Valdés, *La nada cotidiana*, 21; Valdés, *Yocandra*, 7. *La nada cotidiana* mimics Revolutionary *testimonios* such as *Biografía de un cimarrón* (González Abellás, *Visiones*, 23), the first-person account of former slave Esteban Montejo compiled by Miguel Barnet as a portrait of the "new" Revolutionary subject. Yet *La nada cotidiana* departs from its predecessor in marshaling intimate details about Patria's life to condemn (rather than support) the status quo.

15. Valdés, *La nada cotidiana*, 26; Valdés, *Yocandra*, 12. As commemorated in Goya's famous painting of this name, "El dos de mayo de 1808" (2 May 1808) is the date of Spaniards' unsuccessful uprising against the French forces then occupying the nation.

16. Bhabha, *The Location*, 86.

17. The protagonist's name also serves as a reference to the newspaper published by nineteenth-century writer José Martí while in exile: *Patria*.

18. Valdés, *La nada cotidiana*, 183–84.

19. Valdés, *Yocandra*, 153.

20. La Gusana marries a Spaniard as a ticket out of Cuba. For further discussion of the ways in which Cuban writers treat the topic of women who marry to leave the island, see Eisterer-Barceló, "Cuerpos en venta"; for discussion of *jineteras* in Cuba, see Fusco, "Hustling for Dollars."

21. Valdés, *La nada cotidiana*, 133; Valdés, *Yocandra*, 108. Original emphasis.

22. Quiroga, *Cuban Palimpsests*, 115. Original emphasis. While Patria references the Spanish film *Mujeres al borde de un ataque de nervios* [*Women on the Verge of a Nervous Breakdown*] (Pedro Almodóvar, 1988) (105), she does not mention any Cuban films (González Abellás, "Aquella isla," 46). Nonetheless, *La nada cotidiana* does share certain characteristics with Cuban films such as *Fresa y chocolate* [*Straw-*

berry and Chocolate] (Tomás Gutiérrez Alea and Juan Carlos Tabío, 1994; Ramblado Minero), as well as *Adorables mentiras* [*Adorable Lies*] (Gerardo Chijona, 1992) and *La vida es silbar* [*Life is to Whistle*] (Fernándo Pérez, 1998).

23. Publics are created through reading and reading-like practices, as is the "imagined community" invoked by Anderson; publics, however, are multiple rather than singular.

24. Warner, *Publics and Counterpublics*, 119. The counterpublic described here differs from the publics described in earlier chapters in reference to Reina María Rodríguez and her collaborators, or to the Palenque poets, as these groups are not characterized by the same lack of decorum as the protagonists of *La nada cotidiana*.

25. Warner, *Publics and Counterpublics*, 119.

26. Rojas, *Tumbas*, 363. Rojas identifies three "políticas de la escritura en la narrativa cubana actual: la política del cuerpo, la de la cifra y la del sujeto" [politics of writing in contemporary Cuban narrative: the politics of the body, of the cipher, and of the subject] (*Tumbas*, 363; see also 362–71). Rojas maintains that Valdés employs the politics of the body in *Te di la vida entera* (and, I would add, in *La nada cotidiana*; *Tumbas* 363).

27. Valdés, *La nada cotidiana*, 44; Valdés, *Yocandra*, 26.

28. Valdés, *La nada cotidiana*, 46–7; Valdés, *Yocandra*, 28.

29. Valdés, *La nada cotidiana*, 47; Valdés, *Yocandra*, 29.

30. Valdés, *La nada cotidiana*, 144.

31. Valdés, *La nada cotidiana*, 156; Valdés, *Yocandra*, 128.

32. Valdés, *La nada cotidiana*, 162–63; Valdés, *Yocandra*, 133. Original emphasis.

33. Valdés, *La nada cotidiana*, 162; my translation.

34. San Martín Moreno and Muñoz de Baena Simón, "La Habana real y la Habana imaginada," 223.

35. Molinero, "La morfología del lagarto," 129. Bataille writes: "We are discontinuous beings, individuals who perish in isolation in the midst of an incomprehensible adventure, but we yearn for our lost continuity. [. . .] [with eroticism] the concern is to substitute for the individual isolated discontinuity a feeling of profound continuity." Bataille, *Eroticism*, 15.

36. Valdés, *La nada cotidiana*, 143–44; Valdés, *Yocandra*, 117–18. For a discussion of the connection between Valdés and the writers, including Lezama Lima, associated with the journal *Orígenes* (1944–56), see Álvarez Borland.

37. Valdés, *La nada cotidiana*, 150; Valdés, *Yocandra*, 123.

38. Valdés, *La nada cotidiana*, 151; Valdés, *Yocandra*, 124.

39. Santí, "Plante con Zoé Valdés," 406.

40. Rojas, *Isla sin fin*, 196–97. Original emphasis.

41. Valdés, *La nada cotidiana*, 171; Valdés, *Yocandra*, 142. Similarly, el Gigante [the Giant], who is mentioned only once (alongside el Pianista and el Dentista [the Pianist and the Dentist]), is excluded from the novel because of his size (136).

42. Rojas, *Isla sin fin*, 203.

43. de Man, *Blindness and Insight*, 207.

44. Timmer, "Dreams," 194.

45. Valdés, *La nada cotidiana*, 99.

46. Valdés, *La nada cotidiana*, 66; Valdés, *Yocandra*, 45. Patria notes that el Traidor's manuscript recalls *The Shining* (Stanley Kubrick, 1980), in which a wife discovers that her husband has been repeatedly writing "All work and no play . . ." for weeks as he goes insane. Valdés, *La nada cotidiana*, 69. The surfeit of words also belies the scarcity of paper in 1990s Cuba, as detailed in Strausfeld, *Nuevos narradores cubanos*.

47. Benjamin, "The Work of Art."

48. Valdés, *La nada cotidiana*, 39; Valdés, *Yocandra*, 21.

49. On the possible meanings of the name Yocandra, see Quiroga, *Cuban Palimpsests*; Rozencvaig, "La complicidad del lenguaje."

50. Valdés, *La nada cotidiana*, 185; Valdés, *Yocandra*, 154. Original emphasis.

51. Rozencvaig contends that the introduction sums up the nation's entrapment ("La complicidad del lenguaje," 430).

52. Faccini, "El discurso político de Zoé Valdés."

53. The CD bears the subtitle "Soundtrack of Zoé Valdés's novel: 'I Gave You All I Had.'"

54. Valdés, "to Cuban mothers," 5. The introduction and liner notes to the CD are published in English and Spanish; I quote the English here.

55. For Ramsdell, in contrast, "The lyrics contained in the narrative thus function as code for fellow Cubans, both on and off the island, who can relate to the range of sensations and emotions that the songs evoke. Valdés' valorization and recollection of these songs, therefore, is testimony to her own Cubanness" ("Life Is a Bolero," 117).

56. Zavala, *El bolero*, 117.

57. On the need to challenge traditional readings of the bolero, see Quiroga, *Cuban Palimpsests*, 127.

58. Zavala, *El bolero*, 117.

59. Valdés states that the novel is intended to be a tribute to the women of her mother's generation, and homage to Guillermo Cabrera Infante and to Pedro Almodóvar, who uses songs by la Lupe in *Mujeres al borde de un ataque de nervios*. See Santí, "Plante con Zoé Valdés," 395–96.

60. *Te di la vida entera* also tells of Cuca's eventual (albeit brief) reunion with Uan.

61. Pérez, *On Becoming Cuban*, 201.

62. de Maeseneer, "Denzil Romero, Enriquillo Sánchez y Zoé Valdés a ritmo de bolero," 49–50.

63. Valdés, *Te di la vida entera*, 21; Valdés, *I Gave You*, 9.

64. *Te di la vida entera* is one of a series of contemporary novels by Caribbean authors that destabilize desire and the nation through the lyrical. See also Pedro Vergés's *Sólo cenizas hallarás (bolero)* [*Ashes (Bolero)*] (1980); Luis Rafael Sánchez's *La importancia de llamarse Daniel Santos* [*The Importance of Being Called Daniel Santos*] (1998); and Mayra Santos-Febres's *Sirena Selena vestida de pena* [*Sirena Selena: A Novel*] (2000).

65. Whitfield, *Cuban Currency*.

66. Zavala, *El bolero*, 117.

67. Valdés, *Te di la vida entera*, 13.

68. Navarrette, "The songs," 9.

69. Valdés, *Te di la vida entera*, 13.

70. Valdés, *Te di la vida entera*, 13; Valdés, *I Gave You*, 3.

71. Valdés, *Te di la vida entera*, 28; Valdés, *I Gave You*, 13. Original emphasis.

72. Valdés, *Te di la vida entera*, 28; Valdés, *I Gave You*, 13.

73. Valdés, *Te di la vida entera*, 28; Valdés, *I Gave You*, 13. Original emphasis.

74. Valdés, *Te di la vida entera*, 143; Valdés, *I Gave You*, 87. Original emphasis.

75. Valdés, *Te di la vida entera*, 156; Valdés, *I Gave You*, 95. Original emphasis.

76. Navarrette, "The songs," 15.

77. Valdés, *Te di la vida entera*, 338; Valdés, *I Gave You*, 217.

78. Valdés, *Te di la vida entera*, 338; Valdés, *I Gave You*, 217.

79. Valdés, *Te di la vida entera*, 338; Valdés, *I Gave You*, 217.

80. Quoted in Valdés, *I Gave You*.

81. Pugh, "Island Movements," 10.

82. Quoted in García, "Zoé Valdés, a Pen Like a Whip," n.p.

83. Valdés, *El todo cotidiano*, 298.

84. Quoted in Armas, "Zoé Valdés," n.p.

85. Valdés, *El todo cotidiano*, 292.

86. Valdés, *El todo cotidiano*, 294.

87. Valdés, *El todo cotidiano*, 301.

Conclusion

1. See Duany, "Cuban Migration: A Postrevolution Exodus Ebbs and Flows."

2. Blizzard and Batalova, n.p.

3. For an insightful analysis of Mota's novel, see Price, *Planet/Cuba*.

4. "The Movimiento San Isidro challenges Cuba's regime," n.p.

5. Lage (1979–) is generally considered one of the foremost voices of the Generación Cero [Generation of the Zero Years]. His work includes *El color de la sangre diluida* [*The Color of Diluted Blood*] (2007), *Vultureffect* (2011), *Carbono 14. Una novela de culto* [*Carbon 14. A Cult Novel*] (2010), *La autopista: the movie* [*The Highway: The Movie*] (2014), and *Everglades* (2020).

6. Aguilera, "Jorge Enrique Lage, la memoria portátil," 99.

7. Román Maldonado, "Memoria portátil y estética de base de datos," n.p.

8. Lage, *Archivo*, 26.

9. Lage, *Archivo*, 9.

10. Lage, *Archivo*, 25.

11. Martínez, "The Archipelago and the Archive: Transnational Archival Modes and Mediums in Caribbean Literatures and States," n.p.

12. "Cuban anti-Communist anthem featuring Gente de Zona goes viral, sparks state fury," n.p.

13. Posts to social media such as Instagram from the San Isidro Movement (@mov_sanisidro) chronicle the jailing of members as well as their protests.

Appendix of Interviews

1. Lionnet and Jean-François, "Literary Routes," 1223.

2. Lionnet and Jean-François, "Literary Routes," 1223.

3. "Patterns of migration are accelerating. The United Nations estimates that one-sixth of the world's population will be migrants by the end of the next decade: one billion people by 2030. [. . .] Writers and visual artists [. . .] give us the human-interest stories that pull us into the concrete lives of individual migrants and their families." Lionnet and Jean-François, "Literary Routes," 1223.

4. Lionnet and Jean-François, "Literary Routes," 1234.

Works Cited

Abreu Arcia, Alberto. "'For Blacks in Cuba, the Revolution Hasn't Begun,' una lectura a partir del rumor." *Afromodernidades* (4 April 2013). *Afro Hispanic Review* 33, no. 1 (Spring 2014): 15–18.

———. "La vanidad es indecente." Interview with Rito Ramón Aroche. Accessed 25 October 2021. https://afromodernidades.files.wordpress.com/2010/04/entrevista-a-rito-la-vandidad-es-indecente.pdf.

"Acerca de Bokeh." Accessed 8 June 2018. https://bokehpress.com/acerca-de/.

Afrocubaweb. http://www.afrocubaweb.com/.

Aguilera, Carlos A. "Jorge Enrique Lage, la memoria portátil." Interview with Jorge Enrique Lage. In Lage, *Archivo*, 95–100. Reprinted from *El Nuevo Herald*, 5 January 2017.

———. "Ramón Hondal habla sobre *Scratch*, el segundo de una trilogía." Interview with Ramón Hondal, 25 April 2019. *El Nuevo Herald*. Accessed 11 October 2021. https://www.elnuevoherald.com/vivir-mejor/artes-letras/article229375059.html.

Aldama Ordóñez, Celia de. "Entre Ruinas: La Habana de Antonio José Ponte." *Letral* 18 (2017): 101–11. Accessed 27 October 2021. doi: https://doi.org/10.30827/rl.v0i18.6052.

Alonso, Carlos J. "La escritura fetichizadora de Antonio José Ponte." *Revista de Estudios Hispánicos* 43, no. 1 (January 2009): 93–108.

Alvarez Borland, Isabel. "Exilios secretos y sujetos invisibles: Guillermo Cabrera Infante y Antonio José Ponte." *South Atlantic Review* 81, no. 3 (2016): 129–45. Accessed 27 October 2021. https://www.jstor.org/stable/soutatlarevi.81.3.129.

———. "La lengua nómada: *Orígenes* y la diáspora de los 90." *Encuentro de la Cultura Cubana* 33 (Summer 2004): 265–74.

———. "'Soy un ciego empeñado en leer blancos': Liminaridad y posmemoria en *La fiesta vigilada* de Antonio José Ponte." *Caribe: Revista de Cultura y Literatura* 13, no. 2 (2010): 111–28.

Amaya, Hector. "The Cultures of Anonymity and Violence in the Mexican Blogosphere." *International Journal of Communication* 11 (2017): 3815–31. Accessed 27 October 2021. https://criticalracedigitalstudies.com/wp-content/uploads/2018/01/Amaya_Culture-of-Anonymity.pdf.

Anderson, Benedict. *Imagined Communities*. London: Verso, 1983.

"Anthology." *Oxford Living Dictionaries*. Accessed 20 October 2016. https://en.oxforddictionaries.com/definition/us/anthology.

"Archipelago." *Oxford English Dictionary*. Accessed 14 September 2021. https://www-oed-com.proxy.libraries.rutgers.edu/view/Entry/10387?redirectedFrom=archipelago#eid.

Arcos, Jorge Luis. "Una nueva visión." *Encuentro de la Cultura Cubana* 30–31 (2003): 41–44. Accessed 27 October 2021. https://rid.unrn.edu.ar/bitstream/20.500.12049/4748/1/Una%20nueva%20visi%C3%B3n.pdf.

Armas, Armando de. "Zoé Valdés: 'celebré, continúo celebrando y celebraré mientras viva la muerte de

Fidel Castro.'" Radiotelevisiónmartí.com. 15 December 2016. Accessed 21 October 2021. https://www.radiotelevisionmarti.com/a/zoe-valves-celebro-y-celebrare-muerte-de-fidel-castro-/135487.html.

Austin, Elisabeth. "Monstrous Progeny: Fragile National Ideologies in José Martí's *Lucía Jérez*." In *Exemplary Ambivalence in Late Nineteenth-Century Spanish America*, 101–42. Lewisburg: Bucknell University Press, 2013.

"Azotea de Reina." *La Habana Elegante (segunda* época*)*. Accessed 10 May 2019. http://www.habanaelegante.com/Summer98/Azotea.htm.

Bachelard, Gaston. *The Poetics of Space* [*La poétique de l'espace*], edited by Daniel Boulagnon. Accessed 20 September 2016. https://gastonbachelard.org/wp-content/uploads/2015/07/BACHELARD-Gaston-La-poetique-de-l-espace.pdf.

———. *The Poetics of Space: The Classic Look at How We Experience Intimate Places*. Translated by Maria Jolas. Boston: Beacon, 1994.

Barnet, Miguel. *Biografía de un cimarrón*. La Habana: Academia, 1996.

Basile, Teresa. "Las trampas del imperio." In *Cuentos de todas partes del imperio*. Antonio José Ponte. Leiden: Bokeh, 2017. 81–112.

Bataille, Georges. *Eroticism*. Translated by Mary Dalwood. London: Marion Boyars, 1998.

Behar, Ruth. "After the Bridges." In *The Portable Island: Cubans at Home in the World*, edited by Ruth Behar and Lucía M. Suárez, 3–8. New York: Palgrave MacMillan, 2008.

Behar, Ruth, and Lucía M. Suárez, eds. *The Portable Island: Cubans at Home in the World*. New York: Palgrave MacMillan, 2008.

Bejel, Emilio. *Gay Cuban Nation*. Chicago: University of Chicago Press, 2001.

Belnap, Jeffrey Grant, and Raúl A. Fernández, eds. *José Martí's "Our America": From National to Hemispheric Cultural Studies*. Durham: Duke University Press, 1998.

Benítez-Rojo, Antonio. *The Repeating Island: The Caribbean and the Postmodern Perspective*. 1992. Translated by James E. Maraniss, 2nd ed. Durham: Duke University Press, 2001.

Benjamin, Walter. *The Origin of German Tragic Drama*. Translated by John Osborne. London: Verso, 1998.

———. "The Work of Art in the Age of Mechanical Reproduction." In *Film Theory and Criticism*, edited by Leo Braudy and Marshall Cohen, 791–811. New York: Oxford University Press, 2004.

Bethell, Leslie, ed. *Cuba: A Short History*. New York: Cambridge University Press, 1993.

Bhabha, Homi K. *The Location of Culture*. 1994. London: Routledge, 2003.

"Bibliografía de Zoé Valdés." Instituto Cervantes. Accessed 18 October 2021. https://www.cervantes.es/imagenes/File/biblioteca/bibliografias/valdes_zoe_bibliografia_2015.pdf.

Birkenmaier, Anke. "Antonio José Ponte (Cuba, 1964)." In *The Contemporary Spanish American Novel. Bolaño and After*, edited by Will H. Corral, Juan E. de Castro, and Nicholas Birns, 170–85. New York: Bloomsbury, 2013.

———. "La Habana y sus otros: Presencias fantasmagóricas en *La fiesta vigilada* de Antonio José Ponte y *La neblina del ayer* de Leonardo Padura." *Cultura y Letras Cubanas En El Siglo XXI*, edited by Araceli Tinajero, 245–58. Iberoamericana Editorial Vervuert; Vervuert Verlagsgesellschaft Iberoamericana, 2010.

Blizzard, Brittany, and Jeanne Batalova. "Cuban Immigrants in the United States." Migration Information Source. 11 June 2020. Accessed 17 April 2021. https://www.migrationpolicy.org/article/cuban-immigrants-united-states-2018.

BlogBang Cuba. Director Claudio Peláez Sordo. 2014.

Blum, Hester. "Introduction: Oceanic Studies." *Atlantic Studies: Global Currents* 10, no. 2 (2013): 151–55. Accessed 27 October 2021. https://doi.org/10.1080/14788810.2013.785186.

Bonilla, Yarimar, and Max Hantel. "Visualizing Sovereignty: Cartographic Queries for the Digital Age." *Small Axe* (2016). http://smallaxe.net/sxarchipelagos/issue01/bonilla-visualizing.html.

Brady, Erika. *A Spiral Way: How the Phonograph Changed Ethnography*. Jackson: University Press of Mississippi, 1999.

Brock, André. "From the Blackhand Side: Twitter as a Cultural Conversation." *Journal of Broadcasting & Electronic Media* 56, no. 4 (2012): 529–49. Accessed 27 October 2021. doi:10.1080/08838151.2012.732147.

Brock, André, Lynette Kvasny, and Kayla Hales. "Cultural Appropriations of Technical Capital." *Information, Communication, and Society* 13, no. 7 (2010): 1040–59. Accessed 27 October 2021. doi:10.1080/1369118X.2010.498897.

Broussard, Meredith. "Preserving News Apps Presents Huge Challenges." *Newspaper Research Journal* 36, no. 3 (2015): 299–313. Accessed 27 October 2021. https://doi.org/10.1177/0739532915600742.

Bustamante, Michael. "Cold War Paquetería: Snail Mail Services Across (and Around) Cuba's 'Sugar Curtain.'" Presentation at LASA, Barcelona, 23 May 2018. Panel titled "Cuban Diasporas Across Time: Dialogue and Divergence."

Cabezas Miranda, Jorge. *Proyectos poéticos en Cuba (1959–2000): algunos cambios formales y temáticos.* Alicante: Universidad de Alicante, 2012.

Caché. Directed by Michael Haneke. Paris, France: France 3, 2005.

Cámara, Madeline. "Del barroco a la posmodernidad: Parodia de la picaresca en *La nada cotidiana*." *Confluencia* 18, no. 1 (2002): 139–54. Accessed 27 October 2021. https://www.jstor.org/stable/27922890.

Campoalegre, Rosa. Panel titled "Racial Inequalities in Contemporary Cuba: New Research Directions and Scholarship." Presentation at LASA, Barcelona, 25 May 2018.

"Un carpintero cubano en México narra cómo fue una de las fugas de emigrantes en Chiapas." DDC. 28 May 2019. *Diario de Cuba.* Accessed 17 October 2021. https://diariodecuba.com/cuba/1559033871_46609.html.

Casamayor Cisneros, Odette. "Huellas del esclavizamiento en la carne de la mujer negra caribeña: aproximaciones literarias y audiovisuales." Presentation at LASA, Barcelona, 24 May 2018. Panel titled "Nuevas miradas sobre esclavitud y abolición en las culturas caribeñas. Parte II."

Casanova, Pascale. *The World Republic of Letters.* Translated by M. B. DeBevoise. Cambridge: Harvard University Press, 2004.

Cassin, Barbara. "Introduction." Translated by Michael Wood. In *Dictionary of Untranslatables: A Philosophical Lexicon*, edited by Barbara Cassin, translated by Steven Rendell, Christian Hubert, Jeffrey Mehlman, Nathanael Stein, and Michael Syrotinski. Translation edited by Emily Apter, Jacques Lezra, and Michael Wood, xvii–xx. Princeton: Princeton University Press, 2014.

Castro, Fidel. *Palabras a los intelectuales.* 1961. Accessed 28 September 2021. http://www.cuba.cu/gobierno/discursos/1961/esp/f300661e.html.

Cearns, Jennifer H. "'The Mula Ring': Material and Digital Flows between Miami and Cuba." Presentation at LASA, Barcelona, 23 May 2018. Panel titled "Cuban Diasporas Across Time: Dialogue and Divergence."

de Certeau, Michel. *The Practice of Everyday Life.* Translated by Steven Rendall. Berkeley: University of California Press, 1988.

Concepción, José Raúl. "Escaneando el paquete seminal (I) (+ Infografía)." *Cubadebate*, 19 October 2015. Accessed 25 October 2021. http://www.cubadebate.cu/noticias/2015/10/19/el-paquete-semanal-i-infografia/.

———. "Escaneando el paquete seminal (II)." *Cubadebate*, 20 October 2015. Accessed 25 October 2021. http://www.cubadebate.cu/temas/cultura-temas/2015/10/20/el-paquete-semanal-ii/.

Contra las cuerdas. Dir. Amílcar Cárdenas. Thesis, Instituto Superior de Arte, Havana. 2015.

Cruz, Juan. "La revista 'Encuentro de la Cultura Cubana' cumple 10 años." *El País*, 21 June 2006. Accessed 14 October 2021. https://elpais.com/diario/2006/06/22/cultura/1150927206_850215.html.

"'Cuba en USA': Emilio Cueto hace un recuento de la presencia cubana en EEUU." DDC. 25 March 2019. Accessed 16 October 2021. https://diariodecuba.com/cultura/1553539050_45355.html.

"Cuban anti-Communist anthem featuring Gente de Zona goes viral, sparks state fury." 20 February 2021. Accessed 12 April 2021. https://www.reuters.com/article/us-cuba-politics/cuban-anti-communist-anthem-featuring-gente-de-zona-goes-viral-sparks-state-fury-idUSKBN2AK0MA.

"Cúmulo." *Diccionarios.com*. Accessed 5 October 2021. https://www.diccionarios.com/diccionario/espanol-ingles/cúmulo.

Davies, Catherine. *A Place in the Sun?: Women Writers in Twentieth-Century Cuba*. London: Zed Books, 1997.

Dawson, Helen. "Archaeology, Aquapelagos and Island Studies." *Shima: The International Journal of Research into Island Cultures* 6, no. 1 (2012): 17–21.

DeLoughrey, Elizabeth. "'The litany of islands,' The rosary of archipelagoes': Caribbean and Pacific Archipelagraphy." *ARIEL: A Review of International English Literature* 32, no. 1 (2001): 21–51.

———. *Routes and Roots*. Honolulu: University of Hawai'i Press, 2007.

"Del Palenque . . . y para . . ." Blog. 2007–2014. Accessed 23 October 2015. www.delpalenqueypara.blogspot.com.

Después de Paideia. Dir. Mirian Real. 2011.

Diario de Cuba. Accessed 27 October 2021. www.diariodecuba.com.

"Diaspora." *Oxford English Dictionary*. Accessed 25 September 2020. https://www-oed-com.proxy.libraries.rutgers.edu/view/Entry/52085?redirectedFrom=diaspora#eid.

Díaz, Fidel. "Pero los dientes no hincan en la luz." *Temas* 29 (2002): 111–23.

"Digest." Oxford English Dictionary. Accessed 15 April 2019. https://en.oxforddictionaries.com/definition/digest.

Duany, Jorge. *Blurred Borders: Transnational Migration between the Hispanic Caribbean and the United States*. Chapel Hill: University of North Carolina Press, 2011.

———. "Cuban Migration: A Postrevolution Exodus Ebbs and Flows." Migration Information Source. 6 July 2017. Accessed 17 April 2021. https://www.migrationpolicy.org/article/cuban-migration-post-revolution-exodus-ebbs-and-flows.

Duong, Paloma. "Bloggers Unplugged: Amateur Citizens, Cultural Discourse, and Public Sphere in Cuba." *Journal of Latin American Cultural Studies* 22, no. 4 (2013): 375–97. Accessed 27 October 2021. doi:10.1080/13569325.2013.840277.

Dykstra, Kristin. "Afterword: The Only Moment I Will Witness." In *Violet Island and Other Poems*, by Reina María Rodríguez, translated by Kristin Dykstra and Nancy Gates Madsen, 163–204. Los Angeles: Green Integer, 2004.

———. "Dispatch from Havana: Ricardo Alberto Pérez." 2 Jacket, 13 October 2013. Accessed 11 October 2021. https://jacket2.org/article/dispatch-havana-ricardo-alberto-perez.

———. "On Endurance: An Introduction to Writing by Reina María Rodríguez." *Latin American Literature Today*, May 2021. Accessed 14 September 2021. http://www.latinamericanliteraturetoday.org/en/2021/may/endurance-introduction-writing-reina-mar%C3%ADa-rodr%C3%ADguez-kristin-dykstra.

———. "'A Just Image': Poetic Montage and Cuba's Special Period in *La foto del invernadero*." *Mosaic: A Journal for the Interdisciplinary Study of Literature* 41, no. 2 (2008): 55–74. Accessed 27 October 2021. https://www.jstor.org/stable/44029495.

———. "Merging Exile into Diaspora: Other Letters to Milena." *Diálogo* 15, no. 2 (2012): 10–13. Accessed 27 October 2021. doi: 10.1353/dlg.2012.0024.

Dzhyoyeva, Mariya. "Cons(des)trucción del espacio urbano y el discurso identitario en la obra de Antonio José Ponte." *Revista Canadiense de Estudios Hispánicos* 40, no. 2 (2016): 315–32.

Edmond, Rod, and Vanessa Smith. "Introduction." In *Islands in History and Representation*, edited by Edmond and Smith, 1–16. London: Routledge, 2003.

Eisterer-Barceló, Elia. "Cuerpos en venta: El tema de la enajenación corporal en algunos escritores de la diáspora cubana." In *Aves de paso: Autores latinoamericanos entre exilio y transculturación (1970–2002)*, edited by Birgit Mertz-Baumgartner y Erna Pfeiffer, 207–17. Madrid: Iberoamericana, 2005.

"El debate racial en Cuba: Participar desde el respeto a la diferencia." *La Jiribilla*, 12 April 2013. *Afro Hispanic Review* 33, no. 1 (Spring 2014): 169–72.

"Elio Rodríguez. Corridas y venidas." *Wall Street International.* n.d. Accessed 25 October 2021. https://wsimag.com/art/8598-elio-rodriguez-corridas-y-venidas.

"En 2013 y 8225." Blog. yasminsilvia.blogspot.com.

Ette, Ottmar. *José Martí, apóstol, poeta revolucionario: Una historia de su recepción.* Translated by Luis Carlos Henao de Brigard. México, D.F.: Universidad Nacional Autónoma de México, 1995.

———. "Una literatura sin residencia fija. Insularidad, historia y dinámica sociocultural en la Cuba del siglo XX." *Revista de Indias* LXV, no. 235 (2005), 729–54. https://studylib.es/doc/4677447/una-literatura-sin-residencia-fija.-insularidad.

"Exile, n.1." *Oxford English Dictionary.* Accessed 27 September 2021. https://www-oed-com.proxy.libraries.rutgers.edu/view/Entry/66231?rskey=kPPkp4&result=1&isAdvanced=false#eid.

Faccini, Carmen. "El discurso político de Zoé Valdés: *La nada cotidiana* and *Te di la vida entera.*" *Ciberletras* 7 (2002): n.p. Accessed 22 October 2021. http://www.lehman.cuny.edu/ciberletras/v07/faccini.html.

Faguaga Iglesias, María-I. "Vivir la pluralidad aprendiendo a vivir el pluralismo: Pretexto para expulsar a un afrocubano de la estructura de poder." *Afromodernidades,* 10 April 2013. *Afro Hispanic Review* 33, no. 1 (Spring 2014): 159–64. Accessed 27 October 2021. https://www.jstor.org/stable/24585192.

Feraudy, Heriberto. "*The New York Times* y los negros en Cuba." *La Jiribilla,* 30 March 2013. *Afro Hispanic Review* 33, no. 1 (Spring 2014): 79–80.

"Feria Internacional del Libro de La Habana." Accessed 1 March 2021. https://www.ecured.cu/Feria_Internacional_del_Libro_de_La_Haban.

Fernández Retamar, Roberto. *Martí.* Colección Los Nuestros 3. Montevideo, Uruguay: Biblioteca de Marcha, 1970.

Ferrer, Ada. *Insurgent Cuba: Race, Nation, and Revolution, 1868–98.* Chapel Hill: University of North Carolina Press, 1999.

Figueroa, Sylvia, and Néstor E. Rodríguez. "En la casa de la poesía: Encuentro con la escritora cubana Reina María Rodríguez." *Ciberletras* 9 (2003). Accessed 4 October 2021. https://www.lehman.cuny.edu/ciberletras/v09/figueroarodriguez.html.

Figueroa-Vásquez, Yomaira C. *Decolonizing Diasporas: Radical Mappings of Afro-Atlantic Literature.* Evanston: Northwestern University Press, 2020.

Flores, Juan Carlos. *The Counterpunch (and Other Horizontal Poems).* Translated by Kristin Dykstra. Tuscaloosa: University of Alabama Press, 2016.

Foucault, Michel. "Of Other Spaces: Utopias and Heterotopias." Translated by Jay Miskowiec. *Architecture/Mouvement/Continuité* (October 1984): 1–9.

Fowler, Victor Calzada. "Derivas con (por, y desde) Zurbano: dolor, alegría y resistencia." *La Jiribilla,* 6 April 2013. *Afro Hispanic Review* 33, no. 1 (Spring 2014): 129–40. Accessed 27 October 2021. https://negracubanateniaqueser.com/2013/04/10/derivas-con-por-y-desde-zurbano-dolor-alegria-y-resistencia/.

Fuente, Alejandro de la. *A Nation for All: Race, Inequality, and Politics in Twentieth-Century Cuba.* Chapel Hill: University of North Carolina Press, 2001.

Fuentes, Yvette. "Beyond the Nation: Issues of Identity in the Contemporary Narrative of Cuban Women Writing (in) the Diaspora." PhD diss., University of Miami, 2002.

Fusco, Coco. "Hustling for Dollars: Jineteras in Cuba." *The Bodies That Were Not Ours and Other Writings.* London: Routledge, 2001. 137–53.

Gallon, Kim. "Making a Case for the Black Digital Humanities." In *Debates in the Digital Humanities 2016,* edited by Matthew K. Gold and Lauren F. Klein, 42–9. Minneapolis: University of Minnesota Press, 2016.

García, Iván. "Zoé Valdés, a Pen Like a Whip." *Translating Cuba: English Translations of Cubans Writing from the Island.* 9 October 2010. Accessed 21 October 2021. https://translatingcuba.com/zoe-valdes-a-pen-like-a-whip-ivan-garcia/.

Gates, Henry Louis, Jr. *Black in Latin America*. New York: New York University Press, 2011.

Generación Y. Blog. 2007–2021. Accessed 28 October 2021. https://www.14ymedio.com/blogs/generacion_y.

Gillis, John R. "Island Sojourns." *Geographical Review* 97, no. 2 (April 2007): 274–87. Accessed 27 October 2021. https://doi.org/10.1111/j.1931–0846.2007.tb00403.x.

Gitelman, Lisa. *Scripts, Grooves, and Writing Machines: Representing Technology in the Edison Era*. Stanford: Stanford University Press, 1999.

Glissant, Édouard. *Poetics of Relation*. Translated by Betsy Wing. Ann Arbor: University of Michigan Press, 2010.

Goldman, Dara. *Out of Bounds: Islands and the Demarcation of Identity in the Hispanic Caribbean*. Lewisburg: Bucknell University Press, 2008.

Gombrowicz, Witold. *Ferdydurke*. Havana: Torre de Letras and Arte y Literatura, 2015.

Gómez, Ivette. "Simulaciones de la memoria: Antonio José Ponte y Tuguria, la ciudad-ruina." *Habana Elegante* 47 (2010): n.p. Accessed 14 October 2021. http://www.habanaelegante.com/Spring_Summer_2010/Invitation_Gomez.html.

Gómez Tobón, Juan Arturo. "'La Pequeña Habana' es una playa: más de 600 cubanos varados en una localidad colombiana." *Diario de Cuba*. 25 March 2019. Accessed 17 October 2021. https://diariodecuba.com/cuba/1553516091_45349.html.

González Abellás, Miguel. "'Aquella isla': Introducción al universo narrativo de Zoé Valdés." *Hispania* 83, no. 1 (March 2000): 42–50. Accessed 27 October 2021. https://doi.org/10.2307/346112.

———. "El problema del yo: Autor y narrador en la ficción cubana reciente." *Espéculo: Revista de Estudios Literarios* 29 (March 2005). Accessed 18 October 2021. http://webs.ucm.es/info/especulo/numero29/probleyo.html.

———. "Sexo trasnacional: La cubana como mercancía en la obra de Zoé Valdés." *Alba de América: Revista Literaria* 22, no. 41–42 (2003): 277–85.

———. *Visiones de exilio. Para leer a Zoé Valdés*. Lanham: University Press of America, 2008.

"Un grupo de 700 cubanos marcha en caravana hacia EEUU desde Tapachula." DDC. *Diario de Cuba*. 24 March 2019. Accessed 17 October 2021. https://diariodecuba.com/cuba/1553438836_45327.html.

Gutiérrez Aragoneses, Roman. *Trenes van y trenes vienen*. La Maleza, n.d.

Hagimoto, Koichi. *Between Empires: Martí, Rizal, and the Intercolonial Alliance*. New York: Palgrave Macmillan, 2013.

Hau'ofa, Epeli. "Our Sea of Islands." In *A New Oceania: Rediscovering Our Sea of Islands*, edited by Eric Waddell, Vijay Naidu, and Epeli Hau'ofa, 2–16. School of Social and Economic Development, The University of the South Pacific, 1993.

Hay, Pete. "A Phenomenology of Islands." *Island Studies Journal* 1, no. 1 (2006): 19–42. Accessed 27 October 2021. https://www.islandstudies.ca/sites/vre2.upei.ca.islandstudies/files/u2/ISJ-1-1-2006-Hay-pp19–42.pdf.

Heller, Ben A. *Assimilation/Generation/Resurrection: Contrapuntal Readings in the Poetry of José Lezama Lima*. Lewisburg: Bucknell University Press, 1997.

Hernández Salván, Marta. *Mínima Cuba: Heretical Poetics and Power in Post-Soviet Cuba*. Albany: SUNY Press, 2015.

Hidalgo Paz, Ibrahím. *José Martí, 1853–1895: Cronología*. 2nd ed. Havana: Centro de Estudios Martianos, 2003.

Hondal, Ramón. "La Casa Haneke." *la noria* 8 (2015): 35–9. Accessed 27 October 2021. https://incubadorista.files.wordpress.com/2016/07/la-noria-8.pdf.

———. *Diálogos*. Havana: Ediciones Extramuros, 2014.

———. Personal conversation. June 2013.

———. *Scratch*. Leiden: Bokeh, 2019.

Hulme, Peter. "Subversive Archipelagos: Colonial Discourse and the Break-Up of Continental Theory." *Dispositio* 14, no. 36/38 (1989): 1–23. Accessed 27 October 2021. https://www.jstor.org/stable/41491352.

Huyssen, Andreas. *Present Pasts: Urban Palimpsests and the Politics of Memory*. Stanford: Stanford University Press, 2003.

"Instituto Cubano del Libro (ICL)." Ministerio de la Cultura. 10 March 2020. Accessed 2 October 2021. https://www.ministeriodecultura.gob.cu/es/ministerio-2/directorio-de-entidades/institutos-y-consejos.

"Insular." dictionary.com. Accessed 27 October 2021. https://www.dictionary.com/browse/insular.

Klein, Lauren F., and Matthew K. Gold. "Digital Humanities: The Expanded Field." In *Debates in the Digital Humanities 2016*, edited by Matthew K. Gold and Lauren F. Klein. Minneapolis: University of Minnesota Press, 2016.

Labarcena, Dolores. "Re: fechas/pregunta." Received by Elena Lahr-Vivaz. 6 November 2018.

Labarcena, Dolores, and Pedro Marqués de Armas. Personal conversation, 26 May 2018, Barcelona.

LaFrance, Adrienne. "Raiders of the Lost Web." *The Atlantic*, 14 October 2015. Accessed 27 October 2021. https://www.theatlantic.com/technology/archive/2015/10/raiders-of-the-lost-web/409210/.

Lage, Jorge Enrique. *Archivo*. 2015. Editorial Hypermedia, 2020.

Lahr-Vivaz, Elena. "After the Azotea." *Latin American Literature Today*, May 2021. Accessed 14 September 2021. http://www.latinamericanliteraturetoday.org/en/2021/may/after-azotea-elena-lahrvivaz.

——. "'¿Qué cosa eres?': Reading Refractive Melodrama in Humberto Solás's *Cecilia*." *Chasqui* 46, no. 1 (2017): 153–66. Accessed 27 October 2021. https://www.jstor.org/stable/26492151.

——. "Remapping the Borderlands in *¿Quién diablos es Juliette?*" *Border Cinema*, edited by Rebecca Sheehan and Monica Hanna, 112–28. New Brunswick: Rutgers University Press, 2019.

Lefebvre, Henri. *The Production of Space*. Malden: Blackwell Publishing, 1991.

Lewis, Martin. "Dividing the Ocean Sea." *Geographical Review* 89, no. 2 (1999): 188–214. Accessed 27 October 2021. https://doi.org/10.2307/216086.

Lezama Lima, José. *Paradiso*, edited by Eloísa Lezama Lima. Madrid: Cátedra, 2001.

Lionnet, Françoise, and Emmanuel Bruno Jean-François. "Literary Routes: Migration, Islands, and the Creative Economy." *PMLA* 131, no. 5 (October 2016): 1222–38. Accessed 27 October 2021. doi:https://doi.org/10.1632/pmla.2016.131.5.1222.

Lomas, Laura. *Translating Empire: José Martí, Migrant Latino Subjects, and American Modernities*. Durham: Duke University Press, 2008.

Lombard, Eilyn, and Reina María Rodríguez. "'More than a Place, Exile Is a Literary Genre': An Interview with Reina María Rodríguez." *Latin American Literature Today*, May 2021. Accessed 14 September 2021. http://www.latinamericanliteraturetoday.org/en/2021/may/%E2%80%9Cmore-place-exile-literary-genre%E2%80%9D-interview-reina-mar%C3%ADa-rodr%C3%ADguez.

López, Alfred J. "José Martí." *Oxford Bibliographies*. Accessed 14 October 2021. https://www.oxfordbibliographies.com/view/document/obo-9780199913701/obo-9780199913701-0072.xml.

López, Iraida H. *Impossible Returns: Narratives of the Cuban Diaspora*. Gainesville: University Press of Florida, 2015.

López, Magdalena, and Arturo Matute Castro. "*trazos de islas*: (Dis)locaciones narrativas: arte y literatura actual en la República Dominicana y Cuba." *Revista Iberoamericana* LXXIX, no. 243 (2013): 329–34. Accessed 27 October 2021. doi:https://doi.org/10.5195/reviberoamer.2013.7050.

López-Cabrales, María del Mar. "En busca de la palabra bajo una luz acuosa: la poesía de Reina María Rodríguez." *Céfiro* 2 (2002): 62–9.

Luis, William. "Editor's Note." *Afro Hispanic Review* 33, no. 1 (Spring 2014): 5–10. Accessed 27 October 2021. https://www.jstor.org/stable/24585164.

de Maeseneer, Rita. "Denzil Romero, Enriquillo Sánchez y Zoé Valdés a ritmo de bolero." *Iberoamericana* 2, no. 5 (2002): 37–54. Accessed 27 October 2021. doi:https://doi.org/10.18441/ibam.2.2002.5.37-54.

Maldonado-Torres, Nelson. "The Decolonial Turn." In *New Approaches to Latin American Studies: Culture and Power*, edited by Juan Poblete, 111–27. New York: Routledge, 2018.

de Man, Paul. *Blindness and Insight: Essays in the Rhetoric of Contemporary Criticism*. Minneapolis: University of Minnesota Press, 1983.

Mañach, Jorge. *La crisis de la alta cultura en Cuba: indagación del choteo*. Miami: Ediciones Universal, 1991.

Martí, José. "Nuestra América." 1891. Accessed 25 October 2021. http://bibliotecavirtual.clacso.org.ar/ar/libros/osal/osal27/14Marti.pdf.

Martínez, Enmanuel. 2019. "The Archipelago and the Archive: Transnational Archival Modes and Mediums in Caribbean Literatures and States." PhD diss., Rutgers The State University of New Jersey, School of Graduate Studies.

Martínez, Ivan-César. *The Open Wound: The Scourge of Racism in Cuba from Colonialism to Communism*. Kingston: Arawak Publications, 2007.

Martínez-San Miguel, Yolanda. *Caribe Two Ways: Cultura de la migración en el Caribe insular hispánico*. San Juan: Ediciones Callejón, 2003.

———. "Colonial and Mexican Archipelagoes: Reimagining Colonial Caribbean Studies." In *Archipelagic American Studies*, edited by Brian Russell Roberts and Michelle Ann Stephens, 155–73. Durham: Duke University Press. Accessed 27 October 2021. https://doi.org/10.1215/9780822373209-007.

———. "Colonialismo y decolonialidad archipielágica en el Caribe." *Tabula Rasa* 29 (2018): 37–64. Accessed 27 October 2021. doi:https://doi.org/10.25058/20112742.n29.03.

———. *Coloniality of Diasporas: Rethinking Intra-Colonial Migrations in a Pan-Caribbean Context*. New York: Palgrave Macmillan, 2014.

Mateo del Pino, Ángeles, y José Ismael Gutiérrez. "Zoé Valdés: Entrevista." *Hispamérica* 33 (August 2004): 49–60.

Mitchell, Koritha. *Living with Lynching: African American Lynching Plays, Performance, and Citizenship, 1890–1930*. Urbana: University of Illinois Press, 2011.

Molinero, Rita. "'La morfología del lagarto' y el erotismo como redención en *La nada cotidiana* de Zoé Valdés." *Crítica Hispánica* 22, no. 1 (2000): 121–34. Accessed 27 October 2021. doi:10.1007/978-3-476-05728-0_18196-1.

Montero, Oscar. *José Martí: An Introduction*. New York: Palgrave, 2004.

Mora, Javier L., and Ángel Pérez. "La desmemoria: lenguaje y posnostalgia en un *selfie* hecho de prisa ante el *foyer* del salon de los Años Cero (prólogo para una antología definitiva)." In *Long Playing Poetry. Cuba: Géneración Años Cero*, edited by Mora and Pérez, 9–39. Richmond: Editorial Casa Vacía, 2017.

Morales, Esteban. "La Revolución Cubana comenzó en 1959." *La Jiribilla*, 29 March 2013. *Afro Hispanic Review* 33, no. 1 (Spring 2014): 31–33.

Morán, Francisco. "Cuba.com. Escapes, descosidos y reinvención del espacio nacional." *Encuentro de la Cultura Cubana* 40 (2006): 152–8.

Moretti, Franco. *Distant Reading*. Brooklyn, NY: Verso, 2013.

Mota, Erick J. *Habana Underguater*. Atom Press, 2010.

"The Movimiento San Isidro challenges Cuba's regime." 3 December 2020. Accessed 12 April 2021. https://www.economist.com/the-americas/2020/12/03/the-movimiento-san-isidro-challenges-cubas-regime.

Navarrete, William. "Canciones, autores y sitios / The songs, the writers and the places." *Soundtrack of Zoé Valdés's novel: "I Gave You All I Had."* 8–22.

Navarro, Desiderio. "In Medias Res Publica." *Ciberletras* 7 (2002): n.p. Accessed 28 September 2021. https://www.lehman.cuny.edu/ciberletras/v07/navarro.html.

"Negra cubana tenía que ser." Blog. Accessed 27 October 2021. negracubanateníaqueser.com.

Nuez, Ivan de la. "El destierro de Calibán. Diáspora de la cultura cubana en los 90 en Europa." *Encuentro de la cultura cubana* 4/5 (1997, primavera/verano): 137–44.

Obejas, Achy. "From the Guest Editor." Special issue, *Diálogo: An Interdisciplinary Journal Published by* the *Center for Latino Research at DePaul University* 15, no. 2 (2012): 4–5. Accessed 27 October 2021. https://via.library.depaul.edu/dialogo/vol15/iss2/2.

Ortiz, Fernando, and Nicolás Guillén. "Contra los racismos." In *Las vanguardias latinoamericanas-textos programáticos y críticos*. Edited by Jorge Schwartz, 640–3. Madrid: Cátedra, 1991.

Ortiz Ceberio, Cristina. "La narrativa de Zoé Valdés: Hacia una reconfiguración de la na(rra)ción cubana." *Chasqui: Revista de Literatura Latinoamericana* 27, no. 2 (1998): 116–27. Accessed 27 October 2021. https://doi.org/10.2307/29741442.

Osorio, Camila. "'Patria y vida': la canción de rap que irrita al regimen de Cuba." 22 February 2021. Accessed 12 April 2021. https://elpais.com/cultura/2021-02-22/patria-y-vida-la-cancion-de-rap-que-irrita-al-regimen-de-cuba.html.

Pérez, Louis A, Jr. *On Becoming Cuban: Identity, Nationality, and Culture*. New York: The Ecco Press, 2001.

Pérez, Ricardo Alberto. "Los cerdos: retorno a la virtud." n.p.

——. *¿Para qué el cine?* Havana: Ediciones Unión, 2010.

Pérez Firmat, Gustavo. *Bilingual Blues*. Tempe, Arizona, 1995.

Piñera, Virgilio. "La isla en peso / The Weight of the Island." In *The Weight of the Island. Selected Poems of Virgilio Piñera*, 26–47. Translated by Pablo Medina. Middletown, Delaware: Diálogos, 2014.

Pitman, Thea. "En primera persona: Subjectivity in Literary Evocations of Pregnancy and Birth by Contemporary Spanish-American Women Writers." *Women: A Cultural Review* 17, no. 3 (Winter 2006): 355–67. Accessed 27 October 2021. https://doi.org/10.1080/09574040601027504.

Plasencia, Azucena. "Reina María Rodríguez, más allá de la poesía." *Diario de Cuba*, 4 January 2014. Accessed 7 March 2015. http://www.diariodecuba.com/cultura/1388709134_6545.html.

Ponte, Antonio José. "El abrigo de aire." *La Habana Elegante, segunda época*. Spring 2003. Accessed 23 May 2019. http://www.habanaelegante.com/Spring2003/Barco.html.

——. *Un arte de hacer ruinas y otros cuentos*. México, DF: Fondo de Cultura Económica, 2005.

——. *Cuentos de todas partes del imperio*. 2000. Leiden: Bokeh, 2017.

——. "En Manhattan: Cuba, azúcar, tabaco y revolución." *Diario de Cuba*. 17 March 2019. Accessed 17 October 2021. https://diariodecuba.com/de-leer/1552823990_45040.html.

——. "Epílogo." n.p.

——. *La fiesta vigilada*. Barcelona: Anagrama, 2007.

——. "Martí: historia de una bofetada." *Diario de Cuba*, 23 May 2015. Accessed 23 May 2019. https://diariodecuba.com/de-leer/1432187433_14638.html.

——. "Martí: los libros de una secta criminal." *Diario de Cuba*, 2 April 2018. Accessed 23 May 2019. http://www.diariodecuba.com/de-leer/1522603022_38433.html.

——. Personal interview. 11 May 2019.

——. *Tales from the Cuban Empire*. Translated by Cola Franzen. San Francisco: City Light Books, 2002.

——. *Villa Marista en plata: Arte, política, nuevas tecnologías*. 2010. Madrid: Hypermedia, 2014.

Posner, Miriam. "What's Next: The Radical, Unrealized Potential of Digital Humanities." 27 July 2015. Accessed 28 October 2021. http://miriamposner.com/blog/whats-next-the-radical-unrealized-potential-of-digital-humanities/.

Prats Sariol, José. "En el barrio de Reina María." *Encuentro de la Cultura Cubana* 30–31 (2003): 36–40.

Price, Rachel. "Books to Be Looked At." *Revista de Estudios Hispánicos* 51, no. 2 (2017): 297–323.

——. *Planet/Cuba: Art, Culture, and the Future of the Island*. London: Verso, 2015.

Prieto, Abel. "Cuba's National Literacy Campaign." *Journal of Reading* 25, no. 3 (1981): 215–21. Accessed 27 October 2021. https://www.jstor.org/stable/40029025.

Pugh, Jonathan. "Island Movements: Thinking with the Archipelago." *Island Studies Journal* 8, no. 1 (2013): 9–24.

Puñales-Alpízar, Damaris. "La Habana (im) posible de Ponte o las ruinas de una ciudad atravesada por una guerra que nunca tuvo lugar." *Ciberletras* 20 (December 2008). Accessed 16 October 2021. https://www.lehman.edu/faculty/guinazu/ciberletras/v20/punales.html.

Puri, Shalini. "Finding the Field: Notes on Caribbean Cultural Criticism, Area Studies, and the Forms of Engagement." *Small Axe* 17, no. 2 (41) (2013). Accessed 14 September 2021. https://read.duke-press.edu/small-axe/article-abstract/17/2%20(41)/58/98925/Finding-the-Field-Notes-on-Caribbean-Cultural.

Quijano, Aníbal. "Coloniality of Power, Eurocentrism, and Latin America." *Nepantla: Views from the South* vol. 1, no. 3 (2000): 533–80. Accessed 27 October 2021. muse.jhu.edu/article/23906.

Quiroga, José. *Cuban Palimpsests*. Minneapolis: University of Minnesota Press, 2005.

Ramblado Minero, María de la Cinta. "La isla revolucionaria: El dilema de la identidad cubana en *Fresa y chocolate* y *La nada cotidiana*." *Letras Hispanas* 3, no. 2 (Fall 2006): 86–94. Accessed 27 October 2021. http://hdl.handle.net/10344/4237.

Ramsdell, Lea. "Life Is a Bolero: *Te di la vida entera* by Zoé Valdés." *Brújula: Revista Interdisciplinaria Sobre Estudios Latinoamericanos* 3, no. 1 (2004): 113–23.

"Reina María Rodríguez, Premio Nacional de Literatura 2013." *CubaDebate*, 17 December 2013. Accessed 13 March 2014. http://www.cubadebate.cu/noticias/2013/12/17/reina-maria-rodriguez-premio-nacio-nal-de-literatura-2013/#.V7CdWjkrKCQ.

"Ricardo Alberto Pérez Estévez." EcuRed. Accessed 11 October 2021. https://www.ecured.cu/Ricardo_Alberto_P%C3%A9rez_Est%C3%A9vez.

del Risco, Enrique. "Piñera y profecía." *La Habana Elegante* (Fall/Winter 2012).

Rivera-Taupier, Miguel. "Recuperación de la ciudad y de la fiesta en Antonio José Ponte." *Chasqui: Revista de Literatura Latinoamericana* 44, no. 2 (November 2015): 129–37. Accessed 27 October 2021. https://www.jstor.org/stable/24810764.

Roberts, Brian Russell, and Michelle Ann Stephens, eds. *Archipelagic American Studies*. Durham: Duke University Press, 2017.

Roberts, Brian Russell, and Michelle Ann Stephens. "Archipelagic American Studies and the Caribbean." *Journal of Transnational American Studies* 5, no. 1 (2013): 1–20. Accessed 27 October 2021. doi:10.5070/T851019711.

Rodríguez, Reina María. *Bosque negro*. Havana: Ediciones Unión, 2013.

———. "En busca de una voz: los 'Diálogos' de Ramón Hondal." *Rialta Magazine*, 29 May 2017. Accessed 11 October 2021. https://rialta.org/en-busca-de-una-voz-dialogos-ramon-hondal-rialta-magazine/.

———. "first time." Translated by Joel Brouwer and Jessica Stephenson. Accessed 12 March 2021. https://www.poetryfoundation.org/poetrymagazine/poems/54757/first-time.

———. "memory of water." Translated by Joel Brouwer and Jessica Stephenson. Accessed 12 March 2021. https://www.poetryfoundation.org/poetrymagazine/poems/54756/memory-of-water.

———. *Otras mitologías*. Havana: Editorial Letras Cubanas, 2012.

———. "Poesía cubana: tres generaciones." *LL Journal* 7, no. 1 (2012). Accessed 2 October 2021. https://lljournal.commons.gc.cuny.edu/2012-1-rodriguez-texto/.

———. "Re: Torre de Letras." Received by Elena Lahr-Vivaz. 3 November 2013.

———. . . . *te daré de comer como a los pájaros* . . . Havana: Letras Cubanas, 2000.

———. "te daré de comer . . ." Introduction to Casa Vacía edition of book, provided in manuscript form. n.p.

———. *Travelling*. Havana: Editorial Letras Cubanas, 1995.

———. "Vibraciones de R." *Habana Elegante* (2007 Spring). Accessed 11 October 2021. http://www.ha-banaelegante.com/Spring2007/Azotea.html.

———. *Violet Island and Other Poems*. Translated by Kristin Dykstra and Nancy Gates Madsen. Los Angeles, CA: Green Integer, 2004.

Rodríguez, Yusimi. "Interview with Diario de Cuba Editor Pablo Diaz." 14 October 2014. Accessed 28 June 2019. https://havanatimes.org/interviews/interview-with-diario-de-cuba-editor-pablo-diaz/.

Rodríguez Díaz, Oscar. *Compendio insular: islas del mundo*. Havana: Editorial Científico-Técnica, 2015.

Rojas, Rafael. "Hypermedia, Almenara, Bokeh: las otras fábricas del libro." 14 June 2016. Accessed 28 September 2021. http://www.librosdelcrepusculo.net/2016/06/hypermedia-almenara-bokeh-y-otras.html.

——. *Isla sin fin: Contribución a la crítica del nacionalismo cubano.* Miami: Universal, 1998.

——. *Tumbas sin sosiego: Revolución, disidencia y exilio del intelectual cubano.* Barcelona: Anagrama, 2006.

Román Maldonado, Yairamaren. "Memoria portátil y estética de base de datos." *Hypermedia Magazine*, 10 September 2018. Accessed 29 April 2021. https://www.hypermediamagazine.com/critica/memoria-portatil-y-estetica-de-base-de-datos/.

Romay, Zuleica. *Cepos de la memoria: Impronta de la esclavitud en el imaginario social cubano.* Matanzas: Ediciones Matanzas, 2015.

Rozencvaig, Perla. "La complicidad del lenguaje en *La nada cotidiana*." *Revista Hispánica Moderna* 49, no. 2 (1996): 430–33. Accessed 27 October 2021. https://www.jstor.org/stable/30203427.

San Martín Moreno, Araceli, and José Muñoz de Baena Simón. "La Habana real y la Habana imaginada." In *Aves de paso: Autores latinoamericanos entre exilio y transculturación (1970–2002)*, edited by Birgit Mertz-Baumgartner and Erna Pfeiffer, 219–25. Madrid: Iberoamericana, 2005.

Sánchez, Yansy. *Maldita sea.* Dammit, 2006. Included on blog "Del Palenque . . . y para . . ."

Santí, Enrico Mario. "Plante con Zoé Valdés." In *Bienes del siglo: Sobre cultura cubana*, 392–410. México: Fondo de Cultura Económica, 2002.

Schreibman, Susan, Ray Siemens, and John Unsworth, eds. *A Companion to Digital Humanities.* Oxford: Blackwell, 2004. Accessed 28 October 2021. http://www.digitalhumanities.org/companion/.

Schreibman, Susan, Ray Siemens, and John Unsworth. "The Digital Humanities and Humanities Computing: An Introduction." In Schreibman et al., n.p.

Simal, Monica, and Walfrido Dorta. "Literatura cubana contemporánea: lecturas sobre la Generación Cero (introducción)." *Revista Letral* 18 (2017): 2–8. Accessed 27 October 2021. doi:https://doi.org/10.30827/rl.v0i18.6045.

"Statement by the President on Cuba Policy Changes." 17 December 2014. Accessed 18 October 2021. https://obamawhitehouse.archives.gov/the-press-office/2014/12/17/statement-president-cuba-policy-changes.

Steinberg, Philip E. "Of Other Seas: Metaphors and Materialities in Maritime Regions." *Atlantic Studies* 10, no. 2 (2013): 156–69. Accessed 27 October 2021. https://doi.org/10.1080/14788810.2013.785192.

Stephens, Michelle, and Yolanda Martínez-San Miguel, eds. *Contemporary Archipelagic Thinking: Towards New Comparative Methodologies and Disciplinary Formations.* London: Rowman & Littlefield Publishers, 2020.

Stratford, Elaine. "Disciplinary Formations, Creative Tensions, and Certain Logics in Archipelagic Studies." In *Archipelagic Thinking: Towards New Comparative Methodologies and Disciplinary Formations*, edited by Michelle Stephens and Yolanda Martínez-San Miguel, 51–64. London: Rowman & Littlefield Publishers, 2020.

Stratford, Elaine, Godfrey Baldacchino, Elizabeth McMahon, Carol Farbotko, and Andrew Harwood. "Envisioning the Archipelago." *Island Studies Journal* 6, no. 2 (2011): 113–30.

Strausfeld, Michi, ed. *Nuevos narradores cubanos.* Madrid: Ediciones Siruela, 2000.

Suárez, Lucía M. "Our Memories, Ourselves." In Behar and Suárez, 9–16.

Timmer, Nanne. "El cuerpo y la nuda vida en *La nada cotidiana* de Zoé Valdés." In *Escribir el cuerpo: 19 asedios desde la literatura hispanoamericana*, edited by Carmen de Mora and Alfonso García Morales, 327–38. Sevilla: University de Sevilla, 2003.

——. "Dreams That Dreams Remain: Three Cuban Novels of the 90s." In *Cultural Identity and Postmodern Writing*, edited by Theo D'haen and Pieter Vermeulen, 185–205. Amsterdam: Rodopi, 2006.

Uribe Schroeder, Richard, Fernando Zapata López, Bernardo Jaramillo Hoyos, Fabiano Dos Santos Piúba, Mónica Torres Cadena, Juan Carlos Rueda Azcuénaga, Marifé Boix-García, and Mónica Herrero de Consiglio. *Las ferias del libro. Manual para expositores y visitantes profesionales.* Havana: Editorial Científico-Técnica, 2014.

Valdés, Zoé. *I Gave You All I Had.* Translated by Nadia Benabid. New York: Arcade Publishing, 1999.

———. "A las madres cubanas, Escrito bailando / to Cuban mothers written while I'm dancing." Translated by Dolores M. Koch. In *Soundtrack to Zoé Valdés's novel: "I Gave You All I Had,"* 2–11.

———. *La nada cotidiana.* 1995. Barcelona: Ediciones Salamandra, 2006.

———. *Te di la vida entera.* Barcelona: Planeta, 2004.

———. *Te di la vida entera. Grupo Café Nostalgia.* Naïve, 1999. CD.

———. *El todo cotidiano.* Barcelona: Planeta, 2010.

———. *Yocandra in the Paradise of Nada.* Translated by Sabina Cienfuegos. New York: Arcade Publishing, 1997.

———. "Zoé en el metro." Blog. Accessed 21 October 2021. ecodiario.eleconomista.es/blogs/zoe-en-el-metro/.

Venegas, Cristina. *Digital Dilemmas: The State, the Individual, and Digital Media in Cuba.* New Brunswick: Rutgers University Press, 2010.

Vera-León, Antonio. "Narraciones obscenas: Cabrera Infante, Reinaldo Arenas, Zoé Valdés." In *Todas las islas la isla. Nuevas y novísimas tendencias en la literatura y cultura de Cuba*, edited by Janett Reinstädler and Ottmar Ette, 177–91. Frankfurt: Verveurt, 2000.

Vicari, Stefania. "Blogging Politics in Cuba: The Framing of Political Discourse in the Cuban Blogosphere." *Media, Culture & Society* 36, no. 7 (2014): 998–1015. Accessed 27 October 2021. https://doi.org/10.1177/0163443714536082.

Warner, Michael. *Publics and Counterpublics.* Brooklyn, NY: Zone Books, 2005.

Whitfield, Esther. *Cuban Currency: The Dollar and "Special Period" Fiction.* Minneapolis: University of Minnesota Press, 2008.

———. "La narrativa cubana y el ejemplo del exilio: El caso Zoé Valdés." *Exilios y residencias: Escrituras de España y América*, edited by Juana Martínez, 245–54. Madrid: Iberoamericana, 2007.

Wiedorn, Michael. *Think Like an Archipelago: Paradox in the Work of Édouard Glissant.* Albany: SUNY Press, 2017.

Zavala, Iris M. *El bolero: Historia de un amor.* Madrid: Celeste, 2000.

"Zoé Valdés. Biografía." Cervantes.es Bibliotecas y documentación. Accessed 18 October 2021. https://www.cervantes.es/bibliotecas_documentacion_espanol/creadores/valdes_zoe.htm.

"Zoé Valdés." *Biografías y vidas.* Accessed 24 May 2019. https://www.biografiasyvidas.com/biografia/v/valdes_zoe.htm.

Zurbano, Roberto. "For Blacks in Cuba, the Revolution Hasn't Begun." *New York Times.* 23 March 2013. Accessed 28 June 2019. https://www.nytimes.com/2013/03/24/opinion/sunday/for-blacks-in-cuba-the-revolution-hasnt-begun.html.

———. "The Country to Come: And My Black Cuba." AfroCubaWeb 20 June 2013. *Afro Hispanic Review* 33, no. 1 (Spring 2014): 115–8.

———. "Soy un negro más: Zurbano *par lúi-même*." *Afro Hispanic Review* 33, no. 1 (Spring 2014): 129–10. Accessed 27 October 2021. https://www.jstor.org/stable/24585165.

INDEX

Page references with the letters *p* and *t* refer to photos and tables.

Very old recording (*antigua grabación*), 145
Villa Fernández, Ignacio. *See* De Nieve, Bola
Villa Marista in Silver (*Villa Marista en plata*)
   (Ponte), 113, 154
Vinyl records, 65, 66, 69
"Violet Island" (Rodríguez, R.), 43–44
Violet Island and Other Poems (Rodríguez, R.),
   193n53
Virginity, 130, 131
Visibility, 189n33
Visual artists, 52
"The Voices Dialogue" (*"Las voces dialogan"*)
   (Hondal), 64–65
Void, cultural, 59, 60

Walks, 61, 62
Warner, Michael, 38, 86, 125, 130, 192n35
"The Weed" (*"La Maleza"*) (artwork), 70–72, 71p,
   195nn56–58
Weekly packet (*"paquete semanal"*), 76, 196n3
"The Weight of the Island" (*"La isla en peso"*)
   (Piñera), 13–14

"Wet foot/dry foot" policy, U.S., 122, 152, 190n52
Whitfield, Esther, 126, 140
Wikipedia, 98
Wood, 70
*Words to the Intellectuals (Palabras a los intelectu-
   ales)* (Castro, F.), 20–22, 23, 89, 189n40, 191n9
Workshop, literary, 172
World War II, 148

Yocandra in the Paradise of Nada (*La nada
   cotidiana*) (Valdés), 124, 126–27; as allegorical,
   134–35; circularity of, 137; counterpublic of,
   130, 131, 132–33; nothingness in, 128–29; repetition in, 135–36
Yo-Yo Ma, 66

Zamora, Bladimir, 106, 178, 179
Zavala, Iris M., 138, 140, 141–42
Zombies, 154, 155
Zurbano, Roberto, 8, 75, 198nn63–64; essay of, 77,
   95, 96–97, 98–99; on Morro, 28
Zurbano Case, 95–97, 98, 99

ELENA LAHR-VIVAZ is associate professor of Spanish at Rutgers University–Newark. She is the author of *Mexican Melodrama: Film and Nation from the Golden Age to the New Wave*.